Now These Are the Names

Now THESE ARE THE NAMES

A New English Rendition
of the Book of Exodus

TRANSLATED WITH
COMMENTARY AND NOTES BY
Everett Fox

SCHOCKEN BOOKS / NEW YORK

First published by SCHOCKEN BOOKS 1986

10 9 8 7 6 5 4 3 2 1   86 87 88 89

Copyright © 1986 by Schocken Books, Inc.

Library of Congress Cataloging-in-Publication Data

Bible. O.T. Exodus. English. Fox. 1986.
 Now these are the names.
 Bibliography: p. 225
 1. Bible. O.T. Exodus—Commentaries. I. Fox,
Everett. II. Title.
BS1243.F69 1986   222'.12077   86–6690

Design by Peter Oldenburg
Manufactured in the United States of America
ISBN 0–8052–4020–9

To the memory of
PAUL LICHTERMAN
(1945–1983)

אהב ימים לראות טוב

CONTENTS

TRANSLATOR'S PREFACE   xi

ACKNOWLEDGMENTS   xxi

TO AID THE READER   xxiii

ON THE NAME OF GOD AND ITS TRANSLATION   xxv

GUIDE TO THE PRONUNCIATION OF HEBREW

    NAMES   xxvii

ON THE BOOK OF EXODUS AND ITS STRUCTURE   xxix

Now These Are the Names

PART   I. The Deliverance Narrative (1–15:21)   3

The Early Life of Moshe and Religious Biography   4
On the Journey Motif   6
Moshe Before Pharaoh: The Plague Narrative
    (5–11)   8
    Prologue in Egypt (1)   11
    Moshe's Birth and Early Life (2:1–22)   15
    God Takes Notice (2:23–25)   21
    At the Bush: The Call (3:1–4:17)   22
    The Journey Back (4:18–31)   31
    Before Pharaoh (5:1–6:1)   35
    The Promise Renewed (6:2–13)   39
    The Genealogy of Moshe and Aharon (6:14-27)   41
    The Mission Renewed (6:28–7:13)   43
    First Blow (7:14–25)   45
    Second Blow (7:26–8:11)   47
    Third Blow (8:12–15)   49
    Fourth Blow (8:16–28)   49
    Fifth Blow (9:1–7)   51
    Sixth Blow (9:8–12)   53
    Seventh Blow (9:13–35)   53
    Eighth Blow (10:1–20)   57
    Ninth Blow (10:21–29)   59
    The Final Warning (11:1–10)   61

The Tenth Blow in Its Context   63
The Passover Ritual (12:1–28)   65
Tenth Blow and Exodus (12:29–42)   67
Who May Make Passover (12:43–50)   71
Passover and the Firstborn (12:51–13:16)   71
The Route and the Escort (13:17–22)   74
At the Sea of Reeds (14)   75
The Song of God as Triumphant King (15:1–21)   81

PART   II. In the Wilderness (15:22–18:27)   87

Grumbling I (15:22–27)   89
Grumbling II (16)   91
Grumbling III (17:1–7)   95
War with Amalek (17:8–16)   97
The New Society: Yitro's Visit (18)   99

PART   III. The Meeting and Covenant at Sinai
        (19–24)   103

On Covenant   104
On Biblical Law   105
The Meeting and the Covenant (19)   109
The Ten Words (The Decalogue) (20:1–14)   113
Aftermath (20:15–23)   115
On the Laws   117
Laws Regarding Israelite Serfdom (21:1–11)   117
Capital Crimes of Violence (21:12–17)   119
Injuries (21:18-32)   121
Property (21:33–22:14)   123
Laws Concerning Social Relations and Religious
    Matters (22:15–23:19)   125
Epilogue: The Future Conquest (23:20–33)   131
Sealing the Covenant (24:1–11)   133
Moshe Ascends Alone (24:12–18)   135

PART   IV. The Instructions for the Dwelling and
        the Cult (25–31)   137

The "Contribution" (25:1–9)   141
The Coffer (25:10–16)   142

The Purgation-Cover (25:17–22)   143
The Table (25:23–30)   145
The Lampstand (25:31–40)   147
The Dwelling Proper (26:1–14)   147
The Framework (26:15–30)   149
The Curtain and the Screen (26:31–37)   151
The Altar (27:1–8)   151
The Courtyard (27:9–19)   153
The Oil (27:20–21)   155
The Priestly Garments (28:1–5)   155
The *Efod* (28:6–12, 13–14)   155
The Breastpiece (28:15–30)   157
The Tunic (28:31–35)   159
The Head-Plate (28:36–38)   161
Other Priestly Garments (28:39–43)   161
The Investiture Ceremony (29:1–45)   161
The Incense Altar (30:1–10)   169
Census and Ransom (30:11–16)   169
The Basin (30:17–21)   171'
The Anointing Oil (30:22–33)   171
The Incense (30:34–38)   173
Craftsmen (31:1–11)   173
The Sabbath (31:12–17); The Tablets (31:18)   175

PART   V. The Covenant Broken and Restored (32–34)   177

The Sin of the Molten Calf (32:1–6)   179
Response: God's Anger (32:7–14)   181
Response: Moshe's Anger (32:15–29)   183
After the Purge (32:30–33:6)   185
Moshe at the Tent (33:7–11)   187
Moshe's Plea and God's Answer (33:12–34:3)   189
God Reveals Himself (34:4–9)   191
The New Covenant (34:10–28)   193
Moshe Radiant (34:29–35)   195

PART   VI. The Building of the Dwelling (35–40)   197

The Sabbath Restated (35:1–3)   199
The Contribution Restated (35:4–19)   199

Preparations for the Construction (35:20–36:7)   199
Dwelling II (36:8–19)   203
Boards II (36:20–34)   205
Curtain and Screen II (36:35–38)   205
Coffer and Purgation-Cover II (37:1–9)   205
Table II (37:10–16)   207
Lampstand II (37:17–24)   207
Incense Altar II (37:25–28)   207
Anointing Oil and Incense II (37:29)   209
Altar II (38:1–7)   209
Basin and Pedestal II (38:8)   209
Courtyard II (38:9–20)   209
Accountings (38:21–31)   211
Garments II (39:1)   213
Efod and Breastpiece II (39:2–21)   213
Tunic II (39:22–26)   215
Other Priestly Garments II (39:27–29)   215
Head-Plate II (39:30–31)   215
The Completion of the Parts; Bringing Them to
    Moshe (39:32–43)   215
Final Instructions: Setting Up (40:1–16)   217
The Implementation (40:17-33)   219
The End: God's Glory (40:34–38)   220

APPENDIX A: SCHEMATIC FLOOR PLAN OF THE

DWELLING   223

SUGGESTIONS FOR FURTHER READING   225

TRANSLATOR'S PREFACE

THIS RENDITION of the book of Exodus moves ahead with the approach to biblical texts that I adopted in my translation of the book of Genesis, *In the Beginning* (New York: Schocken, 1983). Briefly stated, the translation attempts to echo the oral, rhetorical character of the Hebrew Bible. The Bible makes extensive use (especially in the Torah) of repetition, allusion, plays on words, and alliteration rhetorically to underscore its meaning. A translation sensitive to this aspect of biblical literature is intended to lead the reader back to the sound structure and form of the Hebrew, and to engage him or her in the process of experiencing and interpreting the text.

The only previous translation to hold consistently to this approach (outside of D. A. Bruno's interesting but forced metrical translation into German) was the German rendition of Martin Buber and Franz Rosenzweig (hereafter abbreviated as B-R), 1925–1962, which has served as a close model for my work. My original intent was to translate B-R directly, but in the course of the work I came to realize that B-R was so tied to the character of the German language, and based on an era of Bible scholarship that predated many important discoveries in philology, that a new start would have to be made. In addition, I have come to recognize the difficulty inherent in the idea that the Bible is, in a formal sense, a type of oral literature. I would now agree with those scholars who see in the biblical text a complex blend of oral, orally based, and written literature, whose boundaries are not always clear (see, for instance, Gunn 1978).

This last point, however, has not shaken my conviction that the sound of biblical texts, when recited, is of the greatest importance in helping the modern reader to enter the world of ancient Israel's literature. Some brief illustrations may help to clarify this. Consider, for example, Exodus 14:11–12. The newly freed Israelites find themselves pursued by their former masters, the Pharaoh and his army; with their backs to the Sea of Reeds, they panic, and bitterly harangue their would-be deliverer, Moshe (Moses). The present translation, attempting to reflect the repetition and structure of the Hebrew original, yields the following:

> they said to Moshe:
> Is it because there are no graves in Egypt
> that you have taken us out to die in the wilderness?

What is this that you have done to us, bringing us out of Egypt!
Is this not the very word that we spoke to you in Egypt,
saying: Let us alone, that we may serve Egypt!
Indeed, better for us serving Egypt
than our dying in the wilderness!

This passage demonstrates several aspects of the "Rhetorical" translation method: the laying out of the text in "cola" or lines meant to facilitate reading aloud; the repetition of "Egypt" (five times) and "wilderness" (twice) to stress the irony of the Israelites' situation (as they see it, Egypt means life, and the wilderness, certain death); and the double use of "serve"—the very word that Moshe constantly drummed into Pharaoh's ears to denote the Israelites' desire to worship God ("Send free my people, that they may serve me"). If we juxtapose the above translation with one from a standard recent version (the New International Version), the importance of this approach becomes clear:

> They said to Moses, "Was it because there were no graves in Egypt that you brought us to the desert to die? What have you done to us by bringing us out of Egypt? Didn't we say to you in Egypt, 'Leave us alone; let us serve the Egyptians'? It would have been better for us to serve the Egyptians than to die in the desert!"

Here the rhetorical force of the Hebrew has been ignored. The Hebrew text does not transpose "desert to die" to "die in the desert" at the end (the word order repeats in the Hebrew, for emphasis); it does not distinguish in sound between "Egypt" and "Egyptians"; and it certainly does not read like standard colloquial prose. Indeed, all of Chapter 14 of Exodus testifies to the Bible's use of an intermediate form between poetry and prose, a form designed to instruct as well as to inspire.

But it is not only in narrative that the rhetoric of biblical language makes itself felt. Fully half of the book of Exodus is law or instruction, and one can find there further examples of the importance of sound structure in the Bible. Take, for instance, the law referring to the protection of widows and orphans in 22:23–24. This time I shall first present the text through the eyes of another translation, the New English Bible:

> You shall not ill-treat any widow or fatherless child. If you do, be sure that I will listen if they appeal to me; my anger will be roused and I will kill you with the sword; your own wives shall become widows and your children fatherless.

Powerful language it is, especially in a law code. But the Hebrew is more so, utilizing as it does a double form of the verb in rare multiple sequence:

> Any widow or orphan you are not to afflict.
> Oh, if you afflict, afflict them . . . !
> For (then) they will cry, cry out to me,
> I will hearken, yes, hearken to their cry.
> my anger will rage
> and I will kill you with the sword,
> so that your wives become widows, and your children, orphans!

The division of the text into lines resembling blank verse, noted above as essential to this kind of translation, functions to isolate rhetorical units of text—here, the three double verbs—by in effect slowing the reader down and focusing attention on the unfolding of the particular point of the passage.

Perhaps the most important application of rhetorical translating is what Buber called the *"Leitwort"* (leading word) method. In this approach, the translator pays careful attention to the recurrence of a Hebrew word (especially in verbal form) throughout textual units of different sizes, and tries to echo the repeating sound in English. Such a word both highlights themes and motifs in the narrative or law and structurally unifies the text—much as themes and motifs may do in classical music (hence the similarity of Buber's term to Richard Wagner's word *Leitmotif*). This often occurs on a large scale (for a list of some of the leading words in Exodus, see "On the Book of Exodus," below), but it may also operate within a relatively short passage, as in the following case: the command to observe the Sabbath in 31:13–17, the longest of several such passages in the book, makes use of several leading words to stress its point. First, the verb *shamor*, "keep," forms the backbone of the passage:

> However: my Sabbaths you are to keep!
> . . . . . .
> You are to keep the Sabbath,
> . . . . . .
> The Children of Israel are to keep the Sabbath. . . .

More tellingly, it is the verb *'asoh*, "do/make," that in its fivefold occurrence plays the leading role in the passage:

> Aye, whoever makes work on it

. . . . . .
For six days is work to be made,
. . . . . .
whoever makes work on the Sabbath day is to be put-to-death, yes, death
. . . . . .
to make the Sabbath-observance throughout their generations
. . . . . .
YHWH made the heavens and the earth. . . .

Note how different shades of meaning all enter—and that is exactly the way that conventional translations render the verb, idiomatically (the New Jewish Version translates *'asoh,* if we take each occurrence in order, as: "does," "done," "does," "observing," "made"). But thereby the intimate connection between human "ceasing" (Heb. *shabbat,* used eight times in this passage as proper noun and verb) and parallel divine action is severed. Retaining this connection is crucial for an understanding of Exodus as a whole; it will be noted at length below how "making," legitimate and illegitimate, is the key theme of the entire second half of the book. Its highlighting at the crucial juncture in Exodus 31—right before the Golden Calf episode—is most appropriate.

A final advantage of rhetorical translation may be cited here, with a brief example. The biblical text in general is highly allusive. It suggests interconnections of ideas and characters by isolating particular words or combinations of words, leaving the reader/listener free to make the connection if he or she wishes. A powerful example of this occurs near the beginning of the book. Baby Moshe, floating precariously yet fetuslike on the Nile, is one of the enduring images in Exodus, as children will attest. Modern English readers, however, are seldom aware that the Hebrew word for Moshe's floating cradle—rendered by virtually all standard translations as "basket"—is the same as the one used in Genesis 6:14ff. to describe Noah's famous vessel (*teva*). To preserve the connection between the two, as I have tried to do in Exodus with "little-ark" (and, incidentally, as the authors of the King James Version did with "ark"), is to keep open the play of profound meaning that exists between the two stories.

From the above examples it may appear that it is not difficult to carry out the Buber-Rosenzweig principles in a translation. In practice, however, the translator who wishes to bring the language spoken by his audience into consonance with the style of the Hebrew text runs the risk of doing violence to that language, forced as he or she is into "hebraizing."

There will of necessity be a certain strangeness and some awkward moments in such a translation. Buber and Rosenzweig themselves came under fire for creating a strange new kind of German; one critic in 1933 accused them of "unusual affectations." My own rendition of Genesis (*In the Beginning*, 1983), while limited in what it wreaks with the English language by both my cautiousness and the less pliable nature (than German) of English, has been liable to similar characterization.

This problem, however, is inherent in this kind of undertaking, and I have accepted its risks willingly. In the last generation there have been any number of clear, smooth-reading translations of the Bible, all aimed at making the text readily accessible to the reader. I have taken a different road, arguing (along with Buber and Rosenzweig) that the reader must be prepared to meet the Bible at least halfway and must become an active participant in the process of the text, rather than a passive listener. To this end, there is no alternative but to force the translated language to become the instrument through which the Hebraic voice of the text speaks.

Reading the Bible in the literary, rhetorical manner just explicated is grounded in certain assumptions about the text we have before us. I do not in my translation make extensive use of the by-now traditional division of the Pentateuch into clear-cut "sources" (termed J, E, P, and D by the Bible scholars of the past century), if only because this remains a theoretical construct. Indeed, the very enterprise of tracing the origins of discrete parts of a work of literature can be problematic, given that the work presents itself as a whole. That in the Torah we are dealing with a set of different traditions which have been artfully combined does seem clear; this can often explain contradictions and inconsistencies in the text. But the final product is more than the sum of its parts. While, therefore, I am not committed to refuting the so-called Documentary Hypothesis after the manner of such Bible scholars as Benno Jacob and Umberto Cassuto, I am most interested in focusing on biblical books as artistic wholes and in cautiously determining their structural integrity. Where the tools of conventional Bible scholarship are illuminating to the end—uncovering demonstrable cognates in other ancient Semitic languages, pointing out parallels between ideas and institutions of Israel and the ancient Near East, suggesting historical situations as the background to various stories and laws, consulting proposed solutions from the past to gnawing textual difficulties—they are useful and even crucial for the translator and the commentator. But one who is concerned with the text's message must also be prepared to press on, beyond the endless and ever-changing debates of conventional scholarship. *Now These Are the Names,* then, deliberately stays close to the basic Masoretic-type text of Exodus, that is, the vocalized text that has been with us for certain for only a millennium. Deviations from that text in the interest of solving textual problems are duly mentioned in the Notes. In following the traditional Hebrew text, I am presenting to the English reader a book that is not the product of a single author in the modern sense, but a book which nevertheless speaks with a certain inner integrity. Whether that is the inner integrity of the Exodus texts, narrative or legal, in their "original" settings—that is, in earlier, separate traditions—will probably never be determined by the methods of scholarship. (For a fuller discussion of these issues, see Greenstein 1985, and Kikawada and Quinn 1985.)

A number of readers of *In the Beginning,* the predecessor to this volume, have asked me to clarify the relationship of my translation to the Buber-Rosenzweig German editions (plural here because there were two editions of the Pentateuch, 1927 and 1930). This is easily done. From B-R I have taken the basic approach, as briefly sketched above: the general layout, attention to the rhythm and syntax of the Hebrew and the repetition of words and phrases, and a number of specific renderings. In some cases, which I have made it a point to note, I have retained the interpretation of B-R fully—either because I believe it to be correct or because I find their interpretation to be of special interest. In addition, I mention some of their readings in the Notes (as "B-R: . . .").

From this point, however, I have set out on another path. I have frequently departed from Buber's arranging of lines and major text divisions, relying on my own sense of sound and meaning; I have read many Hebrew verses differently from a syntactical point of view; and I have used different renderings of Hebrew words and phrases, based on more recent biblical and Semitic philology. In addition, I have indented purely poetic passages, something B-R did not generally do, and I have occasionally loosened the practice, sometimes overdone in B-R, of always reproducing a Hebrew root by a single translated equivalent.

Finally, I have included here the one element that many readers of B-R felt was sorely lacking: notes and commentary. Every translation of the Bible requires notes to explain choices and difficult passages; even more so, it requires a commentary to help bridge the gap between ancient text and modern reader. *Now These Are the Names* is the kind of work that especially requires such an apparatus—both to explain its translation technique and to show how it may fruitfully be used in explicating the text. Along with the translation itself, the explanatory material presents a methodology for studying and teaching the Bible.

This volume is therefore the child of B-R, with all the links and independent features that a parent–child relationship implies. It may be viewed as an attempt to bring the work of B-R into a new era of Bible scholarship, and as an artistic endeavor in its own right.

Now These Are the Names is heavily indebted to B-R, but there is also a contemporary context in which it may be viewed. One can now speak of a literary movement in Bible studies, a phenomenon which was fragmentary until a few years ago. From the early twentieth-century work of Cassuto, Buber, and Meir Weiss in Israel, and Benno Jacob in Germany, such literary Bible scholars in America as James Muilenberg (coiner of the term "Rhetorical Criticism"), Edwin Good, James Ackerman, and such literary critics as Robert Alter (United States) and Meir Sternberg (Israel) have produced full-scale analyses of biblical texts in the rhetorical vein. The list of responsible scholars in the field has grown to the point that, as of this writing, there is a whole new generation of scholars committed to complementing historical Bible study with the fruits of their labors. Many of their names and works appear in "Suggestions for Further Reading" at the end of this book. While my first volume in this project, *In the Beginning*, was pursued largely independent of parallel efforts, the present work has benefited much more directly from the work of colleagues. It is to be hoped that our work will not be seen as antagonistic to the old school of Bible research, but as the uncovering of another side of the Bible's meaning. As a number of scholars have stressed in recent years, it is only when the full spectrum of disciplines is brought to bear on the biblical text that we can begin to get an accurate picture of the totality and greatness of the literature that lies before us.

A final word needs to be said about the way in which I think these translations should be viewed by the reader. They are "performances" in the sense that they represent one person's view of a text over a relatively brief period of time. They are therefore provisional, part of an ongoing work of learning and teaching the text, just as a musician's performance of a particular piece is provisional and time-bound. Of course, what differentiates the translator from the musician is that the latter may change his or her interpretation from day to day, or at least from year to year, based on the experience of performing, whereas the former is fated by the exigencies of the printed word to have his or her performance frozen for a long time.

To what extent can any translation of the Bible be said to be more "authentic" than another? Because of lack of information about the various original audiences of our text, the translator can only try to be as faithful as the information will allow. This is particularly true where a work as universally known as the Bible is concerned. Even if the precise circumstances surrounding its writing and editing were known, the text would still be affected by the interpretations of the centuries. It is as if a Beethoven symphony were to be performed on period instruments, using nineteenth-century performance techniques: would it still sound as fresh and radical to us as it did in Beethoven's own day? Thus I would suggest that it is almost impossible to reproduce the Bible's impact on its contemporaries; all that the translator can do is to perform the task with as much honesty as possible, with a belief in his artistic intuition and a consciousness of his limitations.

Yet how is one to distinguish the point where explication ends and personal interpretation begins? From the very moment of the Bible's editing and promulgation, there began the historical process of interpretation, a process which has at times led to violent disagreement between individuals and even nations. Everyone who has ever taken the Bible seriously has staked so much on a particular interpretation of the text that altering it has become close to a matter of life and death. Nothing can be done about this situation, unfortunately, and once again the translator must do the best he can. Art, by its very nature, gives rise to interpretation—else it is not great art. The complexity and ambiguity of great literature invites interpretation, just as the complexities and ambiguities of its interpreters encourage a wide range of perspectives. The Hebrew Bible, in which very diverse material has been juxtaposed in a far-ranging collection spanning centuries, rightly or wrongly pushes the commentator and reader to make inner connections and draw overarching conclusions. My interpretations in this book stem from this state of affairs. I have tried to do my work as carefully and as conscientiously as I could, recognizing the problems inherent in this kind of enterprise. I hope the result is not too far from what the biblical editors had intended.

The best a new performance of a great work can hope to accomplish is to startle the audience into rehearing and rethinking the work and encourage them to probe it anew. It is in this spirit that *Now These Are the Names* is offered. I have approached my task in the hope that the reader here, like the concert-goer, will experience old sounds with new meaning and new pleasure, and that he or she will discover, as I have in the course of my work, the ongoing value in hearing and wrestling with the rich words of the book of Exodus.

EVERETT FOX

Brookline, Massachusetts
April 1986
Nisan 5746

ACKNOWLEDGMENTS

AS THE SECOND in a series of five books, *Now These Are the Names* has drawn nourishment from many of the same sources that were instrumental in launching the entire project. These sources have been acknowledged in the corresponding section of *In the Beginning*. Nevertheless, there are a number of individuals for whose input I am particularly grateful as regards the present volume.

Pride of place goes to Prof. Arthur Waskow, who in the summer of 1977 aggressively encouraged me to continue my translation work past Genesis. My wife, Cherie Koller-Fox, has continued in her role as my staunchest supporter and helped to keep me consistent with my own principles. I would also like to thank my son, Akiva Fox, for enabling me to see again the attraction and depth of meaning that the Exodus stories hold even for the very young; his siblings, Leora and Ezra, have helped as well in their own ways.

Professor Edward L. Greenstein served as special editor for this volume, going over my manuscript and making numerous helpful suggestions. Through his attention to detail, he has added to my information on Semitic linguistics and has kept me close to the Buber-Rosenzweig approach, sometimes against my initial inclinations. If his name appears at various times throughout this book, it is because I have come to share with him strong convictions about the nature and interpretation of biblical texts.

Bonny Fetterman of Schocken Books has been an ideal editor both for myself and for this project. She has been at once supportive, searching, and properly goading.

I am grateful to readers of *In the Beginning* who have had the kindness to voice their enthusiasm and their criticisms by telephone or letter. In addition, I have profited greatly from seminars and conferences at which, over the years, I have had the opportunity to present my translation and interpretation work-in-progress. These include the Society for Biblical Literature's Section on Narrative Research and the Conference for Alternatives in Jewish Education (CAJE); I should also mention stimulating experiences I have had lecturing at Wellesley, Swarthmore, and Kenyon Colleges. In that connection, I would like to thank Prof. Arthur Gold of Wellesley College, for helping to stimulate my rethinking of issues pertaining to oral literature.

There are several individuals whose ongoing support and interest I would particularly like to note: Cliff Anderson, Baruch Frydman-Kohl, and Craig Eisendrath. I would like to thank Mr. Louis Seligsberger for his help as a specialist in clarifying the Hebrew *tahash* in Exodus 25:25 and elsewhere. I also wish to note Prof. Nahum M. Sarna's graciousness in allowing me to see his manuscript of *Exploring Exodus*, the inclusion of which in the present Notes and Readings gives the reader a valuable tool for understanding important aspects of Exodus.

My last expression of acknowledgment, an explanation of the dedication, should normally be a joyous task, but instead is the most grievous of all the work that has gone into this volume. Paul Lichterman, attorney, teacher, and friend, died in a tragic accident on December 26, 1983. In him were combined many of the good and great qualities of which all religious literature speaks: a passionate concern for the oppressed; a love of sacred text; an appreciation of the music of ethnic traditions; an ability to direct prayer and to enter into it meaningfully; and finally, a deep feeling of connectedness to the solitude and strength experienced in Nature. He embodied the Hebrew Bible's ideal of involvement in this world in a way that connects to the Source of all life and values. What his family, friends, and associates received from him they will never lose, but what was lost with him can never be replaced.

TO AID THE READER

GIVEN the illustrious predecessors that any translator/interpreter of Exodus follows, I have not sought to provide here either a comprehensive commentary or an all-encompassing system of notes. Rather, I have tried to suggest some fruitful avenues for thought and discussion in the Commentary, and to provide such information in the Notes as will be helpful to the nonspecialist. Naturally, the selection of material for these purposes is entirely mine; others may single out different details and different aspects of the text.

Since I have espoused the "Rhetorical" approach to biblical texts in my work, I have decided to limit myself largely to literary remarks in the Commentary: indicating themes and motifs as they appear and are developed in Exodus and elsewhere in the Bible; pointing out structural aspects of the text; and treating issues of character development in the narrative. I have by and large eschewed historical issues, in the belief that these highly theoretical matters are treated comprehensively in the standard works such as Driver (1911), Childs (1974), and Sarna (1986). More detailed information on ancient Near Eastern parallels to Exodus can be found, for instance, in Cassuto (1967) and Sarna (1986). Readers whose interest is primarily archeological will also seek the appropriate works.

From the Table of Contents on, I have divided the text of the book into certain segments, large and small. These may or may not have been in the minds of the biblical writers and editors, but they are useful for an analysis of the book. The traditional chapter divisions are also somewhat artificial, the work of medieval Christian exegetes who took them from the Latin Vulgate. They have been retained so as not to deprive the reader of a universally accepted system of reference.

I have appended brief excurses on selected topics such as Moshe's Biography and the Plague Narrative to my introductions to various parts of the book to further focus on issues of importance that could not be treated adequately in Notes and Commentary.

The Notes themselves, which are keyed to specific verses, deal basically with textual matters. They are designed to convey both the richness and the difficulties of biblical Hebrew, and include the following:

—literary observations about small segments of text, often derived from the research of other scholars

—explanations of concepts or institutions through folklore or comparative study

—clarifications and nuances of specific Hebrew words and phrases

—elucidation of terms or ideas utilizing other biblical passages

—indications of difficult Hebrew syntax or obscure Hebrew words
("Heb. difficult")

—pointing out sound plays in the Hebrew, especially those I have been
unable to reflect in the English translation

—alternative translations that could have been used ("Or . . .")

—readings from other translations that are quite different from mine, or
otherwise interesting ("Others . . .")

—different readings of the Hebrew text (via emendation of vowels or
consonants, and based on the likelihood of scribal errors)

—traditional English renderings of Hebrew names ("Trad.
English . . .")

Authors referred to in the Notes and Commentary are listed, with the
appropriate works, in "Suggestions for Further Reading" at the end of
this book.

ON THE NAME OF GOD AND ITS TRANSLATION

THE PERSONAL NAME of the biblical God, which has been transcribed here by the letters YHWH, has undergone numerous changes in both its writing and translation throughout the history of the Bible. At an early period the correct pronunciation of the name was either lost or deliberately avoided out of a sense of religious awe. Jewish tradition came to vocalize and pronounce the name as "Adonai," that is, "the/my Lord," a usage that has remained in practice since late antiquity. Another euphemism, regularly used among Orthodox Jews today, is "Ha-Shem," literally, "The Name."

Historically, Jewish and Christian translations of the Bible into English have tended to use "Lord," with some exceptions (notably, Moffatt's "The Eternal"). Both old and new attempts to recover the "correct" pronunciation of the Hebrew name have not succeeded; neither the some-times-heard "Jehovah" nor the standard scholarly "Yahweh" can be con-clusively proven.

For their part, Buber and Rosenzweig sought to restore some of what they felt was the name's ancient power; early drafts of their Genesis trans-lation reveal a good deal of experimentation in this regard. They finally settled on a radical solution: representing the name by means of capital-ized personal pronouns. The use of YOU, HE, HIM, etc., stemmed from their conviction that God's name is not a proper name in the conventional sense, but rather one which evokes his immediate presence. Buber and Rosenzweig—both of whom wrote a great deal about their interpretation (see Buber 1958)—based it on their reading of Exodus 3:14, a text in which another verbal form of YHWH appears, and which they translated as "I will be-there howsoever I will be-there" (i.e., my name is not a magical handle through which I can be conjured up; I am ever-present). For more on this passage, and the name, see the Commentary and Notes in the text below.

The B-R rendering has its attractiveness in reading aloud, but it is on doubtful ground etymologically. It also introduces an overly male empha-sis through its constant use of "HE," an emphasis which is not quite so pronounced in the Hebrew. I have therefore decided to follow the practice of printed Hebrew Bibles, which leave the name YHWH unvocalized. As the translation is read aloud, the reader should pronounce the name according to his or her custom, or use one of the standard options found above, such as "the Lord." While the effect of this is jarring at first, it has the merit of approximating the situation of the text as we now have it, and of leaving open the unsolved question of the pronunciation and meaning of God's name.

Readers who are uncomfortable with the maleness of God in these texts may wish to substitute "God" for "he" in appropriate passages. While, as a translator, I am committed to reproducing the text as faithfully as I can, it is also true that the ancient Hebrews viewed God as a divinity beyond sexuality, and modern readers as well may see fit to acknowledge this.

GUIDE TO THE PRONUNCIATION
OF HEBREW NAMES

THE PRECISE pronunciation of biblical Hebrew cannot be determined with certainty. The following guide uses a standard of pronunciation which is close to that of modern Hebrew, and which will serve adequately for the purpose of reading the text aloud.

> *a* (e.g., Aharon, Mara) as in f*a*ther
> *e* (e.g., Levi, Elim) as the *a* in c*a*pe
> *o* (e.g., Yaakov, Moshe) as in h*o*rn
> *u* (e.g., Shur, Hur) as in B*u*ber

When *e* occurs as the second letter of a name (e.g., Yehuda, Betzalel), it is often pronounced like the *a* in *a*go.

> *kh* (e.g., Yissakhar) is to be sounded like the *ch* in Johann Sebastian Ba*ch*.
> *h* (e.g., Hur) most often indicates Hebrew *het*, pronounced less heavily than *kh* but not as the English *h*.

The system for transcribing Hebrew words used in this volume follows the above model, rather than standard scholarly practice (e.g., *karev* instead of *qrb*, *sharatz* instead of *šr.s*), in the interests of the general reader. For this reason, I also do not distinguish between the Hebrew letters *alef* (') and *ayin* (') in transcription.

Some names in the English text have kept their traditional English spelling; they refer to well-known terms whose familiarity might be missed. These include Israel (Heb. *Yisrael*), Pharaoh (*Par'o*), Sinai (*Seenai*), and Egypt (*Mitzrayim*). Otherwise, I have indicated the familiar English forms of biblical names in the Notes, under the rubric "Trad. English. . . ."

ON THE BOOK OF EXODUS AND ITS STRUCTURE

THE BOOK of Exodus is Israel's second book of origins. Genesis had concerned itself with the beginnings of the world, of human beings and their institutions, and of the people of Israel as a tribal family. Exodus continues this thrust as it recounts the origin of the people on a religious and political level (here inseparable as concepts). A number of biblical ideas receive their fullest early treatment in this book: God's acting directly in history; making himself "known" to both Israelites and foreigners; covenant as a reciprocal agreement between God and humans; law as an expression of total world view; and the use of sacred structure (Tabernacle or "Dwelling") as a vehicle for and expression of perceived truths about the world. In addition, several biblical institutions make their first appearance in Exodus: Passover, Sabbath, rudimentary leadership/government, and cult/priesthood. All this is presented in a general narrative framework, raising the question as to whether what we have here is story or history. Is Exodus a fanciful reconstruction of what happened to Moshe (Moses) and his generation, riddled with anachronisms? Or is it a faithful and reliable handing-down of eyewitness data which only the cynical or irreligious would doubt?

For the first position there are several supports. We possess virtually no extrabiblical references to the events recorded in our book, either in Egypt or elsewhere. Then, too, there seem to be inconsistencies of time within the story (Chapters 16 and 18 appear to presuppose laws which were given later), and patterns within the telling of the tale that are too symmetrical (the Plagues) or too stereotyped (the constant use of Deuteronomic language) to be simple reporting of fact. Finally, Exodus is lacking in the citation of personal and geographical names, especially as compared to the books that precede and follow (*Genesis* and *Numbers*).

For the second position, that of Exodus as a reliable historical record, there exist no methods of proof other than evaluation of literary form—that is, accepting that oral literature is able to preserve facts without later coloration. But even if it could be shown that Exodus is oral literature—an evaluation which is too sweeping, given the present form of the book—

modern scholarship has come to cast doubt on the absolute historical reliability of oral tradition (see Vansina 1965).

Despite these observations, there is still something unsettling about writing Exodus off as a work of fiction, however pious that fiction may have been. For the rest of the Hebrew Bible abounds in emotional references to the experience of the exodus. At every stage of biblical literature, that experience is invoked for the purpose of directing behavior (see especially Judges 2, I Samuel 8, II Samuel 7, II Kings 17, Nehemiah 9, and Psalm 78; and most of Deuteronomy is rhetorically grounded in it). The entire structure and emotional force of biblical law rest upon such exhortations as "A sojourner you are not to oppress:/ you yourselves know (well) the feelings of the sojourner,/ for sojourners were you in the land of Egypt" (Ex. 23:9) and such situations as that of the Hebrew serf (Ex. 21:1ff.). Apparently the experience of the exodus period was crucial in forming the group consciousness of the Israelites, and ever since it has provided a model from which both later Judaism and Christianity were to draw frequently and profoundly.

A hypothetical analogy, based on American history, may help to shed light on the historicity of Exodus. Imagine a book based on the following outline: first, a section on the American Revolution, with some biographical material on a few of the Founding Fathers, focusing mostly on the outbreak of the war and key battles; second, a description of the Constitutional Convention, including some of the more important speeches and discussions; third, the text of the Constitution itself; and finally, L'Enfant's original blueprints for the building of the new capital, Washington, D.C., interspersed with accounts of the first few presidents' inaugural addresses. What would be the underlying message of such a book? We are certainly dealing here with more than a straight journalistic description of the events, more than a legalistic discussion of constitutional law, and more than a technical presentation for architects. Such a book would actually be presenting the ideals of America's self-image: a nation founded on the willingness to fight for particular rights against Old World tyranny, established under democratic laws based on reason and providing governmental checks and balances, and whose ideals would be embodied in the construction of a brand-new, centrally located capital city that used classically grounded forms of architecture to express grace and reason as the basis for the new society.

Now this portrayal is very simplistic, but it gets its point across (and I would be willing to wager that, somewhere in this country, there exists a school textbook written along these lines). In a similar manner, although with much more weight given to God's role in the process, the book of Exodus unfolds. The dramatic story of Israel's deliverance from bondage, coupled with Moshe's own early development, is only the first part of the book, and accounts for less than half of it. It is followed by several stories of desert wanderings, and then by a presentation of the covenant made between God and Israel at Sinai, against a stunning natural backdrop. The second half of the book enumerates a series of laws which constitute the covenant, and the details of construction of a portable sanctuary designed both to symbolize and actually to accommodate God's presence among the Israelites (with the interruption of a major rebellion). So, like our theoretical American model, Exodus conveys far more than information about events. It is, rather, the narration of a world view, a laying out of different types of texts bearing the *meaning* of Israel's historical experience.

I stress the word "experience" because that is what is at stake here. Human memory is always selective. We remember what we wish to remember, giving weight to particular emotions, sometimes over and above the facts (or, as the poet Maya Angelou puts it autobiographically, "The facts sometimes obscure the truth"). The same thing appears to be true of group memory. What a people remembers of substance is not nearly as important as how they process their experience.

In our Exodus text one can perceive a characteristically Israelite process at work. The book emerges as a mix of historical recollection, mythical processing, and didactic retelling, what Buber and others have called a "saga." What is preserved in the book of Exodus, therefore, is a Teaching (Heb. *Torah*) based on a set of experiences, which became history for ancient Israel. Hence, to understand better the workings of the book, we need to turn to its themes and its structure. This will be more fruitful than trying to find the exact location of the Sea of Reeds or Mount Sinai, or the "Lost Ark," or Moshe's burial site—whose location "no man knows even today" (Deut. 34:6). These have all receded into archeological oblivion. What has survived of ancient Israel is its approach to history and to life, and its literature. In that sense, the book of Exodus is an attempt to distill history and to learn from it, using echoes from the past to shape the present and the future.

When we turn to a closer consideration of the structure of Exodus, we must proceed on the assumption that a work of art stems from both artful and unconscious design. Therefore, any structuring of such a book can only be hypothetical and must not limit itself to ironclad categories.

With that said, a number of potential divisions of our book present themselves. The first emerges from a close look at the subject matter of the text. Strikingly, Exodus appears to be arranged in groups of a few chapters each (bearing in mind that the chapter divisions are historically late), resulting in the following scheme:

1. Prologue in Egypt (Chap. 1)
2. Moshe's Early Life and Call (Chaps. 2–4)
3. Moshe's Mission in Egypt (5:1–7:13)
4. The First Nine Plagues (7:14–10:29)
5. The Tenth Plague and the Exodus (Chaps. 11–13)
6. In the Wilderness I: The Deliverance at the Sea (14:1–15:21)
7. In the Wilderness II: Early Experiences (15:22–18:27)
8. Covenant at Sinai (Chaps. 19–20)
9. The Terms (Laws) and Conclusion of the Covenant (Chaps. 21–24)
10. Details of the Tabernacle (Chaps. 25–27)
11. Details of the Cult (Chaps. 28–31)
12. Rebellion and Reconciliation (Chaps. 32–34)
13. The Building of the Tabernacle, Priestly Vestments (Chaps. 35–39)
14. Conclusion (Chap. 40)

Such a measured shifting of focus helps to maintain the flow of the text and our interest in it.

A glance through this list will also lead to the positing of larger structures. The traditions collected in Exodus fall naturally into both geographical and thematic divisions. The first part of the book takes place in Egypt (1:1–15:21), the second in the wilderness (15:22–40:38); this could alternatively be viewed as the events preceding Mount Sinai (Chaps. 1–17/18) and those that take place there (Chaps. 18/19–40). One could also combine the geographical and thematic aspects, resulting in the structure (1) Israel in Egypt (1:1–15:21), (2) Israel in the Wilderness (15:22–24:18), and (3) Tabernacle and Calf (Chaps. 25–40).

My own preference for structuring Exodus also combines these aspects, as follows:

I. The Deliverance Narrative (1:1–15:21)
II. In the Wilderness (15:22–18:27)
III. Covenant and Law (Chaps. 19–24)
IV. The Blueprints for the Tabernacle and Its Service (Chaps. 25–31)

V. Infidelity and Reconciliation (Chaps. 32–34)

VI. The Building of the Tabernacle (Chaps. 35–40)

These divisions exhibit a great deal of overlapping. In Part I, Israel's life in Egypt (Chap. 1) paves the way for Moshe's early years (Chaps. 2–4), then the account of his mission before Pharaoh and the Plagues (Chaps. 5–13), and the final victory (Chaps. 14–15); Part II is anticipated by some of what happens after the exodus itself (Chap. 14), and leads to Sinai (Chap. 19); the covenant and laws of Part III naturally lead to other prescriptions, this time the building instructions for the Tabernacle (Chaps. 25–31); planning the sacred structure in Part IV is followed by the making of a forbidden construction, the Golden Calf (Chaps. 32–33); and the reconciliation between God and Israel (Chap. 34) restores Israel's capacity to return to the actual building of the Tabernacle, and to complete it (Chaps. 35–40). So despite the presence of what must have been several very diverse traditions behind the final text of Exodus, it has been skillfully woven together to form a coherent whole. In addition to the above structures, it can be said that the book of Exodus rests on several textual backbones, inner structures and recurring themes and motifs that help to create a unified work. These may be listed by category:

1. There are various climaxes which serve to highlight the action—the Encounter at the Bush (Chaps. 3–4), the Tenth Plague and Exodus (12:29–42), the Deliverance at the Sea (14–15:21), the Revelation at Sinai (Chaps. 19–20), the Calf Episode (Chap. 32), and Completion of the Tabernacle (Chap. 40). Anchoring these dramatic scenes, at the center of the book, is the Sinai Revelation. The Binding of Yitzhak (Isaac) in Chapter 22 of Genesis serves much the same focusing function.

2. There exist three strategically placed accounts of God's Presence accompanying the Israelites (13:21–22, 24:15–18, 40:34–38) which share a common vocabulary. Key words in these passages are "move on," "day/ night," "cloud," "fire," "dwell," "Glory," "cover," "go up," and "in the eyes of the Children of Israel/before the people" (it should be noted that not every passage uses all of these terms). These words chart God's movement: first, following the Exodus; second, following the concluding of the covenant; and third, following the erection of the Tabernacle, at the end of the book. A variation of these Presence accounts occurs in Numbers 9:15–23, where it rounds out the picture—for it is at this point that the Israelites finally depart from Sinai (having spent about a year there), on their journey toward the Promised Land.

3. Several leading words recur throughout the book and give it a sense of unity:

serve—The Israelites pass from "servitude" to Pharaoh into the "service" of God; laws are given that warn against "serving" other gods, that specify how a "serf" is to be treated, and that detail the "service" (i.e., construction and dismantling) of a sanctuary where God is to be properly "served."

Glory—Liberated from Pharaoh's "stubbornness" (Heb. *koved lev*), the Israelites experience God's "Glory" (Heb. *kavod*) at the Sea of Reeds, and encounter it again at Sinai (Chap. 24) and when the Tabernacle is completed (Chap. 40). When Israel falters in Chapter 32, Moses begs to see God's "Glory" as a sign of reassurance. This is one of the central issues of the book, receiving its clearest formulation in Chap. 17:7—"Is YHWH in our midst, or not?" Without the accompanying Presence, the Israelites can survive neither in Egypt nor in the wilderness. That the book ends with the "Glory" taking up residence in the Tabernacle is a sign that all is well in this regard.

know—The Plagues and the liberation take place so that Egyptian and Israelite alike will acknowledge God as the true ruler (who "knows" the slaves' sufferings). The book as a whole portrays a God who is "known" by his compassion toward the oppressed.

see—God "sees" and rescues the people early in the book (Chap. 3); they "see" his deliverance at the sea (Chap. 14) and the awesome display at Sinai (Chaps. 19–20); the Tabernacle blueprint is given to Moshe to "see" (Chaps. 25ff.).

4. Aside from theme words, there are also several thematic threads that run through the book. These may be listed as well:

distinction—The Israelites learn what it is to be separated out, first for oppression and later for God's service. This process occurs during the Plagues and throughout the legal sections, which are often based on the making of distinctions (the Hebrew word for "holy," *kadosh*, may originally have had this connotation). In general, Exodus is a book that abounds in polarities and distinctions: between God and Pharaoh, life and death, slavery and freedom, Egyptianness and Israeliteness, city and wilderness, visible gods/magic and an invisible God who is not conjurable, doubt and trust.

construction—The Israelites are enslaved as builders of Egyptian cities; they go on to build a society, a calf-god, and a Tabernacle.

rebellion—From the beginning, God and Moshe are often unheeded, as the Israelites seek to maintain or return to their status as dependent slaves in Egypt (Chaps. 2, 5, 14, 15–17, 32).

Sabbath—As a newly freed people, Israel is to adapt to a rhythm of work and sacred cessation, which celebrates both creation and freedom. The Sabbath is at issue immediately after liberation (Chap. 16) and is commanded three times (Chaps. 20, 31, 35); and the account of the Tabernacle's completion echoes the vocabulary of God's completed creation in Genesis 2, a passage which serves as one justification for observing the Sabbath (see Ex. 20:11).

origins—We are told of the beginnings of the new covenant (distinct from that concluded with Abraham), the law system, the cult/priesthood, and the sacred calendar, but with the significant omission of the monarchy.

covenant—God establishes a relationship with the people of Israel: if they will obey him and observe his laws, he will protect them and treat them as his "firstborn son." This form of covenant is different from the ones in Genesis, and plays a significant role in subsequent books of the Bible.

God in History—The God of Exodus actively intervenes to rescue a people, defeating their oppressors in battle; he leads them through the wilderness, meets them, and makes a covenant with them.

5. The above themes are specifically Israelite themes. There are, however, motifs in Exodus that have a more universal ring. One could term these anthropological, since they employ standard aspects of human experience to convey the overall messages of the book.

Fire is used frequently and in varied contexts (at the Burning Bush and later back at Mount Sinai, in the desert trek, in the Tabernacle service, and at the Calf incident), usually to make a statement about God. In contrast to conventional fire gods (e.g., the Norse trickster Loki), the God of Exodus is most often associated with the more positive aspects of fire: constancy, purity, and transformation. The fire at Sinai does not destroy Moshe and the people, but rather turns them into something new. At the same time it should not be forgotten that fire is used regularly to connote anger in the Bible, especially God's, and especially in the later wilderness narratives.

Water appears throughout Exodus, not as a backdrop but as an active medium which most often signifies life and death simultaneously. The Nile, into which the enslaved Hebrews' babies are thrown, gently bears the infant Moshe to safety; the Nile, the giver of life in Egypt, is changed into blood, itself a major signifier of life in the Bible but useless here because it is undrinkable; the Sea of Reeds acts as a passageway of birth for the Israelites but as a graveyard for their Egyptian pursuers. The availability of water becomes a central issue in the wilderness, as an instrument for survival and for the testing of the Israelites' faith. Finally, water creates the ritual purity necessary for the people at Sinai and their priests in the Tabernacle to approach God.

Desert/Wilderness is the scene of the crucial second part of the book. Only in the desert, away from the massive influence of age-old Egyptian culture, can the new Israelite society be forged. Moshe, like many other real-life and fictional heroes, demonstrates this in his own early life. The desert acts as a purifying agent for him, changing the Egyptian prince into a member of his own true people. Similarly, the Israelites begin the process of transformation from bondage to self-rule, a process which is taught in the harsh reality of desert life and which will take an entire generation to complete.

In point of fact, all these media—fire, water, and desert—suggest change as a major concern of the book of Exodus. Our text chronicles the start of Israel's journey as a nation, a transformative journey which takes vastly changed circumstances, a whole generation in time, and indeed several books of recounting to complete. Exodus is very concerned with topography—not for the purposes of historical recollection (as Genesis was, apparently) but as an account of an inner journey. Thus the people travel to the boundary between Egypt and the desert, through the sea, to the great fiery mountain; and we know that they cannot but be on their way to a final goal. That goal, the Promised Land, will not be realized in Exodus, because in this book we stand only at the beginning of the journey. Change does not occur quickly, and the true molding of a people, like that of an individual, requires formative experiences over time. In Exodus, then, the People of Israel begins in adolescence, as it were. It has survived infancy in Genesis, a period marked by constant threats of physical extinction, and must now begin the tortuous process of learning to cope with adulthood—that is to say, peoplehood—in a hostile world.

That process will take us past the present text. Exodus stands at the beginning of a trilogy in the middle of the Torah. It takes us from slavery up to Sinai, inaugurating the law-giving process. Leviticus will concentrate almost exclusively on laws (of "holiness"), never budging geographically, while Numbers will see the conclusion of the Sinai experience and the traveling toward (and actually reaching) the land of Israel. Exodus is thus of great importance in the overall five-book pattern, introducing key

elements of the wilderness books: law, institutions, rebellion, and—
Moshe himself. It serves as a bridge between the great narratives of Genesis and the priestly code of Leviticus and the wanderings of Numbers
(Greenberg 1972 notes how the opening of Exodus points back, to Genesis
46; and the closing points forward, to Numbers 9). It in fact contains
elements of all three books.

Exodus is the basis not only of what follows in the Torah, but also sets
the stage for the rest of the Hebrew Bible. What Israel understood of its
God, and what that God expects of them, are set forth most directly and
unforgettably in the memories enshrined in the book of Exodus.

NOW THESE ARE THE NAMES

PART I The Deliverance Narrative (1–15:21)

T HE FIRST PART of the book of Exodus is presented as a continuation of the Genesis narratives, by abbreviating the genealogy of the immigrant Yaakov from Gen. 46:8–25. We find here the same centrality of God, the same kind of sparse but powerful biographical sketch of the human hero, and a narrative style similar to that of the previous book.

And yet Exodus introduces a new and decisive element into the Hebrew Bible, which becomes paradigmatic for future generations of biblical writers. The book speaks of a God who acts directly in history, blow by blow—a God who promises, liberates, guides, and gives laws to a people. This is, to be sure, an outgrowth of a God who brings the Flood and disperses the Babel generation, but it is also a decisive step forward from a God who works his will in the background, through intrafamily conflicts (which comprise most of Genesis). This deity frees his people, not by subterfuge, but by directly taking on Egypt and its gods. Pharaoh and the Nile, both of which were considered divine in Egypt, are in the end forced to yield to superior power. Surely it is no accident that the ending of Part I—the Song of Moshe at the Sea—hails YHWH as Israel's true king, a king whose acts of "leading," "redeeming," and "planting" his people are exultingly affirmed in the body of the Song.

Part I receives its structural coherence in a number of ways. For one, it encompasses a straight chronological narrative, moving from Israel's enslavement to its liberation and triumph over its oppressors. The ending, Chapter 15, is rhetorically and stylistically fitting (see Gaster 1969), celebrating as it does the mighty deeds of God. For another, Part I carefully paces its climaxes, building up from the Burning Bush to various stages of Plagues, to the Tenth Plague/exodus and finally the great scene at the sea. There are also a number of key words that help to tie together various sections of the narratives: "know," "serve," and "see." All of these go through interesting changes in meaning, through which one can trace the movement of central ideas (see the Commentary).

In the area of vocabulary, David Daube (1963) has made the interesting observation that the Deliverance Narrative uses a number of verbs that occur regularly in biblical law regarding the formal release of a slave: "send free" (Heb. *shale'ah*), "drive out," (*garesh*), and "go out" (*yatzo'*). In addition, the motif of the Israelites' "stripping" the Egyptians (3:22, 12: 36) links up with the regulation of release in Deut. 15:13. " . . . you are not to send him free empty-handed." Daube sees our text as bearing the stamp of Israelite social custom: Pharaoh is made to flout "established social regulations."

Finally, several scholars (Kikawada 1975, Ackerman 1974, Fishbane 1979, and Isbell 1982) have pointed out that the vocabulary of the first few chapters of the book foreshadows the whole of Part I. This use of sound and idea helps to create unity in these narratives (despite their possibly diverse origins), and is also of importance in viewing the biographical material in the first four chapters.

The Early Life of Moshe and Religious Biography

Dominating the early chapters of Exodus, more than the description of bondage itself, is the figure of the reluctant liberator, Moshe. The portrayal of his beginnings contrasts strongly with the classic hero stories of the ancient world.

This is not immediately apparent. Moshe's birth narrative parallels that of King Sargon of Akkad; his flight from Egypt and return as leader are reminiscent of Jephthah and David in the Bible, and of the Syrian king Idrimi (as recounted in Akkadian texts) as well. In addition, half a century ago Lord Raglan attempted to demonstrate common elements in hero biographies by compiling a list of up to thirty key motifs. Those relevant to Moshe include: the father a relative of the mother, an attempt made to kill him at birth, his escape through the action of others, being raised by foster parents, little information about his childhood, his traveling to his "future kingdom" upon reaching adulthood, promulgating laws, losing favor with the deity, dying on the top of a hill, not being succeeded by his children, and a hazy death/burial. Moshe therefore shares with Oedipus, Hercules, Siegfried, and Robin Hood, among others, a host of common elements; his point total according to Raglan's scheme puts him toward the top of the list as an archetypal traditional hero. It must be concluded that, far from being a factual account, his biography is composed largely of literary constructs.

When one looks closer at the biblical portrayal of Moshe, however, the purpose and particularly Israelite thrust of these constructs becomes clear. Almost every key element in Moshe's early life—e.g., rescue from death by royal decree, rescue from death by water, flight into the desert, meeting with God on the sacred mountain—foreshadows Israel's experience in the book of Exodus. The key theme of the distinction between Israel and Egypt, so central to the Plague Narrative and to Israelite religion as a whole, is brought out beautifully in the depiction of Moshe's development from Egyptian prince to would-be liberator to shepherd in the wilderness, the latter an ancestral calling (cf. Nohrnberg 1981, who also discusses Yosef as developing in exactly the opposite direction—from Israelite shepherd boy to Egyptian viceroy, complete with Egyptian appearance, wife, and name). What is important in these early chapters of Exodus, then, is not the customary focus on the young hero's deeds (e.g., Hercules strangling serpents in the cradle) or his fatal flaw (although there is a hint of this too!), but on what he shares with his people, or, more precisely, how he prefigures them.

Another aspect of these stories removes them from the usual realm of heroic biography. Elsewhere in the Bible, individual hero types are at least partially overshadowed by the true central "character": God. This appears to be true in Exodus as well. Moshe develops only so far; he recedes as a full-blown personality during the Plague Narrative, to emerge sporadically in later encounters with the people (e.g., Chapters 16 and 32–33; the portrait expands in the narratives of the book of Numbers). No wonder that later Jewish legend (and further, Christian and Muslim stories as well) found it necessary to fill in the tantalizing hints left by the biblical biographer, with sometimes fantastic tales. But in the Exodus text, it is God who holds sway. In this context, one is reminded that Israelite thinking had room neither for worship of human heroes nor interest in the biography of God (i.e., divine birth and marriage) on the model of surrounding cultures. The biblical portrayal of both God and Moshe has been reduced in our book to only such facts as will illuminate the relationship between Israel and its God. Thus we learn from the Moshe of Exodus much about the people themselves, and about prophecy (cf. Chaps. 3–4); from the God of Exodus, how he acts in history and what he demands of the people. More than that is not easily forthcoming from our text (interestingly, the Passover Haggadah picked up on the Bible's direction and all but omitted Moshe's name in the celebration of the holiday).

As we have suggested, later Jewish legend—some of which may actually be of great antiquity—sought to fill in various aspects of Moshe's life that are missing from the Exodus text. A perusal of Ginzberg (1937) will uncover rich legendary material, dealing with Moshe's childhood, family identity, experience in Midian and elsewhere as a hero. While this material does not always illuminate the biblical story, it does demonstrate how folk belief includes a need for heroes in the classic Raglan mold; the Midrashic portrait of Moshe corresponds nicely to what we find in other cultures.

Turning to stylistic characteristics of these early chapters, we may note that a good deal of repetition occurs, as if further to highlight the themes. Baby Moshe is saved from death twice; three times he attempts acts of opposing oppression; twice (Chaps. 2 and 5) he fails in his attempts to help his enslaved brothers; and twice (Chaps 3 and 6) God reassures him with long speeches that center around the Divine Name. This kind of continuity is artfully literary, but it is also an echo of real life, where people often live out certain themes in patterns.

Finally there is the matter of recurring words. Most important is the telling use of "see," from the loving gaze of Moshe's mother (2:2), through to the auspicious glance of Pharaoh's daughter (2:6), then to Moshe's sympathetic observing of his brothers' plight (2:11); all this seems to be linked to the episode at the Burning Bush, where God "is seen" by the future leader (3:2), and where the climax of this whole development takes place: God affirms that he has "seen, yes, seen the affliction of my people that is in Egypt . . . . and I have also seen the oppression with which the Egyptians oppress them" (3:7, 9). Thus Moshe's biography leads to, and is an outgrowth of, the people's own situation.

In sum, Moshe's early biography leads us to ponder the "growing up" process through which the people of Israel must pass on their way out of Egypt. The narratives that deal with his leadership of the people in the wilderness period, from Exodus 16 on, will help to round out our picture of him as a real personality, with the tragedies and triumphs that are a part of human life but magnified in the case of great individuals.

On the Journey Motif

World literature is dominated by stories involving a journey. More often than not, these tales are framed as quests for holy or magical objects (e.g., the Golden Fleece, the Holy Grail), or for eternal youth/immortality (Gilgamesh). The classic pattern, as Joseph Campbell (1972) has described it,

calls for the hero to make a kind of round trip, crossing dangerous thresholds (monsters, giants, unfriendly supernatural beings) both on the way
toward the goal and on the way home. Either at the middle or at the end of
the journey stands the goal, which often entails meeting with the divine
and/or obtaining a magical or life-giving object (e.g., the Golden Fleece).

Such stories mirror our own longings for accomplishment and accep-
tance, as well as our universal desire to overcome the ultimate enemy,
Death. In the hero's triumphs, we triumph; his vanquishing of death
cathartically becomes our own.

This mythic substructure has penetrated the biblical tales, but it has
been toned down for human protagonists, to suppress the idea of the
mortal hero in favor of the divine one. Thus all the Patriarchs except
Yitzhak (Isaac) go on fateful long journeys (his is reserved for the three-
day trip to Moriah in Genesis 22), yet there is none of the color and
adventure that we find, for example, in Greek mythology. Outside of
Yaakov's encounter with the mysterious wrestler in Genesis 32, there is
little in Genesis to suggest hero tales on the classic mold. In Exodus, too,
Moshe makes a significant journey—to Midyan—one might say, within
himself, to find his true identity and calling, but it is highly muted,
containing virtually no details. The round trip contains two thresholds of
death, with Moshe first threatened by Pharaoh's justice (2:15) and, on the
way back to Egypt, by God himself (4:24–26). The initial goal is attained
at the "mountain of God" "behind the wilderness," where, meeting with
divinity amid fire, he is finally able to integrate his own past, present, and
future (as he will return to this mountain with the entire people in Chaps.
19ff). At the Burning Bush, the Egyptian prince, the Israelite shepherd,
and the Hebrew liberator coalesce, investing Moshe with unique qualifica-
tions for his task.

But it is to a larger journey framework that we must look to understand
the "hero" content of Exodus, and with it, that of the Torah as a whole.
The major journey undertaken is, of course, that of the people of Israel,
from slavery to Promised Land. It is also a journey from death to life, from
servitude to god-king to the service of God as king; along the way, death
serves to purify an entire generation. And yet even this most obvious of
journey stories differs markedly from those of gods and heroes so familiar
in Western culture. The people of Israel function as a collective antihero,
an example of precisley how *not* to behave. They play no active role
whatsoever in their own liberation, use neither brawn nor wits to survive
in the wilderness, constantly grumble about wanting to return to Egypt,

and at both Sinai and the threshold of the Promised Land (in the book of
Numbers), their chief form of behavior is first fear and later rebellion.

Moshe's own journeys parallel those of the entire people later on. Like
them, he flees from Pharaoh into the wilderness, meets God at flaming
Sinai, and has trouble accepting his task but must in the end. Here is
where Moshe shines as the true leader: he epitomizes his people's experience and focuses and forges it into something new.

Moshe Before Pharaoh: The Plague Narrative (5–11)

The heart of the Exodus story sets out the confrontation between the
visible god-king, Pharaoh, who embodies the monumental culture of
Egypt, and the invisible God of Israel who fights for his ragtag people.
The drama is conveyed by means of alternating conversations/confronta-
tions and events. The narrator has built his account, bracketed by the
early approach of Moshe and Aharon (Aaron) to Pharaoh, which fails
(Chap. 5), and the extended construct of the Tenth Plague (11–13); in
between fall the schematically arranged first nine plagues.

Three overall stages characterize this latter section. The first is indicated
by the oft-repeated demand, "Send free my people, that they may serve
me!"; the second is the "hardening" of Pharaoh's heart; and the third, the
unleashing of each plague. Further, it can be shown that the plagues are
presented via a variety of structures and substructures (see Greenberg
1969 and the chart in Sarna 1986). Some commentators divide them into
five thematic groups of two apiece—1 and 2, the Nile; 3 and 4, insects; 5
and 6, disease; 7 and 8, airborne disaster; and 9 and 10, darkness/death
(Plaut 1981). Also fruitful is the following threefold division: 1, 4, and 7,
God's command to confront Pharaoh in the morning; 2, 5, and 8, God
says, "Come to Pharaoh"; 3, 6, and 9, no warning is given to Pharaoh. Yet
another grouping of themes is possible (Bar Efrat 1979): 1–3, God vs. the
magicians of Egypt; 4–6, stress on the distinction between Israel and
Egypt; 7–9, the most powerful plagues.

This utilization of order, symbolized by "perfect" numbers such as 3
and 10, finds a parallel in the creation story of Genesis 1 (where the key
number, of course, is 7, 3 + 3 + 1, whereas here we have 3 + 3 + 3 + 1).
Both texts display a desire to depict God as one who endows nature and
history with meaning. The poetic tradition about the plagues, as represented, for instance, by Psalm 78, was content to describe the plagues in
brief, within the setting of a single poem. The narrator of the Pentateuchal
traditions, however, has a different point to make, and structured exposi-
tion is the best way to do it.

There is another structural tendency that one may observe in the Plague Narrative. Repeating words and motifs comprise over twenty shared and discrete elements in the story. Since the vast majority of these occur by the end of the fourth plague, this leaves the narrator free to develop plagues 7 and 8 with particular intensity, using a full palette of descriptions, with the addition of the theme that these were the worst of their kind ever to take place in Egypt. It will be useful here to list a few of the key words and phrases, and motifs, that can be found in the Plague Narrative:

Words/phrases: Go to Pharaoh; send . . . free; know; throughout the land of Egypt; plead; distinguish; tomorrow; man and beast; not one remained; heavy [i.e., severe] as YHWH had said.

Motifs: Moshe's staff; Aharon as agent; magicians; death.

It is important to note here that the structuring of the plagues is not a perfectly balanced one. The narrative varies between exact repetition of elements and phrases and nonrepetition (Licht 1978). By thus using sounds and ideas in variation, the narrator is able to weave a tale whose message constantly reinforces itself, and which holds the audience's attention without getting tedious.

I have deliberately omitted the question of Pharaoh's heart above, as a separate issue. A host of expressions is used in the text to describe Pharaoh's stubbornness: "harden" (Heb. *hiksha*), "make heavy-with-stubbornness" (*hakhbed*), and "strengthen" (*hehezik/hazzek*), with the resultant "refused" and "did not hearken." This motif is the only one that occurs in all nine plagues, and therefore stands at the very heart of our narrative. When one notes the pattern within—that Pharaoh does the hardening at the beginning, God at the end—the intent begins to become clear. The Plague Narrative is a recounting of God's power, and Pharaoh's stubbornness, which starts out as a matter of will, eventually becomes impossible to revoke. The model is psychologically compelling: Pharaoh becomes trapped by his own refusal to accept the obvious (in biblical parlance, to "know"). Despite the prophetic idea that human beings can be forgiven, we find here another one—that evil leads to more evil, and can become petrified and unmovable.

A final note about the backdrop of these stories. Cecil B. DeMille did it differently, and in the difference lies the gap between Western culture and biblical culture. In the movie *The Ten Commandments* (a strange title, given the actual content of the film!), DeMille's own 1956 remake of his earlier silent film, great stress is put on the physical, visual trappings of Pharaoh's court. Apparently no expense was spared to bring in costumes, sets, and extras, and the result causes the audience to focus on the splendor of Egyptian culture, despite the fact that it is peopled by the villians of the story. In contrast, the Bible says practically nothing about the visual backdrop of the Plague Narrative. Just as Genesis made reference to the mighty culture of Babylonia by parodying it (for instance, in the Babel story of Chapter 11), Exodus strips down Egyptian culture by making it disappear, and by ridiculing its gods. The book saves descriptive minutiae for the Tabernacle (Chaps. 25ff.), preferring to stress the positive and simply to omit what it found as negative. This profoundly "anticultural" stance (see the intriguing analysis by Schneidau 1976) was characteristic of Israel's world view and was a mystery to the Greeks and Romans who centuries later conquered the land; it was to stand the people of Israel in good stead in their wanderings through the centuries.

1:1 Now these are the names of the children of Israel coming to Egypt,
    with Yaakov, each-man and his household they came:
2 Re'uven, Shim'on, Levi and Yehuda,
3 Yissakhar, Zevulun and Binyamin,
4 Dan and Naftali, Gad and Asher.
5 So all the persons, those issuing from Yaakov's loins, were seventy persons,
    —Yosef was (already) in Egypt.

6 Now Yosef died, and all his brothers, and all that generation.
7 Yet the Children of Israel bore fruit, they swarmed, they became many, they grew powerful—exceedingly, yes, exceedingly;
    the land filled up with them.

8 Now a new king arose over Egypt, who had not known Yosef.
9 He said to his people:

Prologue in Egypt (1): Rather than being presented as a totally separate story, the book of Exodus opens as a continuation of the Genesis saga. This is true both specifically and generally: the first five verses echo and compress the information about the descent of Yaakov's family into Egypt that was given in Gen. 46:8–27, while "Now these are the names" (v.1) recalls the oft-repeated formula "Now these are the begettings," which forms the structural background of Genesis. At the same time one might note that the main subject matter of our chapter, life and death (or, threatened continuity), is central to the thematic content of Genesis (see my *In the Beginning*, "On the Book of Genesis and Its Structure").

Kikawada (1975) and Ackerman (1974) have shown that the opening chapters of Exodus reflect other Genesis material as well. For instance, the five verbs in verse 7 mirror the language of creation (Gen. 1:28 and 9:1–2),

1:1 **children of Israel:** Or "sons," though it should be noted that the Hebrew *b'nei* can denote members of a group in general, not just family. In this verse, "children" has been printed with a lowercase "c"; by verse 7 the whole expression comes to mean a nation, and so a capital "C" has been utilized (Hebrew writing does not make this distinction). **Yaakov:** Trad. English "Jacob."

2–4 **Re'uven, Shim'on, Levi, Yehuda, Yissakhar, Zevulun, Binyamin, Dan, Naftali, Gad, Asher:** Trad. English "Reuben, Simeon, Levi, Judah, Issachar, Zebulun, Benjamin, Dan, Naphtali, Gad, Asher."

5 **issuing:** The same Hebrew verb (*yatzo'*) is later used to describe the Israelites' "going out" of Egypt (e.g., 12:31, 41). **loins:** A figurative expression denoting the genitals. **seventy:** A number expressing perfection or wholeness in the thought of many ancient cultures; see Gen. 46:8–27 for the original passage.

6 **Now Yosef died . . . :** Note the rhythmic lilt of this verse; such devices are often used in biblical style when a key event is portrayed. **Yosef:** Trad. English "Joseph."

7 **Yet:** Despite the disappearance of the politically influential generation of Yosef, the Israelites' success continues (Cassuto 1967). **swarmed:** This verb is usually applied to animals (see Gen. 1:20) (Greenberg 1969). Here the term is positive, as part of God's plan; shortly, it will carry a negative connotation for Pharaoh. **grew powerful:** Others, "grew numerous." This reflects the promise of God to Avraham in Gen. 18:18 (to become "a powerful nation") (Keil and Delitzsch 1968).

8 **a new king:** His name is not given, even though later biblical books do refer to foreign rulers by name. This is perhaps another example of the biblical text's playing down history in favor of stressing the story and its lesson. **who had not known Yosef:** Just as his successor will say "I do not know YHWH" (5:2), and will continue the oppression begun here.

9 **his people . . . this people:** Pharaoh states the case as the conflict between one national entity and another.

Here, (this) people, the Children of Israel, is many-more
numerous and powerful than we!

10 Come-now, let us use-our-wits against it,
lest it become many-more,
and then, if war should occur,
it too be added to our enemies
and make war upon us
or go up away from the land!

11 So they set gang-captains over it, to afflict it with their
burdens.
It built storage-cities for Pharaoh—Pitom and Ra'amses.

12 But as they afflicted it, so did it become many, so did it
burst forth.
And they felt dread before the Children of Israel.

13 So they, Egypt, made the Children of Israel subservient with
crushing-labor;

14 they embittered their lives with hard servitude in loam and
in bricks and with all kinds of servitude in the field—
all their service in which they made them subservient with
crushing-labor.

15 Now the king of Egypt said to the midwives of the Hebrews
—the name of the first one was Shifra, the name of the
second was Pu'a—

16 he said:
When you help the Hebrew women give birth, see the supporting-stones:
if he be a son, put him to death,
but if she be a daughter, she may live.

where a similar vocabulary of fecundity signals the divine desire to "fill the
earth." It is as if Israel's "becoming many" in Exodus fulfills the plan of
history inaugurated at creation, at the same time reminding us of God's
promise to Avraham, to make his descendants as numerous "as the stars in
the heavens and [as] the sand that is on the shore of the sea" (Gen. 22:17).

This leads to the predominant issue of Chapter 1: Pharaoh's paranoid
fears about Israel's growth. What for God was a sign of blessing (cf. the
"swarming" of creatures in Gen. 1:20f.) is for Pharaoh a sign of disaster, a
feeling of being overwhelmed by what is alien. The birth of the Israelite

nation is thus placed in a vivid context, completely physical in its description. And because birth, and not the economic aspects of slavery, is central, the actual description of the oppression of the Hebrews has been reduced to a bare minimum here. Contrary to DeMille's spectacular and stereotyped portrayal of the Israelites' sufferings, the Bible limits itself to a few brief verses in the early chapters of the book. The same holds true for parallel depictions of bondage in biblical literature, such as Psalms 78 and 105. It is the experience of being a stranger in Egypt that the Bible has chosen to focus on, rather than on the horrors of slave labor.

In Exodus, the Egyptians cannot stand having aliens among them (this theme has already appeared in Genesis regarding their eating habits—see Gen. 43:32); they dread their presence and fear their increase. A natural plan of attack, to stem the human tide, is genocide. Ironically, because of his fear of war Pharaoh concentrates his worries around the males, ignoring the true source of fecundity. And it is the women in these chapters, as

10 **use-our-wits:** Others, "We must be prudent," "Let us deal shrewdly."
it: The shift from plural to singular to refer to a plural object is not unusual in biblical parlance. **added:** Heb. *nosaf*, like Yosef (Joseph), whose name is interpreted as "May God add . . . another son" at his birth in Gen. 30:24. **go up away:** Heb. unclear.

11 **afflict:** Or "oppress." **Pharaoh:** Heb. *Par'o*. This is an Egyptian title, "(Lord of) the Great House," and not a proper name. One could justifiably translate, as some do, "*the* Pharaoh."

12 **so . . . so:** Heb *ken . . . ken*. Ackerman (1974) interprets this as a rhyming retort to Pharaoh's earlier *pen* ("*lest* he become many more") in 1:10. **burst forth:** The verb (Heb. *parotz*) is connected to fertility and wealth in Genesis (e.g., 28:14).

13 **crushing-labor:** A rare Hebrew word, here translated according to early rabbinic tradition, *perekh* is used rhetorically three times in Leviticus 25 (vv. 43, 46, and 53), where the Israelites are given laws about how to deal with their impoverished countrymen (v.43, "you are not to oppress him with crushing-labor").

14 **in the field:** In Egyptian accounts, the phrase indicates hard labor. **all their service . . . :** The Hebrew syntax is difficult. Here the phrase is taken as the object of "they embittered."

15 **midwives of the Hebrews:** The ambiguity of this phrase raises an ancient question: were they Hebrew or Egyptian? The names seem Semitic (and hence un-Egyptian); then, too, the use of "Hebrew" in the Bible usually occurs when a foreigner is talking about Israelites. Yet the women's answer is verse 19 suggests that they are in fact Egyptians. Abravanel notes that Hebrew women would not be likely to kill Hebrew babies.

16 **supporting-stones:** Some suggest that these were stools or other objects on which to support women in labor, while others see them as a reference to the testicles of the newborn males.

17 But the midwives feared God,
    and they did not do as the king of Egypt had spoken to
        them,
    they let the (male) children live.
18 The king of Egypt called for the midwives and said to them:
    Why have you done this thing, you have let the children
        live!
19 The midwives said to Pharaoh:
    Indeed, not like the Egyptian (women) are the Hebrew
        (women),
    indeed, they are lively:
    before the midwife comes to them, they have given birth!
20 God dealt well with the midwives.
    And the people became many and grew exceedingly power-
        ful.
21 It was, since the midwives feared God, that he made them
        households.
22 Now Pharaoh commanded all his people, saying:
    Every son that is born, throw him into the Nile,
    but let every daughter live.

2:1 Now a man from the house of Levi went and took (to wife) a
        daughter of Levi.
  2 The woman became pregnant and bore a son.
    When she saw him—that he was goodly, she hid him, for
        three months.

many commentators have pointed out (see Exum 1983), who play the
major role in beginning the liberation process. The midwives accomplish a
successful coverup; Moshe's mother and sister, and Pharaoh's daughter,
save the future liberator's life. "If she be a daughter, she may live" (v. 16),
along with four other occurrences of "live" in verses 17–22, underscore
the irony and the certainty of Israelite survival. The use of women—a
group that was often powerless in ancient societies—in these stories makes
the eventual victory of the Israelites all the more striking from a traditional
patriarchal point of view (see Ackerman 1982); the motif returns a number
of times in Israelite literature, as with Jael and Judith.
    Failing in his commissioning of special agents (midwives) to carry out
his genocidal plan, Pharaoh finally must enlist "all his people" (v.22), and

shift the scene to a cosmic setting, the Nile. The stage is thus set for the birth, endangering, and rescue of Moshe.

The historically minded reader may ask: Why would the ruler of a society that is (literally) built on slavery destroy his own workforce? Two answers are possible. First, the story is tied to Chapter 2, the survival of Moshe, and thus must be told to that end (a threat to males). Second, the story does not describe a rational fear, but paranoia—paralleling the situation in Nazi Germany of the of the 1930s and 1940s, where Jews were blamed for various economic and political catastrophes not of their own making and were eliminated from a society that could have used their resources and manpower.

Moshe's Birth and Early Life (2:1–22): Picking up from the last phrase of Chapter 1, "let every daughter live," Chapter 2 opens as a story of three daughters (the word occurs six times here), Moshe's real and foster mothers and his sister.

It has long been maintained that the story of Moshe's birth is a classic "birth of the hero" tale, sharing many features with other heroes of antiquity. (See pp. 4ff.) The parallel most often drawn is that of Sargon of Akkad, whose birth story is set in an era before Moshe but was written

17 **feared:** Worshipped or held in awe. This may be a sound-play on "see" in verse 16: *va-yire'u* ("feared") resembles *va-yir'u* ("saw").

19 **lively:** Another form of the Hebrew would mean "animals," and so B-R combined the two ideas in rendering the word as "lively-like-animals."

20–21 **And the people . . .:** The order here seems confused. "And the people . . ." is perhaps out of place, although the thought is not inappropriate for the context.

22 **all his people:** Specialists (the midwives) are not equal to the task of checking the Israelite population explosion, and so the whole Egyptian population must now be enlisted. **Nile:** Heb. *ye'or*, Egyptian *itrw*, "the great river" (cf. Heb. *ha-nahar ha-gadol*, with the same meaning, used for the Euphrates in Gen. 15:18 etc.).

2:1 **a man . . . a daughter:** Moshe's parents are anonymous, unlike the usual king and queen of the hero myth found in other cultures. The namelessness of all the secondary characters in this chapter—sister, Pharaoh's daughter and her maids—helps us to focus on the protagonist and on his name.

2 **she saw him—that he was goodly:** The parallel in Genesis is "God saw the light: that it was good" (Gen. 1:4). **goodly:** Handsome (so Ibn Ezra, among others), although others interpret the Hebrew *tov* as "healthy," given the context. What is important is the Genesis connection just mentioned. **three months:** Another "perfect" number, which will recur with the Israelites' three-month trip to Mount Sinai (see, 19:1).

3 And when she was no longer able to hide him,
   she took for him a little-ark of papyrus,
   she loamed it with loam and with pitch,
   placed the child in it,
   and placed it in the reeds by the shore of the Nile.
4 Now his sister stationed herself far off, to know what would
      be done to him.

5 Now Pharaoh's daughter went down to bathe at the Nile,
   and her girls were walking along the Nile.
   She saw the little-ark among the reeds
   and sent her maid, and she took it.
6 She opened (it) and saw him, the child:
   here, a weeping boy!
   She pitied him, and she said:
   One of the Hebrews' children is this!
7 Now his sister said to Pharaoh's daughter:
   Shall I go and call a nursing woman from the Hebrews for
      you,
   that she may nurse the child for you?
8 Pharaoh's daughter said to her:
   Go!
   The maiden went and called the child's mother.
9 Pharaoh's daughter said to her:
   Have this child go with you and nurse him for me,
   and I myself will give you your wages.
   So the woman took the child and she nursed him.

down later; similar elements include being separated from the real parents
through a death threat, and being set adrift on the river. Hallo (in Plaut
1981) cites other parallels in Hittite and Egyptian literature, noting at the
same time that "none of them includes all of the elements of the Moses
birth legend."

   If, as I maintained in the introduction ("On the Book of Exodus and Its
Structure"), most of this material has been collected for didactic and not
for historical purposes, we are entitled to ask what this story was intended
to teach. It cannot simply be written off as an attempt to explain away
Moshe's name and origins. Two elements seem crucial. First, the text as
we have it centers around the activity of women—giving birth, hiding,
watching and adopting Moshe. The female principle of life-giving tri-

umphs over the male prerogatives of threatening and death-dealing; the
Nile, source of all life in Egypt, births another child. Second, the story
and its continuation to the end of the chapter set up Moshe as a man of two
sides: Hebrew and Egyptian. He is at once archetypal victim (of Pharaoh's
death decree) and archetypal collaborator, growing up, as he apparently
does, in Pharaoh's palace. What are we to make of this two-sided fate and
personality? It may well have been intended as a reflex of the people of
Israel itself. Often in the Hebrew Bible the hero's life mirrors that of Israel
(see Greenstein 1981), and the case of Moshe is a good example. Moshe
develops into a Hebrew—that is, he eventually recovers his full identity.
This is accomplished, first, through his empathy with and actions on
behalf of "his brothers" (vv.11, 12), then through his exile from Egypt,
and finally through the purifying life in the wilderness as a shepherd.
Thus Moshe's personality changes are wrought by means of separations,
and the same process will characterize the coming Plague Narrative (with
its emphasis on "distinction" between Egypt and Israel) and the entire
Israelite legal and ritual system, which stresses holiness and separation.

The first section of the chapter (vv.1–10) uses a number of repeating
words: "take" appears four times, indicative of divine protection; "child,"

3 **little-ark:** The term used to designate the little basket/boat, *teva*, has
clearly been chosen to reflect back to Noah's ark in Genesis. The implication is that just as God saved Noah and thus humanity from destruction by
water, so will he now save Moshe and the Israelites from the same.
papyrus: A material that floats; it was also used in biblical times for
writing, including biblical texts.   **in the reeds:** Another foreshadowing;
when Moshe grows up, he will lead the liberated people through the Sea of
Reeds. The word *suf* (reeds) appears to be a loan-word from Egyptian.

4 **to know:** Better English would be "to learn." This first occurrence of the
Hebrew word *yado'a* foreshadows the later theme of the Egyptians' and
the Israelites' coming to "know" (or "acknowledge") God's power. For
the moment, and in the story that follows, the issue is one of revealing
information—Moshe's fate (2:4) and the discovery of his crime (2:14).

5 **Pharaoh's daughter:** Her station is important, for it enables Moshe to be
saved and to be brought up in the Egyptian palace (useful both for his
political future and for literary irony of situation).   **girls:** Maidservants.

6 **She opened . . . boy!:** The emphatic, halting syntax of the narrative
brings out the visual drama of seeing, taking, opening, and identifying.
One of the Hebrews' children: How does she know that? The simplest
explanation lies in the situation itself and not in any identifying marks.
Who else but a Hebrew, under the threat of losing her baby, would set
such a child adrift?   **is this:** Or "must this be."

8 **Go:** In biblical Hebrew, a verb repeated from a question is the equivalent
of "Yes," for which there was no other expression.

10 The child grew, she brought him to Pharaoh's daughter,
    and he became her son.
    She called his name: Moshe/He-Who-Pulls-Out;
    she said: For out of the water *meshitihu*/I-pulled-him.

11 Now it was some years later, Moshe grew up;
    he went out to his brothers and saw their burdens.
    He saw an Egyptian man striking a Hebrew man, (one) of
        his brothers.
12 He turned this-way and that-way, and seeing that there was
        no man (there),
    he struck down the Egyptian
    and buried him in the sand.
13 He went out again on the next day, and here: two Hebrew
        men fighting!
    He said to the guilty-one:
    For-what-reason do you strike your fellow?
14 He said:
    Who made you chief and judge over us?
    Do you mean to kill me
    as you killed the Egyptian?
    Moshe became afraid and said:
    Surely the matter is known!

15 Pharaoh heard of this matter and sought to kill Moshe.
    But Moshe fled from Pharaoh's face and settled in the land
        of Midyan;
    he sat down by a well.

seven times (Greenberg 1969); and "see," which as I have mentioned, will
recur meaningfully in Chapter 3. There is also a threefold motif of death
threat in the chapter: at birth, on the Nile, and at the hand of the avenging
Pharaoh. Isbell (1982) notes several items of vocabulary (e.g., "deliver,"
"feared," "amidst the reeds") that return in the victory account at the Sea
of Reeds (Chap. 14).

    From the other two accounts here (vv. 11–14 and 15–22), we learn all we
need to know about Moshe's early personality: he is Hebrew-identifying
but Egyptian-looking; concerned with justice, but impetuous and violent
in pursuit of that goal. It is also ominous that his first contacts with the

Israelites end in rejection, since that will so often be his experience with
them later on. The doubly unsatisfactory situation of confused identity
and impetuous means must be rectified, and it is exile that accomplishes
it. The Midianite wilderness transforms Moshe into shepherd, foreigner,

10 **grew:** His age is not mentioned, but weaning may be inferred (cf. Gen.
   21:8) as the appropriate boundary, and hence the child was probably
   around three (DeVaux 1965).   **he became her son:** A formulaic expression for legal adoption.   **Moshe/He-Who-Pulls-Out:** Trad. English
   "Moses." *Mss* is a well-attested name in ancient Egypt, meaning "son of"
   (as in Ra'amses—"son of Ra"—in Ex. 1:11). Thus it is quite appropriate
   that Pharaoh's daughter names her adopted son in this manner. However,
   there is an explicit irony here, as Buber (1958) and others have pointed
   out. The princess, in a Hebrew folk etymology (one based on sound rather
   than on the scientific derivation of words), thinks that the name Moshe
   recalls her act of "pulling out" the baby from the Nile. But the verb form
   in *moshe* is active, not passive, and thus it is Moshe himself who will one
   day "pull out" Israel from the life-threatening waters of both slavery and
   the Sea of Reeds.
11 **some years later:** Heb. *yamim*, lit. "days," can mean longer periods of
   time, and often years. Here the narrative skips over what it considers
   unimportant, and we are presented with a young man, who already has
   strong identity and opinions.   **his brothers:** Occurring twice in this
   verse, this phrase can only mean that Moshe was aware of his background,
   and concerned with the plight of the Israelites (Heb. *r'h b-*, "see" with a
   specific preposition, indicates not only observation but sympathy).
12 **no man (there):** Although some have interpreted this as "no man around
   to help," the expression taken in context would seem to indicate that
   Moshe was afraid of being seen. This incident reveals Moshe's concern
   and early leanings toward being a liberator, but also demonstrates his
   youthful lack of forethought. In fact, it will take God, not Moshe's own
   actions, to set the liberation process in motion.   **struck down:** This is the
   same verb (Heb. *hakkeh*) that the narrator used in verse 11 to describe the
   fatal beating received by the Israelite slave.
13 **Hebrew men fighting:** A rhyme in Hebrew, *anashim 'ivriyyim nitzim.*
14 **Who made you chief . . .:** One hears here echoes of Moshe's later experiences with his "hard-necked" people, which commences in the book of
   Exodus (Greenberg 1969).   **judge:** Or "ruler." I have retained "judge"
   here in order not to lose the connection with 5:21.
15 **Moshe fled . . . and settled:** The details about what must have been a
   psychologically important journey are not spelled out, as the narrative
   rushes toward its first great climax in Chapter 3. More important than the
   journey motif is that of exile, brought out tellingly in verse 22.   **settled . . . sat:** Adding the "settle down" of verse 21, we hear a threefold
   use of *yashov*, perhaps to stress Moshe's new life.

16 Now the priest of Midyan had seven daughters;
   they came, they drew (water) and they filled the troughs,
   to water their father's sheep.
17 Shepherds came and drove them away.
   But Moshe rose up, he delivered them and gave-drink to
      their sheep.
18 When they came (home) to Re'uel their father, he said:
   Why have you come (home) so quickly today?
19 They said:
   An Egyptian man rescued us from the hand of the shepherds,
   and moreover he drew, yes, drew for us and watered the
      sheep.
20 He said to his daughters:
   So-where-is-he?
   For-what-reason then have you left the man behind?
   Call him, that he may eat bread (with us)!

21 Moshe agreed to settle down with the man,
   and he gave Tzippora his daughter to Moshe.
22 She gave birth to a son,
   and he called his name: Gershom/Sojourner There,
   for he said: A sojourner have I become in a foreign land.

23 It was, many years later,
   the king of Egypt died.
   The Children of Israel groaned from the servitude,
   and they cried out;
   and their plea-for-help went up to God, from the servitude.
24 God hearkened to their moaning,
   God called-to-mind his covenant with Avraham, with Yitz-
      hak, and with Yaakov,

father, and seer—in short, into a son of the Patriarchs (see also "On the
Journey Motif," above).

   Incredibly, the man whose activity is to span four whole books has, it
seems, half his life (or, according to the chronology of 7:7, two-thirds of
his life!) described in a single chapter. Typical of biblical storytelling,
much has been compressed and left out, but enough is told to establish the
person who is to come.

God Takes Notice (2:23–25): Chapter 2 ends on a note that looks forward and backward simultaneously. The fourfold "God" plus verb (vv.24–25) echo the same structure at Creation's first day (Gen. 1:3–5), and suggest that he puts his concern for the people of Israel on a par with his concern

16 **priest of Midyan:** This title has spawned extensive theorizing about the origins of Mosaic religion (sometimes called the "Kenite Hypothesis" after the Kenites, a tribe of smiths connected to Moshe's father-in-law and spoken of favorably at a number of points in the Bible). It has been suggested that Moshe learned the rudiments of his religious or legal system from this source. We do not have enough evidence to make a positive judgment on this theory; biographically, it does make sense for Moshe to marry into a holy family of some sort. **seven daughters:** The requisite "magic" number, as in a good folk tale.

19 **An Egyptian man:** Moshe would have been recognizable as such from his manner of dress and lack of facial hair. In addition, he is not yet fully an Israelite, spiritually speaking.

20 **So-where-is-he:** This is one word in the Hebrew (*ve-ayyo*). The whole verse stands in ironic contrast to Moshe's earlier treatment (v. 14) at the hand of "his brothers" (Childs 1974). There, he was rejected; here, his host cannot welcome him quickly enough. **for-what-reason:** Similarly, this is one Hebrew word (*lamma*). **bread:** As often in both the Bible and other cultures, "bread" is here synonymous with "food."

21 **Tzippora:** Trad. English, "Zipporah." The name means "bird"; such animal names are still popular among Bedouin.

22 **Gershom/Sojourner There:** Related to the Hebrew *ger*, "sojourner" or resident alien. The name more accurately reflects the sound of the verb *garesh*, "drive out" (so Abravanel), which plays its role in the Exodus stories (and in Moshe's recent experience in the narrative). As my student Nancy Ginsberg once pointed out, this naming of sons to express the feelings about exile has already occurred in a more personally positive context—with Yosef (see Gen. 41:50–52). **A sojourner . . . in a foreign land:** The King James Version phrase, "a stranger in a strange land," is stunning, but the Hebrew uses two different roots (*gur* and *nakhor*).

23 **The king of Egypt died./ The Children of Israel groaned:** The change in regime does not prove beneficial to the suffering slaves, but makes it possible for Moshe to return to Egypt, thus impelling the narrative along and reestablishing the link between Moshe and his people. **cried out:** The same verb (Heb. *tza'ok*) is used to describe the "hue and cry" of Sodom and Gomorra (Gen. 18:20; see also the note to 22:22, below).

23–24 **groaned . . . cried out . . . plea-for-help . . . moaning:** As in 1:7, four phrases describe the Israelites' actions. Note also the double use of "from the servitude."

24 **Avraham, Yitzhak, Yaakov:** Trad. English "Abraham, Isaac, Jacob."

25 God saw the Children of Israel,
    God knew.

3:1 Now Moshe was shepherding the flock of Yitro his father-
       in-law, priest of Midyan.
    He led the flock behind the wilderness—
    and he came to the mountain of God, to Horev.
  2 And YHWH's messenger was seen by him
    in the flame of a fire out of the midst of a bush.
    He saw:
    here, the bush is ablaze with fire,
    and the bush is not consumed!
  3 Moshe said:
    Now let me turn aside
    that I may see this great sight—
    why the bush does not burn up!
  4 When YHWH saw that he had turned aside to see,
    God called to him out of the midst of the bush,
    he said:
    Moshe! Moshe!
    He said:
    Here I am.

for creation of light (connoting "good" in folklore). In addition, the four
verbs used here play a prominent role in the entire Deliverance Narrative,
as Isbell (1982) has shown.

At the Bush: The Call (3:1–4:17): The great revelation scene in these two
chapters, so much a classic in the literature of the West, comes as somewhat of a surprise in the close context of our story. Nothing in Exodus so
far has prepared us for such a religious, inward vision on the part of
Moshe; and indeed, Genesis itself contains no meeting between God and a
human being of such a dramatic character. Adam and Avraham converse
with God; Yaakov experiences him, to be sure, in dreams and in the guise
of a wrestler; but nowhere thus far does one find a biblical hero encounter-
ing God with such intensity and purity of vision.

    The shepherd, now in the service of his father-in-law, the "priest,"
comes upon the "mountain of God," "behind the wilderness." The results
are those of an unintended or half-intended journey. Moshe, who had fled
previously, finds himself at the utmost reaches of the wilderness, almost

like Jonah in the bowels of the boat or of the great fish. The sight that Moshe is granted is of unclear nature, but it involves fire, with all its pregnant associations: passion, purity, light, mystery (Greenberg 1969), and here, inextinguishability.

God's initial speech (vv.6–10) contains all the elements basic to the Deliverance Narrative: it identifies him as the ancestral deity, establishes his compassion for the oppressed people, demonstrates his resolve to rescue them, and ends with the commissioning of Moshe to be his emissary. Central here is the verb *see*, whose threefold occurrence (vv.7 and 9) ties together the threads of the previous parts of Moshe's story (see above).

The entire scene is the model for the "call" of the biblical prophet, with

25 **knew:** Others, "took notice," but *yado'a* needs to be noticed throughout the book as a key word.

3:1 **Now Moshe was shepherding . . . :** The Hebrew syntax indicates the beginning of an entirely new story. **shepherding:** A symbol of great power in the ancient Near East; witness the enduring image of King David, sprung from shepherding roots, and of course that of Jesus. **Yitro:** Trad. English "Jethro." It is not clear why other names (Re'uel, Hovav) are also associated with him. The name, if Semitic, means "excellence." **behind:** Others, "to the west side of," "to the far side of," or simply "into," although the word seems to convey a certain mystery. Fairy tales often portray the hero's going deep into a forest and the like. **mountain of God:** Sinai is so designated only several times subsequently in the Pentateuch, suggesting perhaps biblical religion's reluctance to make of it a shrine of permanence. **Horev:** Another name for Sinai, principally used in Deuteronomy (but also twice more in Exodus, 17:6 and 33:6). A related Hebrew root, *harev*, means "dry."

2 **YHWH's messenger:** Traditionally "angel," but the English word stems from the Greek *angelos*, which means "messenger." In Genesis, God appears in somewhat human guise (cf. Chap. 18), and "messenger" indicates an unspecified manifestation of God, open to wide interpretation. **in the flame:** Others, "as a flame." **bush:** Jewish tradition identifies it as a thornbush, but the precise plant remains unknown. The bush, called *s'neh* in Hebrew, perhaps has the added function here of providing assonance with *Sinai*. **the bush is ablaze . . . the bush is not consumed:** The use of tense (plus the opening "here") conveys the immediacy of the vision. **not consumed:** The symbolism of the imperishable bush is left open for the reader; commentators suggest variously Israel and God himself.

3 **let me turn aside:** Despite Moshe's apparent retirement from intervening on behalf of his brothers in Egypt, his reaction here seems active, not passive. He does not shirk from seeking out the strange sight. **burn up:** The same Hebrew verb (*bi'er*) as the one translated as "blaze" above.

4 **Moshe! Moshe!:** The name is repeated for emphasis, as in Gen. 22:11. **Here I am:** The classic response of biblical heroes; see Gen. 22:1, 11; I Sam. 3:4.

5 He said:
  Do not come near to here,
  put off your sandal from your foot,
  for the place on which you stand is holy ground!
6 And he said:
  I am the God of your father,
  the God of Avraham,
  the God of Yitzhak,
  and the God of Yaakov.
  Moshe concealed his face,
  for he was afraid to gaze upon God.
7 Now YHWH said:
  I have seen, yes, seen the affliction of my people that is in
      Egypt,
  their cry have I heard in the face of their slave-drivers;
  indeed, I have known their sufferings!
8 So I have come down
  to rescue it from the hand of Egypt,
  to bring it up from that land
  to a land, goodly and spacious,
  to a land flowing with milk and honey,
  to the place of the Canaanite and the Hittite,
  of the Amorite and the Perizzite,
  of the Hivvite and the Yevusite.
9 So now,
  here, the cry of the Children of Israel has come to me,
  and I have also seen the oppression with which the Egyp-
      tians oppress them.
10 So now, go,
  for I send you to Pharaoh—
  bring my people, the Children of Israel, out of Egypt!
11 Moshe said to God:
  Who am I
  that I should go to Pharaoh,
  that I should bring the Children of Israel out of Egypt?
12 He said:
  Indeed, I will be-there with you,
  and this is the sign for you that I myself have sent you:
  when you have brought the people out of Egypt,
  you will (all) serve God by this mountain.

its emphasis on God's speaking to the fledgling prophet amid a vision and the motif of refusal; of the call scenes in the Bible, this is the longest and most memorable in its starkness. A man is called by God to return to society and serve as God's spokesperson—despite any opposition he may encounter and despite his personal shortcomings. Moshe's reluctance, indeed his almost obsessive need to turn down the commission, is as much indicative of the general nature of prophecy (cf. Elijah and Jeremiah) as it is of Moshe's own personality. The prophet must be prepared "to uproot and tear down, to destroy and overthrow, to build and plant" (Jer. 1:10), and to stand tall against kings if necessary (Jer. 1:13). So it comes as no surprise that the call is met with less than enthusiasm. And this refusal also teaches something about Israel's political conceptions. With such a response as this, there can be no question of personal ambition or inner lust for power. The prophet does what he does out of compulsion: he is driven by forces that he perceives as external to him.

In our text, Moshe refuses the commission five times, and five times God counters. In four of these cases the assurance is given that God will "be-there" with him (3:12, 14; 4:12, 15), and the use of that verb carries in its essence one of the most significant motifs of the Bush Narrative: the interpretation of God's name.

5 **put off your sandal from your foot:** A common form of respect in the ancient East, still practiced by Muslims in worship.

6 **the God of your father:** Hearkening back to the personal and family relationships with God in Genesis (see, for instance, Gen. 26:24, 31:42, 32:10). **Avraham . . . :** The text stresses the Patriarchs, reminding both Moshe and the reader of the promises made to them in Genesis.

7 **I have seen . . . heard . . . known:** Echoing the narrative above, 2:24–25. **the affliction of my people:** Heb. *'oni 'ammi.* **my people:** This fateful designation signals the beginning of the liberation process. The Golden Calf story (Chaps. 32ff.) provides a tragic variation on this phrase.

8 **I have come down:** The phrase indicates God's intervention in human affairs (as, negatively, in Gen. 11:7). **a land flowing with milk and honey:** Or with "goats' milk and date-syrup." This description of Canaan is repeated many times in the three subsequent books of the Pentateuch, but is not found in Genesis. **Canaanite . . . Hittite** [etc.]: These names are the Bible's designation for the indigenous peoples of Canaan at the time of the Israelite conquest. Biblical lists contain varying numbers of peoples, from six to ten.

12 **this is the sign:** The thought is not entirely clear. It may signify that liberation signals Israel's birth as a people, and therefore Moshe's legitimacy as well. **(all):** "You" is plural here. **by:** As opposed to "upon," since the people will not be allowed to trespass its sacred boundaries (see 19:12).

13 Moshe said to God:
    Here, I will come to the Children of Israel
    and I will say to them:
    The God of your fathers has sent me to you,
    and they will say to me: What is his name?—
    what shall I say to them?
14 God said to Moshe:
    EHYEH ASHER EHYEH / I will be-there howsoever I will
        be-there.
    And he said:
    Thus shall you say to the Children of Israel:
    EHYEH/I-WILL-BE-THERE sends me to you.
15 And God said further to Moshe:
    Thus shall you say to the Children of Israel:
    YHWH,
    the God of your fathers,
    the God of Avraham, the God of Yitzhak, and the God of
        Yaakov,
    sends me to you.
    That is my name for the ages,
    that is my title (from) generation to generation.
16 Go,
    gather the elders of Israel
    and say to them:
    YHWH, the God of your fathers, has been seen by me,
    the God of Avraham, of Yitzhak, and of Yaakov,
    saying:
    I have taken account, yes, account of you and of what is
        being done to you in Egypt,
17 and I have declared:
    I will bring you up from the affliction of Egypt,
    to the land of the Canaanite and of the Hittite,
    of the Amorite and of the Perizzite,
    of the Hivvite and of the Yevusite,
    to a land flowing with milk and honey.
18 They will hearken to your voice,
    and you will come, you and the elders of Israel, to the king
        of Egypt
    and say to him:
    YHWH, the God of the Hebrews, has met with us—

so now, pray let us go a three days' journey into the wilderness
and let us make slaughter-offerings to YHWH our God.
19 But I, I know
that the king of Egypt will not give you leave to go,
not (even) under a strong hand.
20 So I will send forth my hand
and I will strike Egypt with all my wonders which I will do
   in its midst—
after that he will send you free!
21 And I will give this people favor in the eyes of Egypt;
it will be that when you go, you shall not go empty-handed:

When Moshe asks God for his name in 3:13, he asks for more than a title
(Buber and Rosenzweig 1936). In the context of Egyptian magic, knowing
the true name of a person or a god meant that one could coerce him, or at
the very least understand his true essence. Moshe foresees that the slaves
will want to be able to call on this power that has promised to deliver
them.

God's answer is one of the most enigmatic and widely debated state-
ments in the Hebrew Bible (the reader will want to consult Childs 1974 for
a full bibliography). What does *ehyeh asher ehyeh* mean? One's suspicions
are aroused from the outset, for the answer is alliterative and hence already

13 **What is his name?:** See Comentary above. B-R: "What is behind his
name?"
14 **EHYEH ASHER EHYEH . . .:** The syntax is difficult. Others, "I am
that I am."
15 **title:** Others, "memorial."
16 **elders:** They are the holders of political power in such a tribal society.
taken account: As per Yosef's promise in Gen. 50:24.
18 **pray let us go:** Interestingly, the initial request made of Pharaoh is not for
emancipation but for permission to observe a religious festival. It eventually becomes clear that Israel cannot be Israel until it is free of Egyptian
hegemony. **make slaughter-offerings:** Offer slaughtered animals to
God.
21 **you shall not go empty-handed:** The despoiling of the Egyptians is reminiscent of obtaining booty in war. At the same time, there is probably a
legal background to this (Daube 1961): the furnishing of a freed slave with
provisions. The follow-up to the despoiling, intended or not, is God's
command that, in Israel's future observance of religious festivals in the
Promised Land, "no one is to be seen in my presence empty-handed" (Ex.
23:15).

22 each woman shall ask of her neighbor and of the sojourner in
    her house
    objects of silver and objects of gold, and clothing,
    you shall put (them) on your sons and on your daughters—
    so shall you strip Egypt!
4:1 Moshe answered, he said:
    But if they will not trust me, and will not hearken to my
        voice,
    indeed, they will say: YHWH has not been seen by
        you. . . !
2 YHWH said to him:
    What is that in your hand?
    He said:
    A staff.
3 He said:
    Throw it to the ground!
    He threw it to the ground, and it became a snake,
    and Moshe fled from its face.
4 YHWH said to Moshe:
    Send forth your hand! Seize it by its tail!
    —He sent forth his hand, took hold of it, and it became a
        staff in his fist—
5 So that they may trust that YHWH, the God of their fathers,
    the God of Avraham, the God of Yitzhak, and the God of
    Yaakov, has been seen by you.
6 YHWH said further to him:
    Pray put your hand in your bosom!
    He put his hand in his bosom, then he took it out,
    and here: his hand was leprous, like snow!
7 Now he said:
    Return your hand to your bosom!
    —He returned his hand to his bosom, then he took it out of
        his bosom,
    and here: it had returned (to be) like his (other) flesh
8 So it shall be, if they do not trust you, and do not hearken to
    the voice of the former sign,
    that they will put their trust in the voice of the latter sign.
9 And it shall be, if they do not put their trust in even these
    two signs, and do not hearken to your voice:

then take some of the water of the Nile
and pour it out on the dry-land,
and the water that you take from the Nile will become blood
    on the dry-land.
10 Moshe said to YHWH:
Please, my Lord,
No man of words am I
not from yesterday, not from the day-before, not (even)
    since you have spoken to your servant,
for heavy of mouth and heavy of tongue am I.

not easy to pin down; the poetics of the phrase indicate both importance
and vagueness or mystery. There is some scholarly consensus that the
name may mean "He who causes (things) to be" or perhaps "He who is."
Buber and Rosenzweig, taking an entirely different tack (of which one
occasionally finds echoes in the scholarly literature), interpret the verb
hayoh as signifying presence, "being-*there*," and hence see God's words as
a real answer to the Israelites' imagined question—an assurance of his
presence. The B-R interpretation has been retained here, out of a desire to
follow them on at least this significant point of theology, and out of my

22 **ask from:** Others, "borrow." **strip:** Here the verb (*natzel*) means
    "strip," perhaps punning on a different form used in verse 8 which means
    "rescue."
4:1 **answered . . . said:** This coupling of verbs is common in Ugaritic and
    Hebrew to denote a new thought on the speaker's part (Cassuto 1967).
6 **bosom:** Others, "upper folds of (his) cloak." **leprous:** Others, "en-
    crusted with snowy scales." According to Cassuto (1967), leprosy was a
    disease common in Egypt. It also was taken as a sign from God, often of
    wrongdoing on the part of the victim.
8 **voice:** Meaning "message," as in Ugaritic usage. **sign:** These were often
    required or used by prophets in the Bible (see the discussion in Deut.
    13:2ff.) (Greenberg 1969).
9 **blood:** Since the Nile was regarded as divine by the Egyptians, not only
    would such a plague be miraculous and devastating, but it would also be a
    direct swipe at the Egyptian religion.
10 **no man of words am I:** Yet this is exactly the quality that Moshe's mission
    requires! (Greenberg 1969). Similarly, Jeremiah (1:6) seeks to evade the
    call, although his refusal is based more on inexperience than on lack of
    eloquence. **yesterday . . . the day-before:** A Hebrew idiom for "the
    past." **heavy of mouth and heavy of tongue:** The nature of Moshe's
    speech impediment is not clear. Curiously, writes Buber (1958), it is the
    stammerer whose job it is to bring down God's word to the human world.

11 YHWH said to him:
Who placed a mouth in human beings
or who (is it that) makes one mute or deaf
or open-eyed or blind?
Is it not I, YHWH?

12 So now, go!
I myself will be-there with your mouth
and will instruct you as to what you are to speak.

13 But he said:
Please, my Lord,
pray send by whose hand you will send!

14 YHWH's anger raged against Moshe,
he said:
Is there not Aharon your brother, the Levite—
I know that *he* can speak, yes, speak well,
and here, he is even going out to meet you;
when he sees you, he will rejoice in his heart.

15 You shall speak to him,
you shall put the words in his mouth!
I myself will be-there with your mouth and with his mouth,
and will instruct you as to what you shall do.

16 He shall speak for you to the people,
he, he shall be for you a mouth, and you, you shall be for
him a god.

17 And this staff, take in your hand,
with which you shall do the signs.

18 Moshe went and returned to Yitro his father-in-law
and said to him:
Pray let me go and return to my brothers that are in Egypt,
that I may see whether they are still alive.

feeling that it also fits the smaller context. For of the several times that
Moshe tries to wriggle out of his mission, God answers him all but once
with the same verb, in the same meaning: "I will be-there with you" (note
the parallel between Moshe and the people again).

It is, however, also possible that *ehyeh asher ehyeh* is a deliberately vague
phrase, whose purpose is antimagical and an attempt to evade the question
(Rosenzweig speaks of this as well), as if to suggest that possession of the
true name cannot be used to coerce this God. In this interpretation, it
would follow that, just as God is magicless (see v.20), he is nameless, at
least in the conventional sense of religion. On the other hand, the name

YHWH, however it may have been vocalized throughout the history of the text, did function as a name in ancient Israel (and possibly outside of Israel as well). It was used in oaths (e.g., Gen. 22:16, II Sam. 12:5), and later, in the Second Temple period, limited in public pronunciation to the high priest on the Day of Atonement. As happens frequently in the history of religion, if we follow a concept long enough it transforms back to the beginning, often in an opposite meaning, and so when the use of YHWH is traced through the Middle Ages one finds it turned into a magical name at the hands of Jewish mystics.

To return to the Bush Narrative as a whole: these chapters introduce a number of important words that will recur throughout the entire Liberation Narrative. These include "trust," "hearken to (my) voice," "staff," "heavy," "go out," "strong," "send," and "blood" (see Isbell 1982). It should also be mentioned that several key words occur in multiples of 7 from 2:23 to 4:31 (Cassuto 1967): "see" (7), "send" (7), "go" (14), "mouth" (7), "speak/word" (Heb. *dabber/davar;* 7). This vocabulary in particular focuses the story around major aspects of prophecy.

In the end, what does Moshe have with which to return from the mount of vision? In the DeMille film version his face and personality clearly change; in the biblical text, however, he comes back with a word—the divine promise—and a staff, "with which you shall do the signs" (4:17). He had previously been a man whose lack of tolerance for injustice produced violence; now he is armed with words and a wonder-working object—not a sword or a helmet, but a shepherd's staff.

The Journey Back (4:18–31): It is clear that something has been inserted into the normal course of our narrative. What follows verse 20 should be verse 27; Moshe, ready to go back to Egypt, is met by Aharon in the wilderness, and they subsequently announce their mission to the Children of Israel. However, the editor has prefaced the brothers' meeting, first

13 **pray send by whose hand you will send!:** That is, find someone else!
14 **raged:** Literally, burned, the normal biblical metaphor for anger.   **Aharon:** Trad. English "Aaron." This is the first mention of the brother whom we later find out was the firstborn.   **the Levite:** Why this designation here? Some theorize that it means "joiner," while others seen it as a tracing of Levite roots as spokespeople in Israel. The phrase could also be translated as, "Is not your brother Aharon the Levite?"
15 **you shall put. . .:** Moshe is to Aharon as God is to a prophet; the latter is to serve principally as a mouthpiece.
16 **a god:** Others, "an oracle."
18 **Yitro:** Here his name appears as *Yeter* in Hebrew.   **Pray let me go:** B-R: "Now I will go."   **my brothers:** This concern has not been heard from Moshe during his years in Midyan, nor has he mentioned his past at all. **whether they are still alive:** Reminiscent of Yosef's cry in Gen. 45:3, "Is

Yitro said to Moshe:
Go in peace!

19 Now YHWH said to Moshe in Midyan:
Go, return to Egypt,
for all the men who sought (to take) your life have died.

20 So Moshe took his wife and his sons and mounted them
upon an ass, to return to the land of Egypt,
and Moshe took the staff of God in his hand.

21 YHWH said to Moshe:
When you go to return to Egypt,
see:
All the portents that I have put in your hand, you are to do
before Pharaoh,
but I will make his heart strong-willed, so that he will not
send the people free.

22 Then you are to say to Pharaoh:
Thus says YHWH:
My son, my firstborn, is Israel!

23 I said to you: Send free my son, that he may serve me,
but you have refused to send him free,
(so) here: I will kill your son, your firstborn!

24 Now it was on the journey, at the night-camp,
that YHWH encountered him and sought to make him die.

25 Tzippora took a flint and cut off her son's foreskin,
she touched it to his legs and said:
Indeed, a bridegroom of blood are you to me!

26 Thereupon he released him.
Then she said, "a bridegroom of blood" upon the circumcision-cuttings.

27 Now YHWH said to Aharon:
Go to meet Moshe in the wilderness!
He went, he encountered him at the mountain of God
and he kissed him.

28 And Moshe told Aharon all YHWH's words with which he
had sent him
and all the signs with which he had charged him.

with a warning to Moshe that his mission will be strongly resisted by Pharaoh, and a warning that Moshe is to deliver to Pharaoh. Then follows a bizarre episode, which, like the Name passage discussed above, has provoked centuries of comment and attempts to explain it. What are we to make of the circumcision story here, especially the last scene, which is unclear not only in import but in details such as pronouns as well?

Buber (1958) explains it as an event that sometimes occurs in hero stories: the deity appears as "divine demon" and threatens the hero's life. Perhaps this underlines the dangerous side of contact between the human and the divine. But there seem to be other reasons for the passage's inclusion at this point in the text. First, it serves as an end bracket to Moshe's sojourn in Midyan. As mentioned earlier, Moshe flees Egypt under pain of death (2:15); here, on his return, he is in mortal danger once more. Second, our passage seems to be an *inclusio* or bracketing passage for the entire Plague Narrative (Kosmala 1962, and others). This is confirmed by the use of verses 21–23 as an introduction. God, designating Israel his firstborn and alluding to the future killing of Pharaoh's/Egypt's firstborn sons, demonstrates his power as life-taker, to be pacified or

my father still alive?" Note that Moshe says nothing to Yitro about what happened to him on the mountain.

19 **all the men:** Moshe need no longer fear for his life at Pharaoh's hands, but he will shortly be threatened by God himself (see vv. 24–26).

20 **mounted them upon an ass:** A stereotyped biblical way of describing setting out on a journey. **staff of God:** In standard hero stories, one would expect to hear a good deal more about this object, which would normally possess magical powers. Here, as usual, such a motif has been suppressed. It surfaces later in Jewish legend, in full mythical garb. The staff is mentioned in this verse, possibly, to provide a dramatic conclusion to the entire revelation account: Moshe sets out for Egypt armed, as it were, with a token from God. This was the missing piece in his activity in Egypt.

21 **portents:** Signs, wonders. **send free:** Others, "let . . . go."

22 **Thus says YHWH:** A formula often used by the prophets to open their pronouncements. The context is similar as well: the prophets stand frequently against the kings of Israel and Judah, arguing for an end to oppression. **my firstborn:** The use of this image is a statement of emotional force, not actual primacy of birth or antiquity, as Israel was a comparative latecomer in the ancient Near East.

24 **to make him die:** To kill him; the means is not specified, but one could surmise that illness is meant.

25 **his:** Whose? Presumably those of Moshe, who is then "released" by God.

26 **released him:** Or "relaxed (his hold upon) him." **circumcision-cuttings:** Others, "on account of the circumcision," "because of the circumcision," "referring to the circumcision."

29 Moshe and Aharon went,
    they gathered all the elders of the Children of Israel,
30 and Aharon spoke all the words which YHWH had spoken
      to Moshe,
    he did the signs before the people's eyes.
31 The people trusted,
    they hearkened
    that YHWH had taken account of the Children of Israel,
    that he had seen their affliction.
    And they bowed low and did homage.

5:1 Afterward Moshe and Aharon came and said to Pharaoh:
    Thus says YHWH, the God of Israel:
    Send free my people, that they may hold-a-festival to me in
      the wilderness!
2 Pharaoh said:
    Who is YHWH, that I should hearken to his voice to send
      Israel free?
    I do not know YHWH,
    moreover, Israel I will not send free!
3 They said:
    The God of the Hebrews has met with us;
    pray let us go a three days' journey into the wilderness,
    and let us make-slaughter-offering to YHWH our God,
    lest he confront us with the pestilence or the sword!
4 The king of Egypt said to them:
    For-what-reason, Moshe and Aharon,
    would you disrupt the people from their tasks?
    Go back to your burdens!
5 Pharaoh said:
    Here, too many now are the people of the land,
    and you would have them cease from their burdens!
6 So that day Pharaoh commanded the slave-drivers of the
      people and its officers, saying:
7 You are no longer to give straw to the people to make the
      bricks as yesterday and the day-before;
    let it be them that go and gather straw for themselves!
8 But the (same) measure of bricks that they have been mak-
      ing, yesterday and the day-before,
    you are to impose on them,

turned away only by a ceremonial blood-smearing—parallel to the Israelites' smearing of blood on their doorposts when their own firstborn are threatened by the Tenth Plague (12:12–13).

Two final points should be noted here. First, it is with the act of his son's circumcision that Moshe finally becomes a true Israelite (that, after all, was the major term of God's covenant with Abraham in Genesis 17). Similarly, Yehoshua (Joshua), Moshe's successor, will circumcise the next generation of Israelites in the process of conquering the Promised Land (Josh. 5:2). And second, it is telling, again, that the person who saves Moshe's life in adulthood is a woman. In a sense, Moshe's early life is now over, having come full circle.

Before Pharaoh (5:1–6:1): Moshe and Aharon's initial efforts to free the people—even temporarily for an act of worship—are unsuccessful, as foretold in the previous chapter. But even though God had predicted failure, we are still left with a portrait of clashing human wills: the liberators', the king's, and the reluctant people's. The narrative appears to be a set-up for the second major revelation of God to Moshe (Chapter 6), which, preceded by expressions of doubt on both Moshe's part and that of

31 **The people trusted . . .:** For the first time in the Torah, Israel responds to God's promises in a positive manner, something which will rarely happen again. The vocabulary and attitude form an *inclusio* (a bracket) with the end of the Liberation Narrative, 14:30–31 (cf. the verbs "trust" and "see").

5:1 **hold-a-festival:** Or "observe a pilgrimage-festival." The Hebrew *hag* is still echoed in the great pilgrimage of Islam, the hajj, in which worshippers make (sometimes long) journeys to Mecca.

2 **Who is YHWH:** This attitude recalls an earlier obstacle to the liberation process, "Who am I" of Moshe (3:11). **I do not know YHWH:** Colloquially, "I care not a whit for YHWH!" To Pharaoh's pointed challenge, the entire narrative that follows is an answer (cf. 14:4, 18).

3 **pray let us go:** A milder phrase than the earlier "Send free my people!" **three days' journey:** Either the magical 3 again, or a standard biblical way of describing a journey (see Gen. 22:4). **lest he confront us:** In the ancient world the gods demanded sacrifices at specified times. "Confront" and "sword" also occur in verses 20–21, nicely balancing this section of narrative.

4 **For-what-reason:** Heb. *lamma*, as distinct from *maddu'a* ("why," with similar meaning).

5 **too many:** Echoing 1:9ff. (Fishbane 1979). **the people of the land:** This phrase occurs here in its wider usage, i.e., the common folk, as opposed to what is found in Gen. 23:7, where the term indicates the landed nobility.

6 **slave-drivers:** In several Semitic languages *nagos* denotes "pressing" or "overpowering" (Ullendorff 1977), hence "driving" here.

you are not to subtract from it!
For they are lax—
therefore they cry out, saying: Let us go, let us make-
   slaughter-offering to our God!
9 Let the servitude weigh-heavily on the men!
They shall have to do it, so that they pay no more regard to
   false words!
10 The slave-drivers of the people and its officers went out
and said to the people, saying:
Thus says Pharaoh:
I will not give you straw:
11 You go, get yourselves straw, wherever you can find (it),
indeed, not one (load) is to be subtracted from your servitude!
12 The people scattered throughout all the land of Egypt,
gathering stubble-gatherings for straw.
13 But the slave-drivers pressed them hard, saying:
Finish your tasks, each-day's work-load in its day, as when
   there was straw!
14 And the officers of the Children of Israel, whom Pharaoh's
   slave-drivers had set over them, were beaten,
they said (to them):
For-what-reason have you not finished baking your alloca-
   tion as yesterday and the day-before,
so yesterday, so today?
15 The officers of the Children of Israel came and cried out to
   Pharaoh, saying:
Why do you do thus to your servants?
16 No straw is being given to your servants, and as for bricks—
   they say to us, Make (them)!
Here, your servants are being beaten, and the fault is your
   people's!
17 But he said:
Lax you are, lax,
therefore you say: Let us go, let us make-slaughter-offering
   to YHWH—
18 so now, go—serve;
no straw will be given to you,
and the full-measure in bricks you must give back!
19 The officers of the Children of Israel saw that they were in
   an ill-plight,

having to say: Do not subtract from your bricks each-day's
    work-load in its day!
20 They confronted Moshe and Aharon, stationing themselves
    to meet them when they came out from Pharaoh,
21 they said to them:
    May YHWH see you and judge,
    for having made our smell reek in the eyes of Pharaoh and in
      the eyes of his servants,
    giving a sword into their hand, to kill us!
22 Moshe returned to YHWH and said:
    My Lord,

the people, harks back to the concerns voiced at the Burning Bush. There
is also a forward-looking figure, Pharaoh, who is a prototype for other
foreign rulers and enemies in the Bible who challenge God (Greenberg
1969).

Chapter 5 contains the Bible's most extended description of the conditions of Egyptian bondage. Not surprisingly, the root "serve" occurs
seven times in verses 9 to 21 (Greenberg 1969), and sound variations on
the Hebrew *ra'* ("ill/evil") three times (vv. 19–23).

9 **so that they pay:** Others, "Let them pay" (Greenberg 1969).
10 **Thus says Pharaoh:** An ironic transformation of the prophetic formula
    noted in verse 1 above, "the language of redemption turned sour" (Green-
    berg).
14 **beaten:** The same Hebrew verb as "striking" in 2:11–13.
16 **your people's:** Heb. *'ammekha*, which some read *'immakh* ("with you").
18 **go—serve:** This phrase will be repeated three times during the Plague
    Narratives (10:8, 24; 12:31), with a different meaning: Go serve God!
    Pharaoh cannot wait to free the Israelites! (Greenberg 1969).
19–21 **saw . . . see:** In these negative usages it is as if the earlier redemptive
    theme of God's "seeing" has gone awry. But all is righted below, in 6:1
    ("Now you will see . . .").
21 **having made our smell reek:** An expression meaning the causing of ha-
    tred or horror. **giving a sword into their hand:** This scenario often
    occurs historically with liberators; initial attempts fail or are rejected.
    Here we have a replay of Moshe's earlier efforts (note the use of "judge"
    there as well, in 2:14). The tension in this chapter may be said to revolve
    around whether God's sword (v.3) or Pharaoh's will prevail.
22 **My Lord:** The Hebrew *Adonai* is used often in the Bible for pleading
    one's case, as before a king (see Gen. 18:27, 30, 31, 32; 19:18, and Ex.
    3:10).

for-what-reason have you dealt so ill with this people?
For-what-reason have you sent me?

23 Since I came to Pharaoh to speak in your name, he has dealt
      only ill with this people,
and rescued—you have not rescued your people!

6:1 YHWH said to Moshe:
Now you will see what I will do to Pharaoh:
for with a strong hand he will send them free,
and with a strong hand he will drive them out of his land.

2 God spoke to Moshe,
he said to him:
I am YHWH.

3 I was seen by Avraham, by Yitzhak, and by Yaakov
as God Shaddai,
but (by) my name YHWH I was not known to them.

4 I also established my covenant with them,
to give them the land of Canaan,
the land of their sojournings, where they had sojourned.

5 And I have also heard the moaning of the Children of Israel,
whom Egypt is holding-in-servitude,
and I have called-to-mind my covenant.

6 Therefore,
say to the Children of Israel:
I am YHWH;
I will bring you out
from beneath the burdens of Egypt,
I will rescue you
from servitude to them,
I will redeem you
with an outstretched arm, with great (acts of) judgment;

7 I will take you
for me as a people,
and I will be for you
as a God;
and you shall know
that I am YHWH your God,
who brings you out
from beneath the burdens of Egypt.

8 I will bring you

into the land (over) which I lifted my hand (in an oath) to
    give to Avraham, to Yitzhak, and to Yaakov.
I will give it to you as a possession,
I, YHWH.

The Promise Renewed (6:2–13): Greenberg (1969) and others have noted
how this section in many respects recapitulates God's speeches at the
Bush. Once again God assures Moshe that he has "heard" and "recalled"
the Israelites and their old covenant; once again he promises to act ("bring
out" resounds four times); once again the promise is linked to an interpretation of God's name; and once again Moshe expresses doubt as to whether
he will be believed or listened to (v.12).

Why the repetition? Perhaps here, as elsewhere, to double is to emphasize. Also, just as Moshe initially failed as a self-appointed liberator in
Chapter 2, only to be sought out by God in the wilderness, he fails as a
leader here as well, followed by God's reassuring speech. There can be no
question from whence the liberation comes.

22–23   **this people . . . this people . . . your people:** Note Moshe's brilliant use
    of psychology in dealing with God, similar to what he will do again in
    32:11–13.
    23   **to speak in your name:** The issue of God's name will become paramount
        in the passage following.
    6:1   **out of his land:** The phrase is also used in connection with "sending free"
        in 6:11, 7:2, and 11:10.
    2   **I am YHWH:** An authority formula in the ancient Near East (as in Gen.
        41:44, where it refers to an earlier Pharaoh) (Greenberg 1969).
    3   **Shaddai:** Heb. obscure; traditionally translated "Almighty," while some
        understand it as "of the mountains." In Genesis the name is most often
        tied to promises of human fertility (see 17:12); a possibly related Hebrew
        word means "breasts." **was not known:** Others, "did not make
        known."
    6ff.   **I will bring . . . :** God's answer comprises verbs of action: "bring out,"
        "rescue," "redeem," "take," and "give." The Hebrew rhymes (*ve-heveti
        etkhem. . . . ve-hitzalti etkhem . . .*).
    6–7   **beneath. . . . beneath:** A more vivid image than merely rescuing them.
    7   **I will take you . . . :** This covenant language recalls the vocabulary of
        marriage in many societies ("take you," "be for/to you"). **you shall
        know:** The verb "know" in the ancient Near East is often part of covenant
        (treaty) language, and so Moshe's task is not only to force Pharaoh to
        acknowledge God, but also to bring the Israelites into a special relation-
        ship with God (see Chaps. 19ff).
    8   **(over) which I lifted my hand . . . :** The promise of the land forms the
        backbone of the book of Genesis, which ends with it as well (Gen. 50:24).

9 Moshe spoke thus to the Children of Israel.
  But they did not hearken to Moshe,
  out of shortness of spirit and out of hard servitude.

10 YHWH spoke to Moshe, saying:
11 Go in, speak to Pharaoh king of Egypt,
   that he may send free the Children of Israel from his land.
12 Moshe spoke before YHWH, saying:
   Here, (if) the Children of Israel do not hearken to me,
   how will Pharaoh hearken to me?
   —and I am of foreskinned lips!
13 YHWH spoke to Moshe and to Aharon,
   and charged them to the Children of Israel and to Pharaoh
      king of Egypt,
   to bring the Children of Israel out of the land of Egypt.

14 These are the heads of their father-households:
   The sons of Re'uven, firstborn of Israel: Hanokh and Pallu,
      Hetzron and Karmi,
   these are the clans of Re'uven.
15 And the sons of Shim'on: Yemuel, Yamin, Ohad, Yakhin
      and Tzohar, and Sha'ul the son of the Canaanite-woman,
   these are the clans of Shim'on.
16 Now these are the names of the Sons of Levi according to
      their begettings:
   Gershon, Kehat and Merari.
   Now the years of Levi's life were seven and thirty and a
      hundred years.
17 The sons of Gershon: Livni and Shim'i, according to their
      clans.
18 And the sons of Kehat: Amram, Yitzhar, Hevron and
      Uzziel.
   Now the years of Kehat's life were three and thirty and a
      hundred years.
19 And the sons of Merari: Mahli and Mushi.
   These are the Levite clans, according to their begettings.
20 Amram took himself Yokheved his aunt as a wife,
   she bore him Aharon and Moshe.
   Now the years of Amram's life were seven and thirty and a
      hundred years.

21 Now the sons of Yitzhar: Korah, Nefeg and Zikhri.

22 And the sons of Uzziel: Mishael, Eltzafan and Sitri.

23 Aharon took himself Elisheva daughter of Amminadav,
Nahshon's sister, as a wife.
She bore him Nadav and Avihu, Elazar and Itamar.

24 Now the sons of Korah: Assir, Elkana and Aviasaf; these are
the Korahite clans.

25 Elazar son of Aharon took himself one of Putiel's daughters
for himself as a wife,
she bore him Pin'has.
These are the heads of the Levite father-groupings according to their clans.

The Genealogy of Moshe and Aharon (6:14–27): At this tension-filled moment in the narrative, in the face of Moshe's self-doubt and the possible
collapse of his mission, there is an unlikely break, at least by Western
storytelling standards. Apparently the genealogy has been inserted to but-
tress Moshe and Aharon's claim to represent the people before the Egyptian crown, and to stress their Levite ancestry (which solidly establishes
them within the priestly class in Israel). Significantly, the genealogy of
Yaakov's sons ends with the third, Levi, and the rest of the list enumerates
the Levite clans. More significantly, the ages mentioned are composed of
patterned numbers such as 3, 7, 30, and 100. As in Genesis, this betokens
a concept of order and meaning in history.

9 **shortness of spirit:** Others, "impatience" (so Ramban), "shortness of
breath" (so Rashi). Also notable is Walzer's (1985) suggestion of "dispirit-
edness." A parallel Ugaritic phrase probably means "wretched."

12 **spoke before:** Appealed to (Orlinsky 1970).   **of foreskinned lips:** Either
Moshe had some physical defect, as legend has it, or he is alluding to his
difficulties as a public speaker (cf. 4:10). The use of "foreskinned" may
express the biblical idea that things in their natural state require sanctify-
ing, as can be seen with firstborn humans and animals, first-fruits, food,
sexuality, etc.

14 **father-households:** Tribal units, listed according to the name of the ancestor.   **sons:** Heb. *banim,* translated above as "children," but here
clearly referring to the males.

16 **seven and thirty and a hundred years:** Here, and in verse 18 and 20, the
life spans of Moshe's family members are composed of "perfect" numbers
in combinations and multiples, as if to say that biography as well as group
history has a preordained meaning.

25 **Pin'has:** Trad. English "Phinehas." He will play an important role in
Num. 25:7 as a zealot for the new faith. The name is Egyptian in origin.

26 That is (the) Aharon and Moshe to whom YHWH said:
   Bring the Children of Israel out of the land of Egypt by
   their ranks;
27 those (were they) who spoke to Pharaoh king of Egypt, to
   bring the Children of Israel out of Egypt,
   that Moshe and Aharon.

28 So it was on the day that YHWH spoke to Moshe in the land
   of Egypt,
29 YHWH spoke to Moshe, saying:
   I am YHWH;
   speak to Pharaoh king of Egypt all that I speak to you.
30 Moshe said before YHWH:
   If I am of foreskinned lips,
   how will Pharaoh hearken to me?
7:1 YHWH said to Moshe:
   See, I will make you as a god for Pharaoh,
   and Aharon your brother will be your prophet.
 2 You are to speak all that I command you,
   and Aharon your brother is to speak of Pharaoh,
   so that he may send free the Children of Israel from his land.
 3 But I,
   I will harden Pharaoh's heart,
   I will make my signs and my portents many in the land of
   Egypt:
 4 Pharaoh will not hearken to you,
   so I will set my hand against Egypt,
   and I will bring out my ranks,
   my people, the Children of Israel,
   from the land of Egypt, with great (acts of) judgment;
 5 the Egyptians will know that I am YHWH,
   when I stretch out my hand over Egypt
      and bring the Children of Israel out from their midst.
 6 Moshe and Aharon did
   as YHWH had commanded them, thus they did.
 7 Now Moshe was eighty years old, and Aharon was eighty-
   three years old, when they spoke to Pharaoh.
 8 YHWH said to Moshe and to Aharon, saying:
 9 When Pharaoh speaks to you, saying: Give, you, a portent,
   then say to Aharon:

Take your staff and throw it down before Pharaoh: Let it
become a serpent.

10 Moshe and Aharon came to Pharaoh,
they did thus, as YHWH had commanded,
Aharon threw down his staff before Pharaoh and before his
servants, and it became a serpent.

11 Pharaoh too called for the wise men and for the sorcerers,
that they too, the magicians of Egypt, should do thus with
their occult arts,

Thus legitimated, Moshe and Aharon can return to the task at hand. It
would seem, then, that the passage is speaking to the Israelites, both in
Egypt and in the audience of later generations.

The Mission Renewed (6:28–7:13): As preparation for the next meeting with
Pharaoh, Moshe is once more reminded that the king will not listen to him.
Taking a page from his speech at the Bush, God instructs Moshe and
Aharon to use the "sign" that had previously served to convince the people:
snake magic. Yet despite Aharon's one-upping the Egyptian magicians in
the warm-up for the plagues, Pharaoh remains unconvinced. This episode

26 **by their ranks:** The term has a military ring, and is used frequently in the
Bible with that connotation.

7:1 **as a god:** Or "oracle," as mentioned in the note to 4:16.

5 **when I stretch out my hand:** In the Plague Narrative, Moshe and Aharon
will do the actual stretching out of hands (see 7:19, 8:1, 12; 9:22; 10:12,
21; and the climactic passage in 14:16, 26).

6 **Moshe and Aharon did/ as YHWH had commanded them, thus they
did:** This construction can be broken up in two ways (with, for instance,
the break at "them"), a syntactical usage found fairly frequently in biblical texts (cf. 39:43). The wording recalls the Flood Narrative in Genesis,
with the same emphasis: the hero obeys God without question.

7 **eighty . . . eighty-three:** Another set of "perfect" numbers, this time
using 40 (and 3) as the base. It occurs here due to the biblical practice of
mentioning age to "mark . . . a milestone in life's journey" (Greenberg
1969).

9 **Give, you, a portent:** That is, "Prove yourselves by working a miracle"
(Hyatt 1971). **your staff:** It is not clear whether the staff is the aforemen-
tioned one of Moshe, or part of another tradition, connected to Aharon.
serpent: Heb. *tanin*, a word indicating a reptile, with possible mythologi-
cal overtones (as in "dragon").

11 **occult arts:** Whereas Aharon needs none, since God performs the miracle
(Greenberg 1969).

12 they threw down, each-man, his staff, and these became
    serpents.
    But Aharon's staff swallowed up their staffs.
13 Yet Pharaoh's heart remained strong-willed, and he did not
    hearken to them,
    as YHWH had spoken.

14 YHWH said to Moshe:
    Pharaoh's heart is heavy-with-stubborness—he refuses to
    send the people free.
15 Go to Pharaoh in the morning, here, he goes out to the Nile,
    station yourself to meet him by the shore of the Nile,
    and the staff that changed into a snake, take in your hand,
16 and say to him:
    YHWH, the God of the Hebrews, has sent me to you, saying:
    Send free my people, that they may serve me in the wilder-
    ness!
    But here, you have not hearkened thus far.
17 Thus says YHWH:
    By this shall you know that I am YHWH:
    here, I will strike—with the staff that is in my hand—upon
    the water that is in the Nile,
    and it will change into blood.
18 The fish that are in the Nile will die, and the Nile will reek,
    and the Egyptians will be unable to drink water from the
    Nile.
19 YHWH said to Moshe:
    Say to Aharon:
    Take your staff
    and stretch out your hand over the waters of Egypt,
    over their tributaries, over their Nile-canals, over their
    ponds and over all their bodies of water,
    and let them become blood!
    There will be blood throughout all the land of Egypt—in the
    wooden-containers, in the stoneware.
20 Moshe and Aharon did thus, as YHWH had commanded
    them.
    He raised the staff and struck the water in the Nile, before
    the eyes of Pharaoh and before the eyes of his servants,
    and all the water that was in the Nile changed into blood.

21 The fish that were in the Nile died, and the Nile reeked,
   and the Egyptians could not drink water from the Nile;
   the blood was throughout all the land of Egypt.
22 But the magicians of Egypt did thus with their occult arts,

helps to prepare for what follows, and indeed contains a virtual glossary of
Exodus words. Some of these are: "speak," "send," "harden," "heart,"
"sign/portent," "hand," "bring out," "know," "staff," "hearken,"
"midst."

First Blow (7:14–25): The first plague uses elements and words common
to many subsequent plagues; in addition to those just mentioned, it introduces "refuse" and "reek" and "throughout all the land of Egypt." More
important is the choice of site and object for the curse: the Nile (a god in

12 **swallowed up:** Leaving no doubt as to whether optical illusion or sleight
   of hand is involved.
14 **heavy-with-stubbornness:** In the Plague Narrative, the root *kaved*,
   "heavy," occurs ten times—five times referring to Pharaoh's heart and
   five referring to the plagues themselves. The latter are perhaps seen as the
   direct outcome of the former.
15 **he goes out to the Nile:** Many interpretations have been proposed for this
   action, which must have had some significance for the biblical narrator. It
   remains unclear whether Pharaoh is involved in a religious rite or a function of state. More charming is the suggestion by Rashi, the medieval
   Hebrew commentator, that Pharaoh went secretly to the river in order to
   relieve himself—so that the Egyptians would not see him as less than a
   god.
17 **change:** Continuing the theme of transformation found in the scene with
   the snake. Overall, the change from slavery to liberation and to responsible society is a major theme in Exodus.
19 **wooden-containers . . . stoneware:** It is unclear what is meant. The
   context seems to suggest "even in their kitchen utensils," reflected in the
   present translation. On the other hand, virtually everywhere in the Bible
   that "wood and stone" occur as a pair in the singular, they refer to idols;
   Cassuto (1967) speaks of the Egyptians' bathing their idols and thus sees
   the passage as another example of Exodus' denigrating Egyptian religion.
20 **He raised the staff:** "He" refers to Aharon. **struck:** The first
   "stroke"—that is the Hebrew term (*makka*) used for what we know in
   English as a "plague."
21 **throughout all the land of Egypt:** One of the refrains used in this section
   of the book (see "On the Book of Exodus and Its Structure," p. xxix).

and Pharaoh's heart remained strong-willed, and he did not
   hearken to them,
as YHWH had spoken.

23 So Pharaoh turned and came into his house, neither did he
    pay any mind to this.

24 But all Egypt had to dig around the Nile to drink water,
    for they could not drink from the waters of the Nile.

25 Seven days were fulfilled, after YHWH had struck the Nile.

26 YHWH said to Moshe:
    Come to Pharaoh and say to him:
    Thus says YHWH:
    Send free my people, that they may serve me!

27 And if you refuse to send them free,
    here, I will smite your entire territory with frogs.

28 The Nile will swarm with frogs;
    they will ascend, they will come
    into your house, into your bedroom, upon your couch,
    into your servants' houses, in among your people,
    into your ovens and into your dough-pans;

29 onto you, onto your people, onto all your servants will the
    frogs ascend!

8:1 YHWH said to Moshe:
     Say to Aharon:
     Stretch out your hand with your staff, over the tributaries,
        over the Nile-canals, and over the ponds,
     make the frogs ascend upon the land of Egypt!

2   Aharon stretched out his hand over the waters of Egypt,
    the frog-horde ascended
    and covered the land of Egypt.

3   Now the magicians did thus with their occult arts—
    they made frogs ascend upon the land of Egypt.

4   Pharaoh had Moshe and Aharon called
    and said:
    Plead with YHWH, that he may remove the frogs from me
       and from my people,
    and I will send the people free, that they may make-
       slaughter-offering to YHWH!

5   Moshe said to Pharaoh:
    Be praised over me:

For when shall I plead for you, for your servants, for your
   people,
to cut off the frogs from you and from your houses,
(so that) only in the Nile will they remain?
6 He said:
For the morrow.
He said:
According to your words, (then)!
In order that you may know
that there is none like YHWH our God.

Egypt), water (source of life for the Egyptians but earlier source of death
for the Hebrew babies), and blood (sign of life and death). No more
effective choice could have been made for this first demonstration of the
far-reaching power of the Israelite God.

As with the first six plagues, the threat is long and the actual carrying-
out brief. Note the relationship, at the end of the episode, between the
uncaring Pharaoh and his own people, who have to scratch for water.

Second Blow (7:26–8:11): The second plague is linked to the first by a
number of elements: the Nile, the magicians, and of course, Pharaoh's
disregard of the threats after it is all over. It is also a full narrative,

25 **YHWH had struck the Nile:** Even though Aharon did the "striking," it
becomes clear here that the brothers are only agents.

27 **frogs:** A symbol of fertility in Egyptian culture (the goddess Heket), and
so the plague might be regarded as an assault on the Egyptian gods again
(Casuto 1967). There may also be an ironic hint here of the "swarming" of
the Israelites in 1:7.

28 **ovens:** A place which, because of its dryness, would be most unlikely to
harbor them (Childs 1974).

8:2 **frog-horde:** The Hebrew uses a collective singular here (likewise with
"insects" in 8:17ff. and "locusts" in 10:4ff.); all other "frogs" in this
plague receive the standard plural.

3 **the magicians did thus:** The theme of Israel's distinctiveness, so prominent in these stories, is delayed. Here the magicians can do the same tricks
as their Hebrew counterparts, although, as noted above, they require the
aid of "occult arts."

5 **Be praised over me:** Others, "Have the advantage over me." The sense is
that Pharaoh will be allowed to choose the precise time of the frogs' removal.

6 **In order that you may know:** The intent of Moshe's words in verse 5 is
now revealed: precise timing, even when chosen at will, demonstrates
God's total power.

7 The frogs shall remove from you, from your houses, from
   your servants, from your people,
   —only in the Nile shall they remain.
8 Moshe and Aharon went out from Pharaoh,
   Moshe cried out to YHWH
   on account of the frogs that he had imposed upon Pharaoh.
9 And YHWH did according to Moshe's words:
   the frogs died away, from the houses, from the courtyards,
   and from the fields.
10 They piled them up, heaps upon heaps, and the land reeked.
11 But when Pharaoh saw that there was breathing-room,
   he made his heart heavy-with-stubbornness, and did not
   hearken to them,
   as YHWH had spoken.

12 YHWH said to Moshe:
   Say to Aharon:
   Stretch out your staff and strike the dust of the land,
   it will become gnats throughout all the land of Egypt!
13 They did thus,
   Aharon stretched out his hand with his staff and struck the
   dust of the ground,
   and gnats were on the man and on beast;
   all the dust of the ground became gnats throughout all the
   land of Egypt.
14 Now the magicians did thus with their occult arts, to bring
   forth the gnats, but they could not,
   the gnats were on man and on beast.
15 The magicians said to Pharoah:
   This is the finger of a god!
   But Pharaoh's heart remained strong-willed, and he did not
   hearken to them,
   as YHWH had spoken.

16 YHWH said to Moshe:
   (Arise) early in the morning, station yourself before Pharaoh—here, he goes out to the water,
   and say to him:
   Thus says YHWH:
   Send free my people, that they may serve me!
17 Indeed, if you do not send my people free,

here, I will send upon you, upon your servants, upon your
   people, upon your houses—
insects,
the houses of Egypt will be full of the insects,
as well as the ground upon which they are!

containing most of the formal aspects of the plagues within itself (see "The
Plague Narrative," above).

The threat of this plague breaks into poetry in a striking passage (v.28)
which uses repeating prepositions. The frogs are literally everywhere.
Also, for the first time Pharaoh asks that God be entreated—that is, he
finally acknowledges his existence (as against which, see 5:2).

Third Blow (8:12–15): With the third plague, the curse becomes more
intimate, affecting the bodies of all living creatures in Egypt (cf. the
refrain in vv.13–14, "on man and on beast"). The narrative uses the
briefest plague formula here, without introduction or warning to Pharaoh.
Yet it results in an Egyptian effort to end the siege, as the magicians term
the plague "the finger of a god" (v.15).

Fourth Blow (8:16–28): Despite its similarity to the previous plague (insects), number four introduces a new and important element into the tale:
the idea that God makes a distinction between Egypt and Israel. It also
involves protracted bargaining between Moshe and Pharaoh over the issue
of allowing the Israelites to worship God.

9 **from the houses . . .:** The threefold repetition of "from" paints a vivid
   picture of the end of this plague. The dead frogs recede like water drying
   up.
12 **gnats:** Other translations vary here. There are many traditions, but it
   seems clear that some kind of small insect is indicated (Hyatt 1971).
15 **the finger of a god:** That is, God's direct intervention in human affairs.
   The only other occurrence of this expression is in Exodus (31:18) and in
   the text that retells that story, Deut. 9:10. In the latter cases it refers to the
   divine writing on the two tablets of Testimony.
17 **upon you . . .:** Similar to the refrain of 7:28–29, with regard to the frogs;
   here, "upon" occurs four times in one line. **insects:** As in the last
   plague, there are many opinions as to what these were (e.g., gnats, gad-
   flies, mosquitos); Bekhor Shor understands the "mixture" (the literal
   meaning of the Hebrew term used here, 'arov) as one of wild animals.

18 But I will make distinct, on that day, the region of Goshen,
      where my people is situated,
   so that there will be no insects there,
   in order that you may know that I am YHWH in the land;
19 I will put a ransom between my people and your people—
   on the morrow will this sign occur.
20 YHWH did thus,
   heavy insect (swarms) came into Pharaoh's house, into the
      houses of his servants, throughout all the land of Egypt,
   the land was in ruins in the face of the insects.
21 Pharaoh had Moshe and Aharon callled
   and said:
   Go, make-slaughter-offering to your god in the land!
22 Moshe said:
   It would not be wise to do thuswise:
   for Egypt's abomination is what we slaughter-offer for our
      God;
   if we were to slaughter Egypt's abomination before their
      eyes,
   would they not stone us?
23 Let us go a three days' journey into the wilderness,
   and we shall make-slaughter-offering to YHWH our God, as
      he has said to us.
24 Pharaoh said:
   I will send you free,
   that you may make-slaughter-offering to YHWH your God
      in the wilderness,
   only: you are not to go far, too far!
   Plead for me!
25 Moshe said:
   Here, when I go out from you, I will plead with YHWH,
   and the insects will remove from Pharaoh, from his servants,
      and from his people, on the morrow,
   only: let not Pharaoh continue to trifle (with us),
   by not sending the people free to make-slaughter-offering to
      YHWH!
26 Moshe went out from before Pharaoh and pleaded with
      YHWH.
27 And YHWH did according to Moshe's words,

he removed the insects from Pharaoh, from his servants and
    from his people,
not one remained.

28 But Pharaoh made his heart heavy-with-stubbornness this
    time as well,
and he did not send the people free.

9:1 YHWH said to Moshe:
Come to Pharaoh and speak to him:
Thus says YHWH, the God of the Hebrews:
Send free my people, that they may serve me!

Fifth Blow (9:1–7): Although this plague spares humans, it is nevertheless
described as "heavy" (v.3). The narrative uses a play-on-words as well:
the Hebrew for pestilence (*dever*) echoes that for thing (*davar*).

18 **region:** Lit., "land" (see Gen. 45:10).   **in the land:** That is, as an active
    force.
19 **ransom:** Heb. *pedut*, usually emended to *pelut*, "distinction," to bring the
    phrase into consonance with verse 18 and with the entire plague section in
    general.
20 **in ruins:** The verb "ruin" (Heb. *shihet*) is often used in the Bible in
    connection with punishment for sin (see, for example, Gen. 6:11–12;
    19:13, 29).
22 **wise . . . thuswise:** Heb. *nakhon . . . ken*.   **Egypt's abomination:** In
    Cassuto's (1967) view, there are two possibilities here: either the animals
    in question were venerated as holy by the Egyptians, or they were actually
    thought of as gods, in which case the Hebrew phrase would be quite
    derogatory (so too Rashi).   **stone:** A widely used form of execution in
    biblical times (e.g., 17:4; 19:13; 21:28, 29, 32 below). It was apparently
    used for very severe crimes, and often connected, logically, to the anger of
    the populace (Greenberg 1962).
24 **only: you are not to go far, too far:** Heb. *rak harhek lo tarhiku*.
27 **not one remained:** Similar words will be used of the Egyptians, drowned
    in the Sea of Reeds (14:28).

2 If you refuse to send (them) free, and continue to hold-on-
    strongly to them,

3 here, YHWH's hand will be on your livestock in the field,
    on the horses, on the asses, on the camels, on the oxen, (and)
       on the sheep—
    an exceedingly heavy pestilence!

4 And YHWH will make-a-distinction between the livestock
    of Israel and the livestock of Egypt:
    there will not die among all that belong to the Children of
      Israel a thing!

5 YHWH set an appointed-time, saying:
    On the morrow, YHWH will do this thing in the land.

6 YHWH did that thing on the morrow—
    all the livestock of Egypt died,
    but of the livestock of the Children of Israel, there died not
      one.

7 Pharaoh sent to inquire, and here: there had not died of the
    livestock of the Children of Israel even one.
    But Pharaoh's heart remained heavy-with-stubbornness,
    and he did not send the people free.

8 YHWH said to Moshe and to Aharon:
    Take yourselves fistfuls of soot from a furnace
    and let Moshe toss it heavenward before Pharaoh's eyes,

9 it will become fine-dust on all the land of Egypt,
    and on man and on beast, it will become boils sprouting into
      blisters,
    throughout all the land of Egypt!

10 They took the soot from a furnace and stood before Pha-
    raoh, and Moshe tossed it heavenward,
    and it became boil-blisters, sprouting on man and on beast.

11 Now the magicians could not stand before Moshe because of
    the boils,
    for the boils were upon the magicians and upon all Egypt.

12 But YHWH made Pharaoh's heart strong-willed, and he did
    not hearken to them,
    as YHWH had said to Moshe.

13 YHWH said to Moshe:

Get-up-early in the morning, station yourself before Pharaoh and say to him:
Thus says YHWH, the God of the Hebrews:
Send free my people, that they may serve me!
14 Indeed, this time I will send all my blows upon your heart,
and against your servants, and against your people,
so that you may know that there is none like me throughout
all the land;
15 indeed, by now I could have sent out my hand and struck
you and your people with the pestilence,
and you would have vanished from the land;
16 however, just on account of this I have allowed you to with-
stand,
to make you see my might,
and in order that they might recount my name throughout
all the land.

Sixth Blow (9:8–12): Just as in the previous "short" plague, number 3, the
magicians come to the fore. No longer do they cry to Pharaoh; they cannot
even take the stage!

Seventh Blow (9:13–35): Long like its corresponding predecessors (numbers 1 and 4), the seventh plague prefaces its occurrence with an emphatic
introduction by God, and its warning gives God-fearing Egyptians a
chance to save themselves (vv.19–21), something new. The description of
the plague itself is fraught with spectacle, presaging Sinai with its use of
thunder and fire. There is also the ominous note, twice in the text (vv.18,
24), that such a plague was unique in Egyptian annals. The plagues, at
least for the Egyptians, now transcend the realms of normal, explainable
experience, as well as of historical recollection.

9:2 **hold-on-strongly:** Both Pharaoh's obduracy and his stranglehold on the
slaves are described with the same verbal root.
5 **an appointed-time:** As before (8:5–6), equally striking to the plague itself
is its precise removal at the time promised.
8 **soot:** The transformation from soot to fine-dust and then boils reflects a
poetic justice, paralleling bricks baked in a kiln (Cassuto 1967). It also
reflects the biblical concept of disease as punishment. **toss:** Moshe will
later "toss" the blood of the covenant on the freed Israelites (24:8).
16 **land:** Others, "earth."

17 (But) still you set yourself up over my people, by not send-
     ing them free—
18 here, around this time tomorrow I will cause to rain down an
     exceedingly heavy hail,
     the like of which has never been in Egypt from the days of
     its founding until now!
19 So now:
     send (word): give refuge to your livestock and to all that is
     yours in the field;
     all men and beasts who are found in the field and who have
     not been gathered into the house—
     the hail will come down upon them, and they will die!
20 Whoever feared the word of YHWH among Pharaoh's ser-
     vants had his servants and his livestock flee into the
     houses,
21 but whoever did not pay any mind to the word of YHWH
     left his servants and his livestock out in the field.

22 YHWH said to Moshe:
     Stretch out your hand over the heavens:
     Let there be hail throughout all the land of Egypt,
     on man and on beast and on all the plants of the field,
     throughout the land of Egypt!
23 Moshe stretched out his staff over the heavens,
     and YHWH gave forth thunder-sounds and hail, and fire
     went toward the earth,
     and YHWH caused hail to rain down upon the land of
     Egypt.
24 There was hail and a fire taking-hold-of-itself amidst the
     hail,
     exceedingly heavy,
     the like of which had never been throughout all the land of
     Egypt since it had become a nation.
25 The hail struck, throughout all the land of Egypt, all that
     was in the field, from man to beast;
     all the plants of the field the hail struck, and all the trees of
     the field it broke down;
26 only in the region of Goshen, where the Children of Israel
     were, was there no hail.
27 Pharaoh sent and had Moshe and Aharon called

and said to them:

This-time I have sinned!

YHWH is the one-in-the-right, I and my people are the ones-in-the-wrong!

28 Plead with YHWH!

For enough is the God-thunder and this hail!

Let me send you free—do not continue staying here!

29 Moshe said to him:

As soon as I have gone out of the city, I will spread out my hands to YHWH,

the thunder will stop and the hail will be no more—

in order that you may know that the land belongs to YHWH.

30 But as for you and your servants,

I know well that you do not yet stand-in-fear

before the face of YHWH, God!

31 —Now the flax and the barley were stricken, for the barley was in ears and the flax was in buds,

32 but the wheat and the spelt were not stricken, for late (— ripening) are they.—

33 Moshe went from Pharaoh, outside the city, and spread out his hands to YHWH:

the thunder and the hail stopped, and the rain no longer poured down to earth.

34 But when Pharaoh saw that the rain and the hail and the thunder had stopped,

he continued to sin: he made his heart heavy-with-stubbornness, his and his servants'.

20 **Whoever feared . . .:** The focus now shifts to the Egyptians in general (at least some of them), who now suspect the real source of their troubles, whereas only the magicians recognized it previously.

24 **fire taking-hold-of-itself:** Heb. difficult; others, "lightning flashed back and forth," "lightning flashing through it." **the like of which had never been:** The phrase here foreshadows the final plague (11:6).

27 **one-in-the-right . . . ones-in-the-wrong:** The terms are drawn from the world of legal, not religious, terminology.

28 **enough is:** Or "enough of their being. . . ."

29 **spread out my hands:** In entreaty.

31 **Now the flax . . .:** An editorial comment, to explain how much harm was done (Cassuto 1967: they used it for cloth and for food).

35 Pharaoh's heart remained strong-willed, and he did not send
    the Children of Israel free,
  as YHWH had spoken through Moshe.

10:1 YHWH said to Moshe:
  Come to Pharaoh!
  For I have made his heart and the heart of his servants
    heavy-with-stubbornness,
  in order that I may put these my signs amongst them
  2 and in order that you may recount in the ears of your son
    and of your son's son
  how I have toyed with Egypt,
  and my signs, which I have placed upon them—
  that you may know that I am YHWH.
  3 Moshe and Aharon came to Pharaoh, they said to him:
  Thus says YHWH, the God of the Hebrews:
  How long will you refuse to humble yourself before me?
  Send free my people, that they may serve me!
  4 But if you refuse to send my people free,
  here, on the morrow I will bring the locust-horde into your
    territory!
  5 They will cover the aspect of the ground, so that one will not
    be able to see the ground,
  they will consume what is left of what escaped, of what
    remains for you from the hail,
  they will consume all the trees that spring up for you from
    the field,
  6 they will fill your houses, the houses of all your servants,
    and the houses of all Egypt,
  as neither your fathers nor your fathers' fathers have seen
  from the day of their being upon the soil until this day.
  He turned and went out from Pharaoh.
  7 Pharaoh's servants said to him:
  How long shall this one be a snare to us?
  Send the men free, that they may serve YHWH their God!
  Do you not yet know that Egypt is lost?
  8 Moshe and Aharon were returned to Pharaoh,
    and he said to them:
  Go, serve YHWH your God!
  —Who is it, who is it that would go?

 9 Moshe said:
    With our young ones, with our elders we will go,
    with our sons and with our daughters,
    with our sheep and with our oxen we will go—
    for it is YHWH's festival for us.
10 He said to them:
    May YHWH be thus with you, the same as I mean to send
       you free along with your little-ones!
    You see—yes, your faces are set toward ill!
11 Not thus—go now, O males, and serve YHWH, for that is
       what you (really) seek!
    And they were driven out from Pharaoh's face.

12 YHWH said to Moshe:
    Stretch out your hand over the land of Egypt for the locust-
       horde,
    and it will ascend over the land of Egypt, consuming all the
       plants of the land, all that the hail allowed to remain.

Eighth Blow (10:1–20): Anticipating Pharaoh's eventual capitulation, the
Egyptians now urge their king to release the Israelites, before Egypt is
truly "lost" (v.7). The request occurs before the plague does. This longest
plague is in many ways the most devastating of all, affecting as it does the
very soil itself. Here the last two plagues are anticipated (v.15, "the
ground became dark"; and v.17, "this death"), and the previous one is
echoed (vv.6, 14, with the reference to past history). Also foreshadowed,
in the locusts' removal, is the final victory at the Sea of Reeds (Chap. 14),
through the mention of the location and the use of a powerful wind.

10:2 **toyed:** Others, "dealt harshly with," "made fools of."
    5 **aspect:** Lit., "eye." **not be able to see:** Foreshadowing the next plague,
       darkness (Plaut 1981).
    8 **Who is it:** Pharaoh qualifies his approval with conditions.
    9 **Moshe said . . .:** The answer is rhythmical, almost ritual. **With our
       young ones . . .:** The addition of children and animals to the request of
       Moshe makes Pharaoh suspect that they will not come back.
   10 **May YHWH be thus with you:** That is to say, may he not be with you!
       your faces are set toward ill: You have evil intentions; "your evil inten-
       tions are written on your faces" (Abravanel).
   11 **O males:** And only the males.

13 Moshe stretched out his staff over the land of Egypt,
    and YHWH led an east wind against the land
    all that day and all night;
        when it was morning, the east wind had borne in the locust-
        horde.
14 The locust-horde ascended over all the land of Egypt,
    it came to rest upon all the territory of Egypt,
    exceedingly heavy;
        before it there was no such locust-horde as it, and after it
        will be no such again.
15 It covered the aspect of all the ground, and the ground
        became dark,
    it consumed all the plants of the land, and all the fruit of the
        trees that the hail had left;
        nothing at all green was left of the trees and of the plants of
        the field, throughout all the land of Egypt.
16 Quickly Pharaoh had Moshe and Aharon called
    and said:
    I have sinned against YHWH your God, and against you!
17 So now,
    pray bear my sin just this one time!
    And plead with YHWH your God,
    that he may only remove this death from me!
18 He went out from Pharaoh and pleaded with YHWH.
19 And YHWH reversed an exceedingly strong sea wind
    which bore the locusts away and dashed them into the Sea of
        Reeds,
        not one locust remained throughout all the territory of
        Egypt.
20 But YHWH made Pharaoh's heart strong-willed, and he did
        not send the Children of Israel free.

21 YHWH said to Moshe:
    Stretch out your hand over the heavens,
    and let there be darkness over the land of Egypt;
    they will feel darkness!
22 Moshe stretched out his hand over the heavens,
        and there was gloomy darkness throughout all the land of
        Egypt, for three days,
23 a man could not see his brother, and a man could not arise
        from his spot, for three days.

But for all the Children of Israel, there was light in their
settlements.

24 Pharaoh had Moshe called and said:
Go, serve YHWH,
only your sheep and your oxen shall be kept back,
even your little-ones may go with you!

25 Moshe said:
You must also give slaughter-animals and offerings into our
hand, so that we may make-them-ready for YHWH our
God!

26 Even our livestock must go with us, not a hoof may remain
behind:
for some of them we must take to serve YHWH our God;
we—we do not know how we are to serve YHWH
until we come there.

27 But YHWH made Pharaoh's heart strong-willed, so that he
would not consent to send them free.

28 Pharaoh said to him:
Go from me!
Be on your watch:
You are not to see my face again,
for on the day that you see my face, you shall die!

Ninth Blow (10:21–29): Little is new here; darkness foreshadows the final plague, death. Yet at the end of the brief episode, as well as in 11:8, we are given a glimpse into the human element, as Moshe and Pharaoh rage in anger against each other.

19 **sea wind:** The story is told from the perspective of the land of Israel, where such a wind means a west wind (Plaut 1981). **wind . . . not one . . . remained:** Foreshadowing the incident at the Sea of Reeds (14:21, 28).

21 **they:** The Egyptians.

24 **only your sheep and your oxen:** Pharaoh still tries to salvage some control of the situation.

28 **Go from me!:** Others, "Out of my sight!," "Leave my presence." **on the day . . . you shall die:** The expression is similar to the one used in reference to Yosef in Gen. 43:3, 5. Despite the finality of the language here, the confrontation between Moshe and Pharaoh continues in 11:4–8 and 12:31–32.

29 Moshe said:
    You have spoken well,
    I will not henceforth see your face again.

11:1 YHWH said to Moshe:
      I will cause one more blow
      to come upon Pharaoh and upon Egypt;
      afterward he will send you free from here.
      When he sends you free, it is over—he will drive, yes, drive
          you out from here.
   2 Pray speak in the ears of the people:
      They shall ask, each man of his fellow, each woman of her
          fellow, objects of silver and objects of gold.
   3 And YHWH gave the people favor in the eyes of Egypt,
      while the man Moshe was (considered) exceedingly great in
          the land of Egypt,
         in the eyes of Pharaoh's servants and in the eyes of the
             people.
   4 Moshe said:
      Thus says YHWH:
      In the middle of the night
      I will go forth throughout the midst of Egypt,
   5 and every firstborn shall die throughout the land of Egypt,
      from the firstborn of Pharaoh who sits on his throne
      to the firstborn of the maid who is behind the handmill,
      and every firstborn of beast.
   6 Then shall there be a cry throughout all the land of Egypt,
      the like of which has never been, the like of which will never
          be again.
   7 But against all the Children of Israel, no dog shall even
          sharpen its tongue, against neither man nor beast,
      in order that you may know that YHWH makes a distinction
          between Egypt and Israel.
   8 Then all these your servants shall go down to me,
      they shall bow to me, saying:
      Go out, you and all the people who walk in your footsteps!
      And afterward I will go out.
      He went out from Pharaoh in raging anger.

9 YHWH said to Moshe:
Pharaoh will not hearken to you,
in order that my portents may be many in the land of Egypt.
10 Now Moshe and Aharon had done all the portents in Pharaoh's presence,
but YHWH had made Pharaoh's heart strong-willed, and he
had not sent the Children of Israel free from his land.

The Final Warning (11:1–10): What seems to be the introduction to the
last plague is made up of motifs common to several of the previous ones. It
also reintroduces the idea of despoiling the Egyptians, which had been
mentioned in Moshe's original commission (3:21–22)—so we know that
redemption is at hand. Artfully, the specification of what "one more
blow" is, is delayed until verse 5. In addition, there is the motif of Moshe's
greatness/fame among the Egyptians, which would appear to be a suppressed remnant of the story (in the face of the desire to glorify God as the
hero). The section ends (vv.9–10) with a summary of the entire Plague
Narrative—or at least of what is to be learned from it.

11:3 **Moshe was (considered) exceedingly great:** Interestingly, at this point in
the narrative it is Moshe and not God who is glorified (see also the note to
verse 8, below).
4 **the middle of the night:** As so often in folklore. The Hebrew word for
"middle" (*hatzi*) is different from the one used for "midst" on the next
line (*tavekh*).
6 **cry:** See also 12:30. The cry of the Egyptians echoes that of the Children
of Israel in 3:7, 9.
7 **sharpen:** Heb. obscure. **no dog:** Much less the "bringer-of-ruin" of
verse 13!
8 **in raging anger:** Somewhat uncharacteristically, the story of this last confrontation reports the emotions of both Moshe and Pharaoh. For a change
we get a glimpse of the human side of the drama.
9–10 **Pharaoh will not hearken . . . :** These two verses serve as a summary of
the entire Plague Narrative. They also help to smoothe out the transition
to Chapter 12.
10 **from his land:** The last occurrence of this phrase.

12:1 YHWH said to Moshe and to Aharon in the land of Egypt,
      saying:

  2 Let this New-Moon be for you the beginning of New-
      Moons,
      the beginning-one let it be for you of the New-Moons of the
          year.

  3 Speak to the whole community of Israel, saying:
      On the tenth day of this New-Moon
      they are to take them, each-man, a lamb, according to their
          father-households, a lamb per household.

  4 Now if there be too few in the house for a lamb,
      he is to take (it), he and his neighbor who is near his house,
          by the assessment according to the (total number of)
          persons;
      each-man according to what he can eat you are to assess for
          the lamb.

  5 A whole, male, year-old lamb shall be yours, from the sheep
      and from the goats are you to take it.

  6 It shall be for you in safekeeping, until the fourteenth day of
      this New-Moon,
      and they are to butcher it—the whole assembly of the com-
          munity of Israel—at twilight.

  7 They are to take some of the blood and put it onto the two
      posts and onto the lintel,
      onto the houses in which they eat it.

  8 They are to eat the flesh on that night, roasted in fire,
      and *matzot,*
      with bitter-herbs they are to eat it.

  9 Do not eat any of it raw, or boiled, boiled in water,
      but rather roasted in fire, its head along with its legs, along
          with its innards.

 10 You are not to leave any of it until morning;
      what is left of it until morning, with fire you are to burn.

 11 And thus you are to eat it:
      your hips girded, your sandals on your feet, your sticks in
          your hand;
      you are to eat it in trepidation—
      it is a Passover-Meal to YHWH.

 12 I will proceed through the land of Egypt on this night

The Tenth Blow in Its Context: With Chapter 12 the narrative leaves the realm of storytelling and enters that of ritual. What has so far been recounted as a story now takes on the aspect of commemorative ceremony. Instead of proceeding from warning (11:1, 4–8) to plague (12:29–30), the tenth plague account has been embedded in a setting of the lengthy de-

12:1 **in the land of Egypt:** The text thereby establishes the antiquity of the ritual.

2 **Let this . . . be . . . let it be:** The rhetoric helps to focus attention on this important section.   **beginning-one:** At least one form of the ancient Hebrew calendar began in the spring; the Torah begins its ritual calendar according to its ritual beginning at Passover. It is significant that the new year of nature and that of the nation's birth coalesce. For extensive discussion of Exodus and the biblical calendar, see Sarna 1986.

3 **whole community of Israel:** This term, "community" (Heb. *'eda*), is used somewhat interchangeably with a host of others in the Torah to indicate the leadership (often, the elders) of the people (Weinfeld 1972a).   **tenth:** there is a parallel important day in the fall, on the tenth day of the seventh month—Yom Kippur, the Day of Atonement (see Lev. 16:29).   **father-households:** See the note to 6:14.

5 **whole:** Or "hale" (Heb. *tamim*), that is, physically unblemished. This primary physical meaning often gives way to a spiritualized one, in reference to human beings (Job, for instance, is described as *tamim*, variously translated as "blameless" and "perfect" in Job 1:1).

6 **you . . . they:** The change in the subject of the sentence, from second to third person, is not unusual in biblical Hebrew.   **fourteenth day:** Close to the full moon.   **at twilight:** Lit., "between the evening-hours." This time is mentioned elsewhere (e.g., 16:12; 29:39, 41; and several places in Numbers) in connection with the sacrifices made by the priests. This perhaps implies that we have here the unusual situation (at least in ancient Israel) of the head of the household performing a priestly function.

8 **roasted in fire:** Not raw or boiled, since what seems to be meant is an imitation of standard sacrifices.   **matzot:** Sing. *matza*, the flat, unleavened bread that resembled present-day "Syrian bread."   **with bitter-herbs:** Others, "on bitter herbs." Gaster (1949) notes the long-standing use of such cathartics as purifiers or demon-ridders (e.g., garlic) in folk cultures. Later Jewish tradition speaks to the herbs as a symbol of the bitterness of Egyptian bondage.

9 **legs . . . innards:** That is, completely consumed.

10 **you are not to leave any of it until morning:** Again, as in the removal of leaven, what is meant is complete destruction.

11 **your hips girded . . .:** Prepared for travel. Passover is still observed in this manner by some Jews originating in Arab lands.   **in trepidation:** Others, "in haste," but the element of fear is also contained in the verb (Heb. *hafoz*).

and strike down every firstborn in the land of Egypt, from
  man to beast,
and on all the gods of Egypt I will render judgment,
I, YHWH.

13 Now the blood will be a sign for you upon the houses where
  you are:
when I see the blood, I will pass over you,
the blow will not become a bringer-of-ruin to you, when I
  strike down the land of Egypt.

14 This day shall be for you a memorial,
you are to celebrate it as a festival-celebration for YHWH,
throughout your generations, as a law for the ages you are to
  celebrate it!

15 For seven days, *matzot* you are to eat,
already on the first day you are to get rid of leaven from your
  houses,
for anyone who eats what is fermented—from the first day
  until the seventh day—: that person shall be cut off from
  Israel.

16 And on the first day, a calling-together of holiness,
and on the seventh day, a calling-together of holiness shall
  there be for you,
no kind of work is to be made on them,
only what belongs to every person to eat, that alone may be
  made-ready by you.

17 And keep the (Festival of) *matzot!*
For on this very day
I have brought out your ranks from the land of Egypt.
Keep this day throughout your generations as a law for the
  ages.

18 In the first (month), on the fourteenth day of the New-
  Moon, at evening, you are to eat *matzot,*
until the twenty-first day of the month, in the evening.

19 For seven days, no leaven is to be found in your houses,
for whoever eats what ferments, that person shall be cut off
  from the community of Israel,
whether sojourner or native of the land.

20 Anything that ferments you are not to eat;
in all your settlements, you are to eat *matzot.*

scription of a festival, thus shifting the time sense of the narrative. The enactment of the ceremony is important both for the characters in the story and for the participants in the audience of later generations. Likewise, the description of the actual leaving of Egypt is followed, not by a detailing of the route or what happened next, but by a series of regulations concerning who may eat the Passover meal (12:43–51) and by rules concerning the dedication of the firstborn (13:1–16).

By means of such editing, the final text was obviously meant to move the Exodus story, with all its historical aspects, into what historians of religion call "mythical time." In our text, history becomes present event; the hearer is no longer "in the audience" but actually acts out the story. That immediacy is meant is demonstrated by the threefold occurrence of the phrase "on this/that very day" (vv.17, 41, 51), which also serves to unite the various parts of the text around the tenth plague and the exodus.

The mixture of law and narrative that we find in Chapters 12 and 13 sets the stage for the Sinai scenes that will take place later in the book (Chaps. 19ff.), and indeed for the rest of the Pentateuch.

The Passover Ritual (12:1–28): The festival depicted in this chapter is, in the opinion of many scholars, a combination of two ancient holy days: a Shepherds' Festival, in which each spring a lamb was sacrificed to the deity in gratitude and for protection of the flock, and a celebration of the barley harvest, at which time all leaven/fermentation products were

13 **pass over:** The exact meaning of Hebrew *paso'ah* is in dispute. Some interpret it as "protect"; others, including Buber (1958), relate it to "limp," suggesting a halting dance performed as part of the ancient festival (perhaps in imitation of the newborn spring lambs). It is possible that there are homonyms here, and that the text is playing on them.

14 **celebrate it as a festival-celebration:** Or "make a pilgrimage" (see the note to 5:1).

15 **seven days:** Similar to the great fall festival, Sukkot, mentioned in Lev. 23:24. **leaven . . . fermented:** the removal of these elements is commonly found in agricultural societies (for more, see Gaster 1949, 1969). **from the first . . . that person . . .:** The two phrases occur in reversed order in the Hebrew.

16 **a calling-together of holiness:** Others, "a holy convocation." It is not entirely clear what is meant. **calling-together . . . no kind of work:** The same rules apply to the fall festival (Lev. 23:33–43). **on them:** The first and seventh days.

17 **matzot:** This probably describes a festival separate from the one connected to the lambs, as indicated above.

20 **not to eat . . . to eat matzot:** The section ends with an emphatic doublet.

21 Moshe had all the elders of Israel called and said to them:
   Pick out, take yourselves a sheep for your clans, and butcher
      the Passover-animal.
22 Then take a band of hyssop, dip (it) in the blood which is in
      the basin,
   and touch the lintel and the two posts with some of the blood
      which is in the basin.
   Now you—you are not to go out, any man from the entrance
      to his house, until morning.
23 YHWH will proceed to deal-blows to Egypt,
   and when he sees the blood on the lintel and on the two
      posts,
   YHWH will pass over the entrance,
   and will not give the bringer-of-ruin (leave) to come into
      your houses to deal-the-blow.
24 You are to keep this word
   as a law for you and for your sons, into the ages!
25 Now it will be,
   when you come to the land which YHWH will give you, as
      he has spoken,
   you are to keep this service!
26 And it will be,
   when your sons say to you: What does this service (mean) to
      you?
27 then say:
   It is the slaughtered-meal of Passover to YHWH,
   who passed over the houses of the Children of Israel in
      Egypt,
   when he dealt-the-blow to Egypt and our houses he rescued.
   The people did homage and bowed low.
28 And the Children of Israel went and did
   as YHWH had commanded Moshe and Aharon, thus they
      did.

29 Now it was in the middle of the night:
   YHWH struck down every firstborn in the land of Egypt,
   from the firstborn of Pharaoh who sits on his throne
   to the firstborn of the captive in the dungeon,
   and every firstborn of beast.
30 Pharaoh arose at night,

he and all his servants and all Egypt,
and there was a great cry in Egypt;
for there is not a house in which there is not a dead man.

avoided (although see Ginsberg [1982], who theorizes a shepherds' festival
with *matza*). Each has numerous parallels in other cultures (see Gaster
1949). What has apparently happened here is that the two days have been
fused together and imbued with historical meaning. In addition, rites that
were originally protective in function have been reinterpreted in the light
of the Exodus story. But whatever its origin, Passover as described in our
text bespeaks a strong sense of Israelite tribal community and of distinctiveness. And it is distinctiveness, which played such an important role in
Israelite religion, that is singled out here, with the striking penalty for
transgressing the boundaries of the festival—being "cut off" (probably
death). One also notes the repetition of the phrase "a law for the ages"
(vv.14, 17, 24). Passover, then, is central both to the Exodus story and to
Israelite ideas as a whole (see Sarna 1986 for a detailed discussion).

Tenth Blow and Exodus (12:29–42): The final blow falls. This most horri-
fying of all the plagues, and the reaction to it, are described in only two
verses, whereas the rest of the narrative concerns itself with preparations
for and actual description of the exodus. Note how, as above, the narrative
is surrounded by ritual concerns—trying to explain the subsequent reason

22 **hyssop:** The leaves are known for having a cooling effect (but some
   understand the Hebrew *'ezov* as meaning "marjoram"). **entrance:** Lit.,
   "opening." This spot of entrance often serves as a figurative threshold in
   folklore; here, it is the separation point between life and death, Israelites
   and Egyptians, home and the outside world. Later, it functions as the
   place of revelation or contact with the holy (e.g., 33:10).
23 **pass over:** Or, following the comments on verse 13, above, "skip over."
25 **service:** Ritual; the Israelites have begun their transformation from serfs
   to divine servants, underscored by the recurrence of "service" in 12:26
   and 13:5.
26 **when your sons say:** This framework is used frequently in Deuteronomy
   (e.g., Deut. 6:20).
27 **when he . . .:** The chiastic structure (*A-B/B-A;* here, a verb-noun/noun-
   verb) ends the speech, a device common in biblical style (Andersen 1974).
29 **captive in the dungeon:** Cf. verse 5, "the maid who is behind the hand-
   mill"; both phrases express the idea of the lowest person in the society.
30 **for there is not a house:** The omission of the perfect tense expresses the
   immediacy of the situation.

31 He had Moshe and Aharon called in the night
    and said:
    Arise, go out from amidst my people, even you, even the
        Children of Israel!
    Go, serve YHWH according to your words,
32 even your sheep, even your oxen, take, as you have spoken,
        and go!
    And bring-a-blessing even on me!
33 Egypt pressed the people strongly, to send them out quickly
        from the land,
    for they said: We are all dead-men!
34 So the people loaded their dough before it had fermented,
        their kneading-troughs bound in their clothing, upon
        their shoulders.
35 Now the Children of Israel had done according to Moshe's
        words:
    they had asked of the Egyptians objects of silver and objects
        of gold, and clothing;
36 YHWH had given the people favor in the eyes of the Egyp-
        tians,
    and they let themselves be asked of.
    So did they strip Egypt.

37 The Children of Israel moved on from Ra'amses to Sukkot,
    about six hundred thousand on foot, menfolk apart from
        little-ones,
38 and also a mixed multitude went up with them,
    along with sheep and oxen, an exceedingly heavy (amount
        of) livestock.
39 Now they baked the dough which they had brought out of
        Egypt into *matzot* cakes, for it had not fermented,
    for they had been driven out of Egypt, and were not able to
        linger,
    neither had they made provisions for themselves.

40 And the settlement of the Children of Israel which they had
        settled in Egypt was thirty years and four hundred years.
41 It was at the end of thirty years and four hundred years,
    it was on that very day:
    All of YHWH's ranks went out from the land of Egypt.

42 It is a night of keeping-watch for YHWH,
   to bring them out of the land of Egypt;
   that is this night for YHWH,
   a keeping-watch of all the Children of Israel, throughout
      their generations.

for eating unleavened bread (which had not been done in verses 15f.,
above). There also returns the important motif of despoiling ("stripping")
Egypt.

The section ends (vv.40–42) with a dramatic summary of Israel's sojourn in Egypt and the importance of the Passover festival, built on repeti-

31 **according to your words:** Pharaoh has never thus conceded before, and
    so we know that this time he is sincere. The same change of heart is
    indicated in the next verse, "And bring a blessing even on me!"
31–32 **even . . .:** The fourfold use of "even" here shows that Pharaoh is finally
    not hedging. He gives permission for *all* the Israelites to leave, without
    preconditions.
33 **Egypt pressed the people strongly:** Contrasting with Pharaoh's "strong-
    willed heart" of 10:27 and previously.
34 **their kneading-troughs bound:** To explain why only *matza* was baked; see
    verse 39, below.
37 **moved on:** The Hebrew (*naso'a*) literally means "pulled out their tent
    pegs." **six hundred thousand . . . menfolk:** That is, there were over
    600,000 men of military age (over twenty). Extrapolating from this several
    million slaves strains the credulity; one might accept either the explana-
    tion put forth in Plaut (1981) that *elef* means, not "thousand," but "troop/
    contingent" (of nine or ten men each), or Cassuto's (1967) designation of
    the number as a "perfect" or folkloric one, built on the numerical system
    of 6/60. For a full discussion Sarna (1986).
38 **mixed multitude:** This is the usual translation in English. The Hebrew is
    'erev rav, "riffraff." **heavy:** Their wealth is a counterpart to Pharaoh's
    previously "heavy" heart (and "heavy" plagues).
39 **were not able to linger,/ neither had they made provisions:** It comes
    almost as a surprise to the Israelites. Here there can be no question of
    military victory, as in a coup; history depends on the incursion of God.
40 **thirty years and four hundred years:** The numbers are patterned as
    usual; although this total disagrees with Gen. 15:13, for instance (which
    reckons it as 400 years), the differences seem to be more over which
    patterned numbers to use and not historical exactitude.
42 **keeping-watch:** Reflecting the play on words in the Hebrew *shamor,* by
    including ideas of both "guarding" and "observing." Cassuto (1967) sees
    shamor as a shepherd's term, appropriate here. Note again, in the tense
    structure, the conflation of narrative and contemporary ritual.

43 YHWH said to Moshe and Aharon:
This is the law of the Passover-meal:
Any foreign son is not to eat of it.

44 But any man's serf who is acquired by money—if you have
circumcised him, then he may eat of it.

45 Settler and hired-hand are not to eat of it.

46 In one house it is to be eaten,
you are not to bring out of the house any of the flesh,
outside.
And you are not to break a bone of it.

47 The entire community of Israel is to do it.

48 Now when a sojourner sojourns with you, and would make
the Passover-meal to YHWH,
every male with him must be circumcised, then he may
come-near to make it, and will be (regarded) as a native of
the land.
But any foreskinned-man is not to eat of it.

49 One Instruction shall there be for the native and for the
sojourner that sojourns in your midst.

50 All the Children of Israel did
as YHWH commanded Moshe and Aharon, thus they did.

51 It was on that very day,
(when) YHWH brought the Children of Israel out of the
land of Egypt by their ranks,

13:1 YHWH spoke to Moshe, saying:

2 Hallow to me every firstborn,
breacher of every womb among the Children of Israel, of
man or of beast,
it is mine.

3 Moshe said to the people:
Remember this day,
on which you went out from Egypt, from a house of serfs,
for by strength of hand YHWH brought you out from here:
no fermentation is to be eaten.

4 Today you are going out, in the New-Moon of Ripe-Grain.

5 And it shall be,
when YHWH brings you to the land of the Canaanite,

tion ("four hundred thirty years," "a night . . . for YHWH," "keeping-watch"). Again, a past event is made immediate for the audience. The powerful religious tones of story and ceremony are established by the threefold reference to night as the setting for both (vv.29–31).

Who May Make Passover (12:43–50): Continuing the immediacy of ritual, the narrative pauses where one would expect it to talk about the Israelites' route, to specify carefully that partaking of the Passover meal, and indeed being a part of the community in general, requires circumcision on the part of the participant. In essence, it creates the new Israelite nation, on the heels of common participation in a historical event. This small passage has been inserted between two occurrences of the same phrase ("that very day"), an editorial device often used in biblical literature.

Passover and the Firstborn (12:51–13:16): To close out the text's celebration of the exodus event, the editor includes a peroration on the firstborn. This too is a reinterpretation of earlier religious practices. Many ancient cultures selected the firstborn as an object for sacrifice to the gods—whether firstborn of fruit, of animals, or of human beings—the grounds for this being that the firstborn represents the best that nature has to offer

43 **foreign son:** Or "foreigner." The English here echoes Hebrew usage and the English idea of "native son" (Edward Greenstein, personal communication).

46 **outside:** Into that area which has the function of being the realm of death in the story.   **you are not to break a bone:** As if to violate its perfection, since the bone was identified as symbolic of the whole (viz., the same Hebrew word used for "bone" and "essence, person"). The biblical idea, found in reference to all animal sacrifices, is that only unblemished ("whole" or "hale") animals may be used for such purposes. In Gaster's (1969) view, the prohibition in this verse was originally instituted to ensure a full flock.

48 **come-near:** This verb (Heb. *karev*) is often used in connection with the priestly cult.

49 **Instruction:** Or "teaching," "priestly ruling." The same word later refers to Moshe's fuller "teaching," and eventually to the entire Pentateuch.

51 **that very day:** The phrase serves to bridge the two chapters here (Plaut 1981).

13:2 **Hallow:** Make holy.   **breaches:** Opens. This should not be confused with a so-called breach birth.

3 **Remember:** Here and again at 20:8, the Hebrew verbal form is an emphatic one.

4 **ripe-grain:** Heb. *aviv*. The month later took on a Babylonian name (Nisan), as did all the months of the Jewish calendar.

of the Hittite, of the Amorite, of the Hivvite and of the
   Yevusite,
which he swore to your fathers to give you,
a land flowing with milk and honey,
you are to serve this service, in this New-Moon:
6 For seven days you are to eat *matzot*,
   and on the seventh day (there is): a festival to YHWH.
7 *Matzot* are to be eaten for the seven days,
   nothing fermented is to be seen with you, no leaven is to be
     seen with you, throughout all your territory.
8 And you are to tell your son on that day, saying:
   It is because of what YHWH did for me, when I went out of
     Egypt.
9 It shall be for you for a sign on your hand and for a memorial
     between your eyes,
   in order that YHWH's Instruction may be in your mouth,
   that by a strong hand did YHWH bring you out of Egypt.
10 You are to keep this law at its appointed-time from year-day
     to year-day!
11 It shall be,
   when YHWH brings you to the land of the Canaanite, as he
     swore to you and to your fathers,
   and gives it to you,
12 you are to transfer every breacher of a womb to YHWH,
   every breacher, offspring of a beast that belongs to you,
   the males (are) for YHWH.
13 Every breacher of an ass you are to redeem with a lamb;
   if you do not redeem (it), you are to break-its-neck.
   And every firstborn of men, among your sons, you are to
     redeem.
14 It shall be
   when your son asks you on the morrow, saying: What does
     this mean?
   You are to say to him:
   By strength of hand YHWH brought us out of Egypt, out of
     a house of serfs.
15 And it was
   when Pharaoh hardened (his heart) against sending us free,
   that YHWH killed every firstborn throughout the land of
     Egypt,

from the firstborn of man to the firstborn of beast.
Therefore I myself slaughter-offer to YHWH every breacher
   of a womb, the males,
and every firstborn among my sons I redeem.
16 It shall be for a sign on your hand and for headbands between your eyes,
for by strength of hand YHWH brought us out of Egypt.

(see Gen. 49:3, where Jacob's firstborn is "beginning of my strength"). The idea of strength is played upon in the reinterpretation of sacrifice: four times, including at the end of the passage, we are told that the firstborn is to be consecrated, "for by strength of hand YHWH brought you out of Egypt" (vv.3, 9, 14, 16).

The chapter has a few notable characteristics. For one, the eating of *matzot* has been integrated into the firstborn material; for another, the language is unmistakably reminiscent of Deuteronomy (vv.5 and 11, "it shall be [a refrain here]/when YHWH brings you to the land of the Canaan-ite . . ."; see Deut. 6:10, 7:1, etc.). This has led some scholars to point to a relatively late date for the material, supporting the idea that Israel in its

9 **sign . . . memorial:** This may have been figurative originally; it became taken literally and gave rise to the phylacteries (*tefillin*) in rabbinic Juda-ism. Notable in this verse is how the body is pressed into the service of memory ("hand . . . eyes . . . mouth"). Rashi draws attention to the par-allel idea of the Song of Songs: "Set me as a seal upon your heart . . . upon your arm" (Song 8:6).

10 **year-day:** Heb. *yamim;* the rendering follows B-R, which took the expres-sion to denote both "year to year" and specifically the holiday.

11-12 **It shall be . . . every breacher:** Returning to the subject of verse 2.

12 **for YHWH:** That is, for sacrifice to him.

13 **ass:** Not one of the "pure" animals fit for sacrifice, and hence its substitu-tion ("redeeming") by a lamb. **break-its-neck:** Others, "decapitate." The intent seems to be that if the animal is not redeemed, one is not allowed to benefit economically from it (Plaut 1981). **firstborn of men . . . redeem:** In this case the male child is symbolically transferred to God; child sacrifice was of course abhorrent to the Bible (see Gen. 22). To this day religious Jews "redeem" their firstborn sons with money given to charity, thirty days after birth (*Pidyon Ha-Ben*).

14 **What does this mean?:** Lit., "What is this?"

16 **headbands:** Others, "frontlets." The meaning is unclear; see the discus-sions in Plaut (1981) and Tigay (1982), from which the present translation is taken.

17 Now it was, when Pharaoh had sent the people free,
    that God did not lead them by way of the land of the Philis-
       tines, which indeed is nearer,
    for God said to himself:
    Lest the people regret it, when they see war,
    and return to Egypt!
18 So God had the people swing about by way of the wilderness
       at the Sea of Reeds.
    And the Children of Israel went up armed from the land of
       Egypt.
19 Now Moshe had taken Yosef's bones with him,
    for he had made the Children of Israel swear, yes, swear,
       saying:
    God will take account, yes, account of you—so bring my
       bones up from here with you!
20 They moved on from Sukkot and encamped in Etam at the
       edge of the wilderness.
21 Now YHWH goes before them,
    by day in a column of cloud, to lead them the way,
    by night in a column of fire, to give light to them,
    to (be able to) go by day and by night.
22 There does not retire
    the column of cloud by day
    or the column of fire by night
    from before the people!

14:1 YHWH spoke to Moshe, saying:
   2 Speak to the Children of Israel,
      that they may turn back and encamp before Pi ha-Hirot,
         between Migdol and the sea,

sixth-century B.C.E. exile in Babylonia looked back to recast the past in its
own image. At any rate, memory is clearly important here, with two
passages stressing the continuity of commemoration through the following
generations (vv.8–10 and 14–16).

The Route and the Escort (13:17–22): The initial exit from Egypt highlights
an ominous fact about the Israelites: God is well aware of their weaknesses
and leads them by a detour, lest they "see war" and seek to recover the
familiar security of being serfs. The section also explains what they are

doing out of the way of the logical route to Canaan (the place names are difficult to identify, but the general stress is clear), and sets up the great final victory of the next chapter.

Two other elements of weight enter in this brief passage. One concerns Yosef's bones, which leave Egypt with his descendants. The body of Yosef seems to anchor early Israelite history: its mummification brings the Genesis stories to a close, its journey here links up Israel's patriarchal past with the radically new deliverance from bondage, and its final interment in the land of Israel formally closes out the conquest of the land under Yehoshua (Joshua) (Josh. 24:32).

Another unifying motif is that of God's accompanying the journeying Israelites in the form of cloud and fire. This passage is the first of what I have called the "Presence Accounts" described in "On the Book of Exodus and Its Structure," above.

At the Sea of Reeds (14): The liberation account ends with two literary masterpieces: the semi-poetic story of Israel's miraculous passage through the Sea of Reeds along with God's smashing of the Egyptian war machine, and the song of triumph that follows in Chapter 15. Taken together, they form a natural conclusion to what has gone before and a bridge to what follows. Chapter 14 marks the Israelites' last contact with the Egyptians, and the beginning of their desert journey.

17 **lead them . . . regret:** A play on words: Heb. *naham . . . yinnahem.*
     way: Some take this to be a proper noun or name: "The Way/Road of the
     Land of the Philistines." **land of the Philistines:** That is, along the
     Mediterranean coast.
18 **Sea of Reeds:** Not "Red Sea," which came from an ancient translation. It
     has more recently been suggested that the term (Heb. *suf*) can be read
     "End [*sof*] Sea," that is, the Sea at the End of the World. This mythologi-
     cal designation is attractive, given the cosmically portrayed events of the
     next chapter, but is not provable. The exact location, in any event, has not
     been established with certainty. **armed:** Heb. (*hamush*) unclear. The
     present rendering is supported by ancient versions; Plaut (1981) raises the
     possibility of "groups of five/fifty."
19 **he had made the Children of Israel swear:** See Gen. 50:25. The bones
     will be reburied, marking the end of the conquest of Canaan, in Josh.
     24:32.
21 **YHWH goes before them:** Others, "went before them." The Hebrew
     idiom here means "to lead," especially in war, and is the classic biblical
     description of a king. **column of cloud:** Heb. *'ammud 'anan.*
     cloud . . . fire: These are seen as physical manifestations of God's pres-
     ence, and are brought back in the narrative at Sinai (19:16, 18).
14:2 **Pi ha-Hirot:** The location is unknown.

before Baal-Tzefon, opposite it, you are to encamp by the
   sea.

3 Now Pharaoh will say of the Children of Israel:
   They are confused in the land! The wilderness has closed
      them in!

4 I will make Pharaoh's heart strong-willed, so that he pursues
      them,
   and I will be glorified through Pharaoh and all his forces,
   so that the Egyptians may know that I am YHWH.
   They did thus.

5 Now the king of Egypt was told that the people fled,
   and Pharaoh's heart and (that of) his servants changed re-
      garding the people, they said:
   What is this that we have done, that we have sent free Israel
      from serving us?

6 He had his chariot harnessed,
   his (fighting-) people he took with him,

7 and he took six hundred selected chariots and every (kind
      of) chariot of Egypt,
   teams-of-three upon them all.

8 YHWH made the heart of Pharaoh king of Egypt strong-
      willed, so that he pursued the Children of Israel,
   while the Children of Israel were going out with (their) hand
      upraised.

9 The Egyptians pursued them and overtook them encamped
      by the sea,
   all of Pharaoh's chariot-horses, his riders, and his forces,
   by Pi ha-Hirot, before Baal-Tzefon.

10 As Pharaoh drew near, the Children of Israel lifted up their
      eyes:
   Here, Egypt moving up after them!
   They were exceedingly afraid.
   And the Children of Israel cried out to YHWH,

11 they said to Moshe:
   Is it because there are no graves in Egypt
   that you have taken us out to die in the wilderness?
   What is this that you have done to us, bringing us out of
      Egypt?

12 Is this not the very word that we spoke to you in Egypt,

saying: Let us alone, that we may serve Egypt!
Indeed, better for us serving Egypt
than our dying in the wilderness!

As if the actual exodus were not dramatic enough, the narrator or editor has included a battle scene at this point in the text. As before, the principal combatants are God and Pharaoh, and as before, we begin with God's hardening the monarch's heart (v.4) to teach him a final lesson ("I will be glorified"). In that vein, some of the plague motifs are repeated, making Chapter 14 a fitting conclusion to the Deliverance account stylistically and thematically (see also Isbell 1982). At the same time the story includes a foreshadowing of Israel's behavior in the wilderness for the next two years, with a detailed account of their complaints against Moshe (and God's miraculous response).

God appears in this story in his most warlike garb, and temporarily resembles many of the gods of antiquity (Cross 1973 uses the term "the divine warrior," relating it to Northwest Semitic imagery). This is not unusual for the Bible, and seems appropriate here, given the climactic nature of the events and the general context of the Deliverance Narrative. Otherwise, the Hebrew God was conceived of as the originator of all

4 **be glorified through:** The Hebrew uses the same stem (*kbd*) earlier in the narrative, as if to suggest that Pharaoh's "heaviness" (stubborness) is answered, not only by "heavy" (severe) plagues, but by God, showing his "heaviness" (glory) at the sea. I did not find a solution in English to the unified use of the one root in Hebrew—a frustrating defeat, given the principles of this translation.

5 **told that the people fled:** As if they were not expecting it; now it is obvious that the Israelites are not leaving simply to observe a religious festival (Plaut 1981).

6 **(fighting-) people:** This reading is supported by Num. 31:32 and Josh. 8:1 (Childs 1974).

7 **six hundred:** A nice counterpart of the 600,000 (or 600 units of) Israelite males mentioned previously. **teams-of-three:** Others, "officers," "warriors," "a picked team."

8 **(their) hand upraised:** Others, "defiantly," "in triumph."

11–12 **they said. . . . wilderness:** The Israelites' complaint has been shaped into a great rhetorical paragraph, with the people's first "grumbling" against Moshe an ominous foreshadowing of what will occur throughout the wanderings. In this construction, the longed-for "Egypt" is repeated five times, and the unknown "wilderness" twice. Note also the stress on Moshe: "you have taken us out. . . . you have done to us."

13 Moshe said to the people:
Do not be afraid!
Stand fast and see
YHWH's deliverance which he will work for you today,
for as you see Egypt today, you will never see it again for the
    ages!
14 YHWH will make war for you, and you—you be still!
15 YHWH said to Moshe:
Why do you cry out to me?
Speak to the Children of Israel, and let-them-move-forward!
16 And you—
hold your staff high, stretch out your hand over the sea
and split it!
The Children of Israel shall come through the midst of the
    sea upon the dry-land.
17 But I,
here, I will make Egypt's heart strong-willed,
so that they come in after them,
and I will be glorified through Pharaoh and all his forces,
his chariots and his riders;
18 the Egyptians shall know that I am YHWH,
when I am glorified through Pharaoh, his chariots and his
    riders.
19 The messenger of God that was going before the camp of
    Israel moved on and went behind them,
the column of cloud moved ahead of them
and stood behind them,
20 coming between the camp of Egypt and the camp of Israel.
Here were the cloud and the darkness,
and (there) it lit up the night;
the-one did not come near the-other all night.
21 Moshe stretched out his hand over the sea,
and YHWH caused the sea to go back
with a fierce east wind all night,
and made the sea into firm-ground;
thus the waters split.
22 The Children of Israel came through the midst of the sea
    upon the dry-land,
the waters a wall for them on their right and on their left.
23 But the Egyptians pursued and came in after them,

things, good and evil, and was of course not compartmentalized into limited tasks as were other gods of neighboring cultures.

From a formal point of view, the sea narrative is among the most formulaic in the Hebrew Bible. That is, it is built entirely upon several phrases that repeat throughout the text, stressing its major themes. These include: God's "making Pharaoh's heart strong-willed" (vv.4, 8, 17); God's "being glorified" through what he does to the Egyptians (vv.4, 17, 18); Israel's going "upon dry-land" (vv.16, 22, 29); the waters' "returning" (vv.26, 27, 28); Israel's marching "through/into the midst of the sea" (vv.16, 22, 23, 27, 29); Pharaoh's "chariots and riders" (vv.17, 18, 23, 26, 28); and a description of the standing waters, "the waters a wall for them to their right and to their left" (vv.22, 29); see also the refrain, "before Pi ha-Hirot . . . before Baal-Tzefon" (v.4) and "by Pi ha-Hirot, before Baal-Tzefon" (v.9). The text is thus much more than a journalistic account of what happened: it is a rhythmic retelling of an experience, strongly conditioned by traditional (probably oral) Israelite forms of storytelling.

The ending (vv.29–31) betrays the influence of Deuteronomy. Using language that mirrors the end of the entire Torah (Deut. 34), the text speaks of seeing, fearing, hand, eyes, and the unique-to-Deuteronomy phrase "Moshe his servant" (see Deut. 34:5). Significantly, then, the final narrative of Israel's relationship to Egypt is cast as a classic ending in general.

What exactly happened at the sea? As I indicated in "On the Book of Exodus and Its Structure," above, such a point is unanswerable, and may not have a great bearing on the meaning of our text. Scholars have scrambled their brains for decades, trying either to reconstruct precisely what

13 **Moshe said . . .:** There follow four rapid-fire verbs of command, to quiet the complaints. **Stand fast and see:** Heb. *hityatzevu u-re'u.* **deliverance:** A word meaning "rescue," but extending to circumstances that appear miraculous to those who experience them.

15–16 **YHWH said . . .:** God echoes Moshe, issuing four commands.

15 **let-them-move-forward:** Countering the "Egypt moving up after them" of verse 10.

16 **and split it!:** As if that were as natural an act as stretching out one's hand!

20 **and (there) it lit up:** Heb. unclear; some read the verb as coming from a different root, meaning "cast a spell on," which, however, weakens the theme of distinction mentioned earlier.

21 **fierce east wind:** Looking back to the "east wind" that rid Egypt of the locusts in 10:13, and forward to God's "fierce-might" in 15:2, after the triumph at the sea. **firm-ground:** In the Flood Narrative, another story of deliverance (and death) by water, the same word appears as a sign that all is well. Similarly, the "dry-land" of the next verse appears in Gen. 8:14.

all of Pharaoh's horses, his chariots and his riders,
into the midst of the sea.

24 Now it was at the morning-watch:
YHWH looked out against the camp of Egypt in the column
    of fire and cloud,
and he stirred up the camp of Egypt,

25 he loosened the wheels of his chariots and made them to
    drive with heaviness.
Egypt said:
I must flee before Israel,
for YHWH makes war for them against Egypt!

26 Then YHWH said to Moshe:
Stretch out your hand over the sea,
and the waters shall return
upon Egypt—upon its chariots and upon its riders.

27 Moshe stretched out his hand over the sea,
and the sea returned, at the face of morning, to its original-
    place,
as the Egyptians were fleeing toward it.
And YHWH shook the Egyptians in the midst of the sea.

28 The waters returned,
they covered the chariots and the riders of all of Pharaoh's
    forces that had come after them into the sea,
not even one of them remained.

29 But the Children of Israel had gone upon dry-land, through
    the midst of the sea,
the waters a wall for them on their right and on their left.

30 So YHWH delivered Israel on that day from the hand of
    Egypt;
Israel saw Egypt dead by the shore of the sea,

31 and Israel saw the great hand that YHWH had wrought
    against Egypt,
the people feared YHWH,
they trusted in YHWH and in Moshe his servant.

15:1 Then sang Moshe and the Children of Israel
this song to YHWH,
they uttered (this) utterance:

I will sing to YHWH,
for he has triumphed, yes, triumphed,

"natural" event this "really" was (e.g., tides, tidal wave), or to identify the exact location of the "Sea of Reeds." While such matters are important to the historian, the Bible itself concentrates on the theme of the story. The narrator was concerned to demonstrate God's final victory and to portray Israel's escape in terms of a birthing (through a path, out of water), and these themes had the most influence both on later biblical tradition and on the generations of inspired Jews and Christians that heeded them.

The Song of God as Triumphant King (15:1–21): Moshe's famous Song at the Sea provides a natural boundary in the book of Exodus. It sets off the Egypt traditions from those of Sinai and the wilderness, and brings to a spectacular close the saga of liberation. This is borne out even in scribal tradition, still observed in the writing of Torah scrolls today, where the Song is written out with different spacing from the preceding and following narrative portions.

A poem is necessary at this point in the story, to provide emotional exultation and a needed break before the next phase of Israel's journey in the book. The Song manages to focus the Israelites' (the audience's?) intense feelings in a way that neither the ritual of Chapters 12–13 nor even the semi-poetic description of God's miraculous intervention in Chapter 14 can do. Only poetry is capable of expressing the full range of the people's emotions about what has happened. This is similar to the effect of the great poems that occur toward the end of Genesis (Chap. 49, the Blessing of Yaakov) and Deuteronomy (Chaps. 32–33, the Song and Blessing of Moshe).

A major concern of the poet is God's kingship, with which he ends the poem (a one-liner—"Let YHWH be king for the ages, eternity!"—contrasting with the doublets and triplets in the body of the poem). This is no accident, nor is it inappropriate; since Chapters 4 and 5 the story of

24 **morning-watch:** Before sunrise; the biblical night was divided into three "watches." **stirred up:** Others, "threw into panic." The phrase is used in the Bible to describe God's effect on his enemies (e.g., Josh. 10:10, Jud. 4:15, I Sam. 7:10) (Hyatt 1971).

25 **heaviness:** Again, possibly a play on Pharaoh's "heaviness" (stubbornness) and God's "glory."

27 **face:** Or "turning," which, however, would have clashed with the frequent "returning" (another Hebrew verb) in these verses. **originalplace:** Others, "bed," "normal depth."

30–31 **saw . . . saw:** The key verb again, echoing back not only to verse 13 but to various narratives throughout the book.

15:1 **uttered (this) utterance:** Giving a wider range of meaning for the Hebrew *va-yomeru le'mor.* **triumphed:** A rendering based on Ugaritic.

the horse and its charioteer
he flung into the sea!

2   My fierce-might and strength is YAH,
he has become deliverance for me.

This is my God—I honor him,
the God of my father—I exalt him.

3   YHWH is a man of war,
YHWH is his name!

4   Pharaoh's chariots and his forces
he hurled into the sea,
his choicest teams-of-three
sank in the Sea of Reeds.

5   Oceans covered them,
they went down in the depths
like a stone.

6   Your right-hand, O YHWH,
majestic in power,
your right-hand, O YHWH,
shattered the enemy.

7   In your great triumph
you smashed your foes,
you sent forth your fury,
consumed them like chaff.

8   By the breath of your nostrils
the waters piled up,
the gushing-streams stood up like a dam,
the oceans congealed in the heart of the sea.

9   Uttered the enemy:
I will pursue,
overtake,
and apportion the plunder,
my greed will be filled on them,

my sword I will draw,
my hand—dispossess them!
10   You blew with your breath,
the sea covered them,
they plunged down like lead
in majestic waters.

11   Who is like you among the gods, O YHWH!
who is like you, majestic among the holy-ones,
Feared-One of praises, Doer of Wonders!

12   You stretched out your right-hand,
the Underworld swallowed them.

Exodus has revolved around just who shall be king (God or Pharaoh) and
just who shall be served. By the end of Chapter 14 this is no longer an
issue. The victorious YHWH can now be acclaimed as king, while we hear
nothing further of Pharaoh. (Has he drowned or merely been written out
of the story? Later generations of Jews enjoyed giving him a role in the
world to come: he stands at the gate of Hell, admonishing evildoers as they
enter; see Ginzberg 1937.)

The attempts to recover what happened at the sea through the poem are
doomed to failure, considering that the piece is constructed out of two
traditional stories, the victory at the sea and the later conquest of Canaan
(vv.1–12, 13–17). Further, it is set in cosmic terms. The words "Oceans"

2 **strength:** Others, "song."   **YAH:** A shortened form (YH) of the name of
God (YHWH), and found often in biblical names (e.g., Uriah).
3 **man of war:** Or "warrior."
6 **right-hand:** As elsewhere in the ancient and medieval world, the right
hand was symbolic of strength.
8 **piled up:** Heb. root *'rm*, found only here.
9 **Uttered the enemy . . .:** The Hebrew uses alliteration, as well as a concentration on "I/my," to express the vividness and urgency of the enemy's
greed: *'amar 'oyev/ 'erdof 'asig/ 'ahallek shallal.* I have tried to use alliptera-
tive English words ("uttered. . . . enemy/I. . . . overtake . . . and apportion") and at least to hint at the poetic force of the Hebrew.   **greed:** The
Hebrew (*nefesh*) means "seat of feelings, emotions"; trad. "soul."
11 **among the gods:** The sea is the scene of YHWH's final triumph over the
gods of Egypt, as it were.
12 **Underworld:** Others, "earth."

13   You led in your faithfulness
        your people redeemed,
        guided (them) in your fierce-might
        to your holy pasture.

14   The peoples heard,
        they shuddered;
        frenzy seized
        Philistia's settlers,
15   and then, terrified,
        Edom's chieftains,
        Moav's "rams"—
        trembling did seize them;
        then melted away
        all Canaan's settlers.

16   There fell upon them
        dread and anguish;
        before your arm's greatness
        they grew dumb like stone.

        Until they crossed—your people, O YHWH,
        until they crossed—the people you fashioned.
17   You brought them, you planted them
        on the mount of your heritage,
        foundation of your (royal) seat
        which you prepared, O YHWH,
        the Holy-Place, O Lord,
        founded by your hands.

(Heb. *tehomot*; vv.5, 8) and "breath" (*ru'ah*; v.8) recall the primeval chaos
at the beginning of Creation itself (Gen. 1:2). This technique is characteristic of much of ancient/religious literature: a great event is told in a way
that reflects the beginnings of the gods/the world (this may include state-
ments about the end of the world as well).

    It should be noted that some scholars point out the close resemblance
between God's victory here and scenes in other ancient Near Eastern
literatures that portray the triumph of a storm god over a sea god. So

however historical the events in Chapters 14–15 may have been, in their biblical retelling they have been patterned after antecedents in myth.

Much has been written concerning the structure of the Song (see, e.g., Cassuto 1967, Cross 1973, and Lichtenstein 1984). I will mention only a few points here. The vocabulary of the poem is extremely concentrated. Major ideas are expressed by clusters of key verbs. Note, for instance, the grouping of "flung," "hurled," "plunged," "shattered," "smashed," "consumed"—a veritable lexicon of military victory. A number of verbs describe divine leadership ("led," "guided," "brought"), and God's establishment of the Israelites in Canaan ("planted," "founded"). The fear of the Canaanites (of Israel and its God) is graphically expanded to "shuddered," "seized with frenzy," "terrified," "seized with trembling," "melted away," ". . . dread and anguish," and "grew dumb." Finally, there are a number of nouns that express weight (cf. Heb. *kaved*, previously discussed): "stone," "dam," and "lead."

The overall effect of the poem is of fierce pride at God's victory, and exultant description of the destruction and discomfort of enemies, whether Egyptian or Canaanite. This general tone parallels many ancient war poems; what is characteristically Israelite about it is God's choosing and leading a people. Therefore the last verse goes far beyond the celebration of a single military victory. The Song constitutes the founding of a theocratic people.

Scholars have long noted the archaic style of the Song, which uses forms characteristic of early biblical Hebrew. Its tone is for this reason even more exalted than is usual in biblical poetry. An imaginative reflection of the effect can be found in Daiches (1975), who paraphrases the Song in the style of early English epic poetry.

Two sections have been appended to the end of the poem. First there is the poetically remarkable summary of the narrative in verse 19, notable for the fact that it is composed wholly from phrases used in Chapter 14. There follows a women's repetition/performance of at least part of the Song complete with dance. Some scholars see this as the "original" form of the poem. Of equal interest is the characterization of Miryam as a "prophet-

13 **holy pasture:** A shepherd's term, which could indicate the entire land of Canaan, and hence support the background of the Conquest in the poem (Childs 1974).

14–15 **Philistia . . . Edom . . . Moav:** Israel's later (and hostile) neighbors, to the west and east.

15 **"rams":** Perhaps, as in Ugaritic usage, a technical term for "chieftains."

17 **mount . . . foundation . . . holy-place:** Probably the Jerusalem Temple of later times, although the entire land is sometimes referred to as "mount of your inheritance" (see Deut. 3:25) (Hertz 1960).

18   Let YHWH be king
          for the ages, eternity!

19 For Pharaoh's horses came with (their) chariots and riders
        into the sea,
      but YHWH turned back the sea's waters upon them,
      and the Children of Israel went upon the dry-land
      through the midst of the sea.

20 Now Miryam the prophetess, Aharon's sister, took a timbrel
        in her hand,
      and all the women went out after her, with timbrels and with
        dancing.
21 Miryam chanted to them:

          Sing to YHWH,
          for he has triumphed, yes, triumphed,
          the horse and its charioteer
          he flung into the sea!

ess." But there may be a structural reason for her appearance as well: the
enterprise of deliverance from Egypt began with a little girl at the Nile,
watching through the reeds to make sure her baby brother would survive;
it ends with the same person, now an adult, a "prophetess" celebrating the
final victory at the Sea of Reeds.

    20 **Miryam the prophetess:** Trad. English "Miriam." This is the first time
        in the narrative that she is mentioned by name, and also the first appear-
        ance of a "prophetess" in the Hebrew Bible.

PART **II** In the Wilderness

(15:22–18:27)

T HE WILDERNESS narratives in the Torah must have been extraordinarily important to the narrator/editor, as evidenced by their placement at this point in Exodus. Why did he/they see fit to insert here material which, chronologically at least, would fit better at a later point—for instance, in the book of Numbers (which reports essentially the same sort of incidents)?

The answer comes from several quarters. The wilderness stories embody a key process for the Torah story: Israel's passage from enslaved childhood to troubled adolescence, with a hopeful glance toward adulthood (the Promised Land). This process starts immediately after liberation; indeed, it is its direct result. Further, the three "desert themes" prominent in Chapters 15–18—"grumbling" against God and Moshe, hostile neighbors, and early self-government—are appropriate to include before the meeting at Sinai, in that they demonstrate dramatically the people's need for reassurance, protection, group solidarity, and institutions (whereby they can live harmoniously). These narratives, therefore, lay out Israel's precarious position and create the hope for a cure. It is only later on in the Torah, in the book of Numbers, that we will discover that the growing-up process in the wilderness could not be accomplished in a single generation.

The portrait of a people (or of an individual, as is often the case in religious literature) undergoing transformation in a place outside of normal geographic/cultural boundaries is a well-known phenomenon in traditional stories. Anthropologist Victor Turner (1969) speaks of the "liminal" experience, where the protagonist or initiant is separated spiritually and geographically from his origins in order to be changed into something new (see Fredman 1983, Cohn 1981). This is paralleled by the process of pilgrimage in the world of ritual, as can still be observed among many communities of the world to this day. The desert is the site of liminality

par excellence: it is a harsh place that contains none of the succoring
elements of human civilization, yet at the same time it leads the wanderer
into truer communication with nature and the divine, metacultural forces
of the universe. It is a place of betwixt and between, which mirrors the
experiencer's psychological state. In the case of Israel, later biblical
sources speak of the wilderness period with striking force, either as an
example of the people's long-standing and deeply ingrained rebelliousness
(e.g., Psalm 95), or fondly, as a kind of honeymoon period between God
and Israel (e.g., Jer. 2:2). In both cases what is evoked is only a stage on
the way, and not the final goal (see Talmon 1966).

Transformation always involves both life and death, and so it is not
surprising that a characteristic theme of the stories before us is lack of food
and/or water. The opening episodes of the section (15:22–17:7) comprise
three scenes of "grumbling" about the difficulties of survival (with the
structure: water–food–water), with a unique biblical twist: God and the
people "testing" each other. And so the transformation depends very
much on God's action on the people's behalf (twice he has to "instruct"
them—the very verb from which the term "Torah" is derived). The
suspension of the life process, or at least its imperiling, is notable also in
the fact that, in contrast to the fertility of the Israelites in Egypt, "the trek
narrative does not relate a single birth" (Cohn 1981). This is especially
striking given the strong birth image of Israel at the Sea of Reeds, which is
still in the reader's mind as the section opens.

22 Moshe had Israel move on from the Sea of Reeds,
   and they went out to the Wilderness of Shur.
   They traveled through the wilderness for three days, and
       found no water.
23 They came to Mara,
   but they could not drink water from Mara, because it was
       mar/bitter.
   Therefore they called its name Mara.
24 The people grumbled against Moshe, saying:
   What are we to drink?
25 He cried out to YHWH,
   and YHWH directed him (to some) wood

which he threw into the water, and the water became
   sweet.—
There he imposed law and judgment for them, and there he
   tested them.
26 He said:
If you will hearken, yes, hearken to the voice of YHWH
   your God,
and what is right in his eyes will do,
giving-ear to his commandments
and keeping all his laws:
all the sicknesses which I have imposed upon Egypt, I will
   not impose upon you;
for I am YHWH, your healer.

Grumbling I (15:22–27): The first of the wilderness narratives is linked to what has gone before via the theme of water. Fresh from their rescue from death at the sea, the Israelites look for water in the desert and find the discovery of unpotable water intolerable. The key word, especially for the many later wilderness traditions such as we find in Numbers, is "grumbled" (Heb. *lyn*), which leads to God's nurturing of the people. Strangely, the theme of undrinkable water recalls the beginning of the plague sequence in Egypt (7:20–21).

Right away in this first desert episode we are told the purpose of Israel's journey: God is testing them, to see if they will "hearken" to what he bids them to do. The language is in the style of Deuteronomy. One should also mention the idea of "law and judgment," indicating another crucial desert theme: Israel's ability or inability to govern itself.

The account ends with an abundance of water in verse 27.

22 **Shur:** Some translate as "Wall" (of Egypt)—the outer fortified boundary of the country, and hence the edge of civilization.
24 **grumbled:** Others, "murmured," which is, however, more alliterative than the Hebrew itself (*va-yilonu*).
25 **There he imposed law and judgment:** Others, "There he made for them statute and ordinance," etc. The force is not clear, but the phrase seems to fit in with the overall section, which, as I have noted, concerns itself with the Israelites' early government.
26 **sicknesses . . . upon Egypt:** A recurring theme in the Torah; see the curse in Deut. 28:60.

27 They came to Elim;
there were twelve springs of water
and seventy palms,
and they camped there by the water.

16:1 They moved on from Elim, and they came, the whole community of the Children of Israel, to the Wilderness of Syn,
which is between Elim and Sinai,
on the fifteenth day of the second New-Moon after their
going-out from the land of Egypt.

2 And they grumbled, the whole community of the Children of
Israel, against Moshe and against Aharon in the wilderness.

3 The Children of Israel said to them:
Would that we had died by the hand of YHWH in the land
of Egypt,
when we sat by the flesh pots,
when we ate bread till (we were) sated!
For you have brought us into this wilderness
to bring death to this whole assembly by starvation!

4 YHWH said to Moshe:
Here, I will make rain down upon you bread from the heavens,
the people shall go out and glean, each day's amount in its
day,
in order that I may test them, whether they will walk according to my instruction or not.

5 But is shall be on the sixth day:
when they prepare what they have brought in,
it shall be a double-portion compared to what they glean day
after day.

6 Moshe and Aharon said to all the Children of Israel:
In the evening
you will know
that it is YHWH who brought you out of the land of Egypt;

7 in the morning
you will see the Glory of YHWH:
when he hearkens to your grumblings against YHWH—
what are we, that you grumble against us?

8 Moshe said:
Since YHWH gives you

flesh to eat in the evening,
and in the morning, bread to sate (yourselves);
since YHWH hearkens to your grumblings which you
  grumble against him—
what are we:
not against us are your grumblings, but against YHWH!
9 Moshe said to Aharon:
Say to the whole community of the Children of Israel:
Come-near, in the presence of YHWH,
for he has hearkened to your grumblings!
10 Now it was, when Aharon spoke to the whole community of
  the Children of Israel,
they faced the wilderness,
and here:
the Glory of YHWH could be seen in the cloud.
11 YHWH spoke to Moshe, saying:

Grumbling II (16): Moving now halfway (in terms of time) to their Sinai destination, the people encounter a new lack: food. This reintroduces the "testing" motif (v.4), with its built-in answer: God provides quails and *mahn* (trad. English "manna"). The story is full-blown, and its repeating vocabulary sets forth the issues clearly: "grumble" occurs seven times, and "command/commandments" four times, linked to the idea of testing.

27 **Elim:** Lit., "terebinths" (great trees already mentioned in Gen. 12:6 and 18:1). **twelve springs . . . seventy palms:** Once again the numbers are obviously typological.

16:1 **whole community:** See the note to 12:3. **Syn:** Pronounced "seen." The present spelling has been adopted to avoid the unfortunate associations of the sound "sin" in English.

3 **Egypt . . . flesh pots . . . :** Notice the endings of each line, which can be grouped into two clusters: "Egypt . . . flesh pots . . . sated" versus "wilderness . . . starvation."

4 **YHWH said:** Notice how God's answer is totally devoid of anger, for the dissatisfaction of the people is to provide them with a "test." **them . . . they:** The pronouns are collective singular in Hebrew.

5 **a double-portion:** For the Sabbath, when no gleaning is permitted.

7 **what are we:** The issue is not between Israel and its human leaders, but really between them and God.

8 **bread:** See the note to 2:20.

9 **Come-near:** See the note to 12:48.

12 I have hearkened to the grumblings of the Children of
      Israel—
    speak to them, and say:
    At twilight you shall eat flesh,
    and in the morning you shall be sated with bread,
    and you shall know
    that I am YHWH your God.
13 Now it was in the evening
    a horde-of-quail came up and covered the camp.
    And in the morning
    there was a layer of dew around the camp;
14 and when the layer of dew went up,
    here, upon the surface of the wilderness,
    something fine,
    scaly,
    fine as hoar-frost upon the land.
15 When the Children of Israel saw it
    they said each-man to his brother:
    Mahn hu/what is it?
    For they did not know what it was.
    Moshe said to them:
    It is the bread that YHWH has given you for eating.
16 This is the word that YHWH has commanded:
    Glean from it, each-man according to what he can eat,
    an *omer* per capita, according to the number of your persons,
    each-man, for those in his tent, you are to take.
17 The Children of Israel did thus,
    they gleaned, the-one-more and the-one-less,
18 but when they measured by the *omer*,
    no surplus had the-one-more, and the-one-less had no short-
      age;
    each-man had gleaned according to what he could eat.
19 Moshe said to them:
    No man shall leave any of it until morning.
20 But they did not hearken to Moshe,
    and (several) men left some of it until morning;
    it became wormy with maggots and reeked.
    Moshe became furious with them.
21 They gleaned it morning after morning, each-man in accor-
      dance with what he could eat,

but when the sun heated up, it melted.
22 Now it was on the sixth day
that they gleaned a double-portion of bread, two *omers* for
(each) one.
All the exalted-ones of the community came and told it to
Moshe.

Indeed, this long story poses the question central to all the wilderness
narratives: ". . . whether they will walk according to my instruction or
not" (v.4).

The manna was important in early Israelite tradition as a witness to
God's nurturing, as attested by the end of the chapter with its ritual
prescriptions regarding it (vv.32–34; note the threefold repetition of
"safekeeping"). But it also sets up an emphasis on a more permanent
institution in Israelite culture: the Sabbath. One notion that this passage
may convey is the antiquity and importance of the Sabbath, preceding the
laws of Sinai as it does here. Also at issue is whether the Israelites can
follow simple rules laid down by God.

14 **something fine:** The *mahn* (trad. English "manna"), described again in
verse 31, below, possibly refers to insect secretions found on the branches
of certain Sinai plants. The question has been asked, however, as to
whether the amount so produced would under normal circumstances be
sufficient to feed a large population—hence the text itself stresses the
divine element, and any attempt to explain it scientifically misses the point
of the biblical story.

15 **Mahn hu:** A folk etymological corruption of the Hebrew *mah hu,* although
there is some support for this form in other Semitic languages. A playful
rendering might be "whaddayacallit" or "what's-its-name."

16 **omer:** A dry measure, approximately 2 ⅓ liters or 2 dry quarts.

17 **the-one:** Or "some of them."

18 **no surplus . . . no shortage:** In the tradition of miracle stories, exactly
the right amount is found for each person.

19 **No man shall leave any of it until morning:** Like the Passover sacrifice in
12:10 and 34:25, or the festival-offering in 23:18. The idea may be not to
disturb the perfection of the offering by risking putrefaction.

22 **exalted-ones:** Or "princes."

23 He said to them:

It is what YHWH spoke about:

tomorrow is a Sabbath/Ceasing, a Sabbath of Holiness for
   YHWH.

Whatever you wish to bake—bake, and whatever you wish
   to boil—boil;

and all the surplus, put aside for yourselves in safekeeping
   until morning.

24 They put it aside until the morning, as Moshe h.
   commanded,

and it did not reek, neither were there any maggots in it.

25 Moshe said:

Eat it today,

for today is a Sabbath for YHWH,

today you will not find it in the field.

26 For six days you are to glean,

but on the seventh day is Sabbath, there will not be (any) on it.

27 But it was on the seventh day

that some of the people went out to glean, and they did not
   find.

28 YHWH said to Moshe:

Until when will you refuse to keep my commandments and
   my instructions?

29 (You) see

that YHWH has given you the Sabbath,

therefore on the sixth day, he gives you bread for two days.

Stay, each-man, in his spot;

no man shall go out from his place on the seventh day!

30 So the people ceased on the seventh day.

31 Now the House of Israel called its name: *Mahn.*

—It is like coriander seed, whitish,

and its taste is like (that of) a wafer with honey.—

32 Moshe said:

This is the word that YHWH has commanded:

An *omer*-full of it for safekeeping throughout your generations,

in order that they may see the bread that I had you eat in the
   wilderness

when I brought you out of the land of Egypt.

33 Moshe said to Aharon:

Take a vat and put an *omer*-full of *mahn* in it,

and put it aside in the presence of YHWH, in safekeeping
throughout your generations.

34 As YHWH had commanded Moshe, Aharon put it aside
before the Testimony, in safekeeping.

35 And the Children of Israel ate the *mahn* for the forty years,
until they came to settled land,
the *mahn* they ate, until they came to the edge of the land of
Canaan.

36 Now an *omer*—a tenth of an *efa* it is.

17:1 They moved on, the whole commmunity of the Children of
Israel, from the Wilderness of Syn,
by their moving-stages, at YHWH's bidding.
They encamped at Refidim,
and there is no water for the people to drink!

2 The people quarreled with Moshe, they said:
Give us water, that we may drink!
Moshe said to them:
For-what do you quarrel with me?
For-what do you test YHWH?

Grumbling III (17:1–7): With the third wilderness story we return to the
water theme. This time the element of "quarreling" with Moshe is added,
in addition to the portrayal of Moshe's eroding patience (v.4). Otherwise it
is a variation on the basic theme (notice, for instance, the similarities
between 16:3 and 17:3). The ending is ominous, reversing the previously
held idea of God's testing Israel.

23 **It is what YHWH spoke about:** Although this speech is not mentioned in
a previous text. This may support the position that the story was originally
placed after Chapter 20 (which contains the command to observe the
Sabbath). **Ceasing:** The root meaning of the Hebrew *shabbat*, "Sabbath."

24 **it did not reek:** Since this time they followed God's orders.

28 **you:** Plural, referring to the people.

31 **Now . . . honey:** A parenthetical comment. For another biblical description of the manna, see Num. 11:8.

34 **Testimony:** The tablets of the covenant mentioned in 25:21 and 31:18;
their citing seems out of place here, but it should be borne in mind that
the Torah is not always chronological, as was already recognized by medieval commentators.

17:2 **For-what:** Why. Notice how the text equates quarreling with Moshe and
testing YHWH. **quarrel:** A verb that often denotes a legal case in biblical texts.

3 The people thirsted for water there,
   and the people grumbled against Moshe, and said:
   For-what-reason then did you bring us up from Egypt,
   to bring death to me, to my children and to my livestock by
      thirst?
4 Moshe cried out to YHWH, saying:
   What shall I do with this people?
   A little more and they will stone me!
5 YHWH said to Moshe:
   Proceed before the people,
   take some of the elders of Israel with you,
   and your staff with which you struck the Nile, take in your
      hand,
   and go!
6 Here, I stand before you there on the rock at Horev,
   you are to strike the rock, and water shall come out of it, and
      the people shall drink.
   Moshe did thus, before the eyes of the elders of Israel.
7 And he called the name of the place: *Massa*/Testing, and
      Meriva/Quarreling,
   because of the quarreling of the Children of Israel,
   and because of their testing of YHWH, saying:
   Is YHWH among us, or not?

8 Now Amalek came and made war upon Israel in Refidim.
9 Moshe said to Yehoshua:
   Choose us men,
   and go out, make war upon Amalek!
   On the morrow I will station myself on top of the hill, with
      the staff of God in my hand.
10 Yehoshua did as Moshe had said to him,
   to make war against Amalek.
   Now Moshe, Aharon and Hur went up to the top of the hill.
11 And it was, whenever Moshe raised his hand, Israel pre-
      vailed, and whenever he set down his hand, Amalek
      prevailed.
12 Now Moshe's hands are heavy;
   so they took a stone and placed it under him, and he sat
      down on it,
   while Aharon and Hur supported his hands, one on this-side
      and one on that-side.

So his hands remained steadfast, until the sun came in.

13 And Yehoshua weakened Amalek and his people, with the
edge of the sword.

14 YHWH said to Moshe:
Write this as a memorial in an account
and put it in Yehoshua's hearing:
Yes, I will wipe out, wipe out the memory of Amalek from
under the heavens!

War with Amalek (17:8–16): In addition to testing/grumbling, conflict with foreigners is a significant wilderness theme (see Num. 20–24). It is perhaps for this reason that it has been included in the pre-Sinai traditions. Its placement here may depend on its use of Moshe's staff; the previous narrative ended with the use of that object, and such linkage was a known form of composition in ancient literature.

The tradition about Israel's relationship with Amalek, however brief, persists as an important one in the Bible. Saul, Israel's first king, is commanded by God to wipe out the Amalekites, as punishment for their opposition of Israel in our passage (I Sam. 15), and centuries later, Haman, the evil Persian councillor who proposes to exterminate the Jews of his country, is portrayed as a descendant of the Amalekite king (Esther 3:1).

Our story, however, is no mere military report, but also a tradition about the power of the "staff of God." In another culture, indeed in later Midrashic literature, such a theme would receive Excalibur-like treatment, but the Bible suppresses the magical side and simply uses it as a tool, expressing God's continuing deliverance of Israel.

3 **me:** Personalizing the complaint.

6 **you are to strike the rock:** See Num. 20:2–13 for the famous variation on this story that proves to be Moshe's undoing.

7 **saying:** Meaning or signifying.

9 **Yehoshua:** Trad. English "Joshua." The name means "God delivers." He appears subsequently as Moshe's personal attendant, but it is significant that the first mention of him is in a military context, since he will ultimately command the invasion of Canaan.

10 **Hur:** He is mentioned again in 24:4 as Aharon's assistant in the governing of the people during Moshe's absence.

12 **sun came in:** Set.

13 **weakened:** Disabled or defeated.

14 **account:** Or "document." **wipe out the memory:** The command demonstrates the depth of Israel's animosity toward Amalek.

15 Moshe built an altar
and called its name: YHWH My Banner.

16 He said:
Yes,
Hand on YAH's throne!
War for YHWH against Amalek
generation after generation!

18:1 Now Yitro, the priest of Midyan, Moshe's father-in-law,
heard
about all that God had done for Moshe and for Israel his
people,
that YHWH had brought Israel out of Egypt.

2 Yitro, Moshe's father-in-law, took
Tzippora, Moshe's wife—after she had been sent home—

3 and her two sons,
of whom the first-one's name was Gershom/Sojourner
There, for he had said: I have become a sojourner in a
foreign land,

4 and the name of the other was Eliezer/God's-Help, for: the
God of my father is my help, he rescued me from Pharaoh's sword;

5 Yitro, Moshe's father-in-law, came with his sons and his
wife to Moshe, to the wilderness, where he was encamped,
at the mountain of God.

6 He (had it) said to Moshe:
I, your father-in-law Yitro, am coming to you, and your wife
and her two sons with her.

7 Moshe went out to meet his father-in-law,
he bowed and kissed him, and each-man asked after the
other's welfare;
then they came into the tent.

8 Moshe related to his father-in-law
all that YHWH had done to Pharaoh and to Egypt on Israel's account,
all the hardships that had befallen them on the journey,
and how YHWH had rescued them.

9 And Yitro was jubilant because of all the good that YHWH
had done for Israel, that he had rescued him from the land
of Egypt.

10 Yitro said:
Blessed be YHWH,
who has rescued you from the hand of Egypt and from the
    hand of Pharaoh,
who has rescued the people from under the hand of Egypt.

The New Society: Yitro's Visit (18): Israel finally reaches the "mountain of God," but this, remarkably, is subordinated to the fact that Moshe and the people meet up with Yitro, whom we recall from Chapters 2–4. The designation "father-in-law" recurs throughout this chapter (thirteen times), perhaps playing up the importance of the relationship in Israelite society. The real concern of the story, however, is Moshe's early attempt to set up a functioning judicial system in Israel (hence the key word *davar*, ten times, translated here as "matter" in the sense of "legal matter"). The chapter thus

15 **altar:** B-R use "slaughter-site" to reflect the Hebrew root *zavo'ah* in this word (*mizbe'ah*), and I followed them in *In the Beginning*. However, this is not fully acceptable, since by the time of the Bible, not only were grain and other nonanimal products offered up on Israelite altars, but the slaughtering of animals for sacrifices took place near and not on them. Hence the familiar English "altar" (which stems from a Latin word denoting "high place") will have to suffice. Where *zavo'ah* occurs in our text as a verb, I have retained the translation "slaughter."

16 **Hand on:** Cassuto (1967) suggests "monument to," following the meaning of *yad* in I Sam. 15:12, II Sam. 18:18, and other instances.   **throne:** Heb. *kes*, either a corruption of the more standard *kisse* or, most probably, a scribal error for *nes*, "banner," as in verse 15.

18:3 **he:** Moshe, in 2:22, above.

4 **Eliezer:** This is the first and only time we hear of this son.   **he rescued me from Pharaoh's sword:** Here, as sometimes occurs in the biblical text, we learn of earlier events or emotions. Moshe's emotional makeup while he was in Midyan (Chaps. 2–4) thus becomes a little clearer.

5 **at the mountain of God:** Another important fact has been casually slipped in at this point, again probably from a narrative taking place later. In the next chapter Israel's arrival at Sinai will be more dramatically heralded.

8 **YHWH had rescued them:** The verb was used above in relation to Moshe, and is a key repeating word in this chapter. Thus the experience of leader and people unite again, and the narrative of deliverance comes full circle. Moshe had begun his mission at Sinai, as a member of Yitro's household, and now the latter meets him in Sinai, on the brink of the confirmation of 3:12 ("you will serve God on this mountain").

9 **jubilant:** Heb. *va-yihd*, from *hdy*, a rare verb.

10 **who has rescued the people:** There is obviously a redundancy in this verse, based perhaps on a scribal error.

11 (So) now I know:
    yes, YHWH is greater than all gods—
    yes, in just that matter in which they were presumptuous
        against them!
12 Yitro, Moshe's father-in-law, took an offering-up and
        slaughter-animals for God,
    and Aharon and all the elders of Israel came to eat bread
        with Moshe's father-in-law, in the presence of God.
13 Now it was on the morrow:
    Moshe sat to judge the people,
    and the people stood before Moshe from morning until
        evening.
14 When Moshe's father-in-law saw all that he had to do for the
        people,
    he said:
    What kind of matter is this that you do for the people—
    why do you sit alone, while the entire people stations itself
        around you
    from morning until evening?
15 Moshe said to his father-in-law:
    When the people comes to me to inquire of God,
16 —when it has some legal-matter, it comes to me—
    I judge between a man and his fellow
    and make known God's laws and his instructions.
17 Then Moshe's father-in-law said to him:
    Not good is this matter, as you do it!
18 You will become worn out, yes, worn out, so you, so this
        people that are with you,
    for this matter is too heavy for you,
    you cannot do it alone.
19 So now, hearken to my voice,
    I will advise you, so that God may be-there with you:
    Be-there, yourself, for the people in relation to God.
    You yourself should have the matters come to God;
20 You should make clear to them the laws and the instructions,
    you should make known to them the way they should go,
        and the deeds that they should do;
21 but you—you are to have the vision (to select) from all the
        people
    men of caliber, fearing God,

men of truth, hating gain,
you should set (them) over them
as chiefs of thousands, chiefs of hundreds, chiefs of fifties,
    and chiefs of tens,
22 so that they may judge the people at all times.
So shall it be:
every great matter they shall bring before you,
but every small matter they shall judge by themselves.
Make (it) light upon you, and let them bear (it) with you.

serves as a good prelude to Sinai, which will include far-ranging legal material (despite the fact that some scholars see it as an insertion from a later
period—cf. verse 16, "God's laws and his instructions").

It has been noted (Cohn 1981) that the "trek narratives" in Exodus and
Numbers have been laid out evenly, with six "stations" between Egypt
and Sinai and another six between Sinai and the land of Israel. Thus here,
Israel has come to the mid-point of its journey. In another perspective,
Moshe himself has come full circle, returning to both the spot and the man
in whose presence the mature adult phase of his life had begun.

11 **in just that matter:** Heb. difficult; others either omit this phrase alto-
    gether, or use complex English constructions to reproduce it (e.g., "for he
    did this to those who treated Israel arrogantly," "for he has routed the
    mighty foes of his folk").   **they were presumptuous:** The Egyptians.
12 **in the presence of God:** An expression that usually carries a cultic mean-
    ing (Levine 1974).
14 **all that he had to do:** Compare verses 8 and 9, where the great "doing" of
    God is accomplished with ease. Perhaps a contrast is being drawn between
    divine and human deeds; Moshe cannot do the "all" that God can.
18 **heavy:** Again the key word that was mentioned earlier (see the note to
    14:4); it aids in linking up stories, as it has occurred in 17:12.
21 **the vision (to select):** The verb "see" in Hebrew (ra'oh) also has the
    connotation of "select" (cf. Gen. 22:8).   **caliber:** A term often used in a
    military context (see Jud. 11:1, 18:2).
22 **at all times:** That is, in minor matters—as we would say, "everyday
    affairs."

23 If you do (thus in) this matter
   when God commands you (further), you will be able to
       stand,
   and also this people will come to its place in peace.
24 Moshe hearkened to the voice of his father-in-law,
   he did it all as he had said:
25 Moshe chose men of caliber from all Israel,
   he placed them as heads over the people,
   as chiefs of thousands, chiefs of hundreds, chiefs of fifties,
       and chiefs of tens.
26 They would judge the people at all times:
   the difficult matters they would bring before Moshe,
   but every small matter they would judge by themselves.
27 Moshe sent his father-in-law off,
   and he went home to his land.

23 **stand:** Endure.
27 **sent . . . off/ . . . went . . . to his land:** A stock biblical farewell passage
    (see Num. 24:25, for instance).

PART **III** The Meeting and
Covenant at Sinai

(19–24)

THE NARRATIVE has returned to its source. At Sinai it had been foretold that when Pharaoh "sends you free, you will serve God on this mountain," and it is at Sinai that Moshe and the people now arrive. The fateful public meeting between the deity and the amassed human community will betoken the formal change of masters: the people, no longer enslaved by the Egyptian crown, now swear fealty to their divine Lord, who imposes rules of conduct upon them in return for his protection and their well-being.

The settings for these events of covenant-making and law-giving are appropriately impressive. The mountain naturally functions as a bridge between heaven and earth (with only Moshe allowed to ascend!), but it is additionally accompanied on this occasion by the powerful manifestations of smoke, fire, cloud, thunder, lightning, and trumpet blasts. To try and pin down exactly to what natural phenomena the story alludes, be they volcano, earthquake, or the like, is somewhat beside the point; what speaks through the text is the voice of an overwhelming experience. Indeed, as Greenberg (1972) points out, the account in Chapter 19 may have been deliberately left ambiguous and contradictory, showing that the editor wished to include all the received traditions about the event.

At the same time, it should be noted that the Sinai revelation resembles the appearance of the storm-god Baal in Canaanite texts, especially in the combining of thunder/lightning and earthquake. Psalm 18:8 portrays a similar scene. So as varied as the phenomena accompanying God's appearance here are, they conform to a known literary pattern (Greenstein 1984c).

As mentioned previously, Sinai stands geographically at the center of the Israelite wanderings. As the textual center of the book of Exodus as well, it anchors the people of Israel on their journey toward the fulfillment of their destiny. But that function is purely a mythic one. Sinai never became an important biblical cult site, and the only later story to take place there, that of Elijah in I Kings 20, clearly stems from the desire to draw a parallel between Elijah and Moshe. The Hebrews apparently could not conceive of God's abiding place's being located outside the land of Israel. On the other hand, it was necessary to demonstrate that Israel's laws and institutions arose, not out of normal settled political and economic circumstances, but rather as the direct gift and stipulation of God himself (see Cohn 1981), and hence the choice of a site wholly removed from the great culture centers of the ancient Near East: the monolithic culture of Egypt, the ancestral heritage of Mesopotamia, and the fertility-based society the people were to encounter in Canaan. Sinai, the originating point of Israel as a self-defined community, had to start everything anew, on a stage in which all other considerations had been stripped away.

Early in the history of biblical exegesis (the Midrash) it was noted that the events on Sinai resemble the conclusion of a marriage ceremony. Such an idea may even have been in the minds of the transmitters of the Exodus traditions. Indeed, the entire book is remarkably reminiscent of a pattern of rescue—courting—wedding with stipulations—home planning—infidelity—reconciliation—and final "moving in" (these stages fit into the general Part divisions I have used throughout the book). Lest this appear to be too Western a model, let it be noted that such analogies occur in the writings of the prophets, where the relationship between God and Israel is likened to that between husband and wife. This constitutes Israel's version of what Joseph Campbell (1972) has termed "sacred marriage" in hero stories—not, as classically, the hero's successful wooing of a goddess or semi-divine creature, but an intimate relationship established between God and his people. As such, it is unique in the ancient world.

On Covenant

Marriage may be one imaginative model for the Sinai experience, but it was covenant that the writers wished to stress above all in these chapters. Here we observe a fascinating phenomenon that occurs again and again in biblical religion: an institution well known in the secular world is given a religious emphasis in the Bible. For covenant (others, "pact") was a widespread form of political bonding in the ancient Near East. Kings and vassals, from Anatolia to Assyria, regularly aligned themselves in treaties involving either freewill granting of privileges or an agreement of mutual obligations between parties. A number of texts laying out the stipulations and ceremonies particular to covenant-making in the ancient Near East have been recovered, and study of them is helpful for an understanding of what we have in Exodus 19–24. Three things are clear. First, the stylistic pattern in our chapters resembles what is found in Hittite treaty texts (Mendenhall 1954); second, the Exodus passages use narrative to express these events, not merely a list of conditions; third, and most important, no other ancient society, so far as we know, conceived of the possibility that a *god* could "cut a covenant" with a people. This last fact leads to the observation that, for Israel, the true king was not earthly but divine— despite the later establishment of a monarchy (Weinfeld 1972b). Hence the narrator's concentration on these chapters, especially considering the dramatic nature of what had gone before (Chaps. 1–15).

The covenant found in Exodus and subsequently in the Torah differs substantively from the two described in Genesis. Noah (Gen. 9) and all living creatures had been promised no further universal destruction, with the stipulation that human beings were not to eat meat with blood or commit willful murder. Avraham, too (Gen. 15, 17), was the recipient of a covenant: God would give him land and descendants, and Avraham was to attend to the circumcision of all his males (yet this is more sign than stipulation). What these early events have in common is the aspect of bestowal—God acts and promises, and human beings are the passive recipients. Exodus introduces the notes of mutuality and conditionality. Both parties are now to have a stake in the agreement, and it can be broken by either (as in Chapter 32; contrast this with the promise to Noah in Gen. 8:21–22, "I will never doom the soil again . . . never shall [natural processes] cease," and Gen. 9:11, "Never again shall there be Deluge. . . .") From the Creator God we have moved to the God of History, who enters into a fateful relationship with the people of Israel (for more on this, see Sarna 1986).

On Biblical Law

A century of modern Bible scholarship has led to far-reaching changes in the perceptions of biblical law. Initial archeological findings, which often included legal documents, had led comparativists to see in the biblical material a pale reflection of its Mesopotamian antecedents. The Code of Hammurabi, for instance, was deemed the source of some of the Exodus material. These early judgments have given way to a view that places more emphasis on what is distinctive about the biblical laws.

For our purposes here, several brief points should be made, drawn from recent research; the reader may find them explored at greater depth in the essays by Greenberg (1970), Greenstein (1984), Paul (1970), and Sarna (1986), and the work of Sonsino (1980). Expressions of law in the ancient Near East, especially in documents from Mesopotamia, reveal a strong economic underpinning, tied to class structure. They also have at times a personal or political function. Hammurabi, for instance, presents his code with the express purpose that the gods and men may see what a just king he is. The laws are listed by category, with religion occupying its own sphere. Finally, the king acts as the enforcer of the laws, having received them from a god—who is nevertheless not their ultimate source. Law exists in the Mesopotamian texts as an abstract value, designed for the smooth functioning of society.

By way of contrast, Hebrew law, as typified by our chapters, displays very different concepts and concerns. Class is hardly alluded to, reflecting a totally different kind of society economically but also expressing an ideal that began in the Genesis creation story with the common ancestor of the human race. The laws are presented as the terms of the covenant (our section is often termed the "Book of the Covenant"), and the motivation behind them is portrayed as historical/psychological (". . . for you were sojourners in the land of Egypt"). Strikingly, the biblical regulations, not only here but in the other major collections as well (in Leviticus and Deuteronomy), blur the distinctions between religious and secular, and treat all law as a matter directly related to God. He is perceived as the source of laws; they are the expression of his will; and breaking them is a direct affront to and act of rebellion against him (contrast, for example, the modern American view).

The key concept behind much of biblical law seems to be that of Ex. 19:6, to make of the people of Israel "a holy nation." This expression, which appears nowhere else in the Bible, combines a secular notion (the Hebrew *goy*, meaning a political body, a state) with a sacral one: this people is to transform all of its life into service of God. There is, therefore, no subject in the code before us—slavery, social relations, torts, cult, or diet—that is not of immediate concern to the biblical God. The first part of 19:6, "a kingdom of priests" (Buber: "a king's-retinue of priests"), would seem to suggest that despite the clear existence of a priestly group in ancient Israel, the ideal approached a more democratic form of religious expression.

This leads us to posit a final question: Are the materials in Ex. 21–24 (and other texts in the Torah that enumerate laws) to be taken as actual regulations or cases, or as something else, rather more didactic? We have little evidence for the former view, and in fact other ancient Near Eastern legal documents such as the Hammurabi Code seem to point in the other (didactic) direction. Given the nature of Torah literature, where narrative has a teaching function rather than a purely historical one, it seems plausible that the legal texts as well were intended to elucidate principles of Israelite belief—to present, as it were, a world view. The other possibility, more in keeping with the history of law, is Daube's (1947) view that "many ancient codes regulate only matters as to which the law is dubious or in need of reform or both." In other words, law in day-to-day Israel was regulated by established precedents, and certainly not by Exodus 21–23, in the main. But in this case, too, our text would be instructive of the biblical mentality. For a fuller treatment of biblical law and its context in the ancient Near East, see Sarna 1986.

Any attempt to describe this section structurally is bound to run into a roadblock; perhaps precisely because of the Bible's desire *not* to distinguish between various categories of life, we do not have a watertight structure. Suffice it to say that, overall, most sections in these chapters begin with the general proposition "When . . ." (Heb. *ki*), and break down the issue under discussion into subsections begining with "If . . ." (Heb. ' *im*), a pattern found commonly in other legal systems as well. Beyond this, and the observation that there are some general categories and logical connections (for which, see the Commentary), one striking stylistic device in the Hebrew should be pointed out. From 21:5 through 23:24 a double verb form appears (infinitive absolute followed by the imperfect) fully twenty-seven times. The effect of this device, which is rhetorically emphatic, is to give a sense of coherence to what are otherwise quite diverse laws.

19:1 On the third New-Moon after the going-out of the Children
         of Israel from the land of Egypt,
      on that day
      they came to the Wilderness of Sinai.
   2 They moved on from Refidim and came to the Wilderness of
         Sinai,
      and encamped in the wilderness.
      There Israel encamped, opposite the mountain.
   3 Now Moshe went up to God,
      and YHWH called out to him from the mountain,
      saying:
      Say thus to the House of Yaakov,
      (yes,) tell the Children of Israel:
   4 You yourselves have seen
      what I did to Egypt,
      how I bore you on eagles' wings and brought you to me.
   5 So now,
      if you will hearken, yes, hearken to my voice
      and keep my covenant,
      you shall be to me a special-treasure from among all peoples.
      Indeed, all the earth is mine,
   6 but you, you shall be to me
      a kingdom of priests,
      a holy nation.
      These are the words that you are to speak to the Children of
         Israel.
   7 Moshe came, and had the elders of the people called,
      and set before them these words, with which YHWH had
         charged him.
   8 And all the people answered together, they said:
      All that YHWH has spoken, we will do.
      And Moshe reported the words of the people to YHWH.
   9 YHWH said to Moshe:
      Here, I am coming to you in a thick cloud,
      so that the people may hear when I speak with you,
      and also that they may have trust in you for ever.
      And Moshe told the words of the people to YHWH.
  10 YHWH said to Moshe:
      Go to the people,

make them holy, today and tomorrow,
let them wash their clothes,

The Meeting and the Covenant (19): The account of God's revelation at Sinai, like the narrative of the tenth plague and exodus, is embedded in a wider setting. After the covenant has been elucidated, the people assent; preparations are made to meet God; and the brief initial meeting is followed by more preparations, including stern warnings against trespassing on the mountain's sanctity. When one takes Chapter 20 into account, the effect of all this is anything but smooth, from a narrator's point of view, and I would agree with Greenberg (1969) that this may be deliberate—stemming from a desire either to include every tradition about this key event that was available to the editor(s), or else to suggest that such things are impossible to describe in normal language and logical sequence (Buber [1968], in another context, once referred to the Creation story of Genesis 1

19:1 **On the third:** The Hebrew omits the usual connecting *vav* ("now," "and," or "but"), and thus signals the start of a new narrative.

2 **There Israel encamped:** The repetition, as in 14:2, suggests poetry, perhaps a remnant of what Cassuto (1967) terms an epic literature here. The rhetorical force alerts the reader that something important is about to follow.

2–3 **the mountain:** It is not necessary to mention its name.

3 **Say thus . . . /(yes,) tell . . .:** A formulaic opening of a speech, highlighting this important address.

4 **eagles' wings:** Most commonly in Western culture, be it ancient Rome, Imperial Europe, the United States, or even Nazi Germany, the eagle is the symbol of strength, independence, and loftiness. Yet here in the Bible it functions primarily as a symbol of God's loving protection—see the nurturing eagle image in Deut. 32:11.

6 **but you:** Or "and you." **kingdom of priests:** Buber (1949) interprets the phrase as meaning a "royal-retinue" around the king, based on the usage in I Chron. 18:17 and II Sam. 8:18.

8 **All . . . we will do:** This phrase, with variations, is repeated in 24:4 and 24:7 to frame the entire covenant and law-giving account.

9 **thick cloud:** Some interpret the cloud as a massive aura, others as a shield to protect mortals from the brilliant divine "Glory" (Heb. *kavod*). **so that the people may hear:** Or "hearken" (i.e., obey). One would expect "so that the people may see," following upon the last phrase, but the narrator apparently wants to make clear that "you saw no image" (Deut. 4:12).

10 **wash:** The Hebrew verb (*kabbes*) is used for the washing of objects, not of people (which is expressed by *rahotz*).

11 that they may be ready for the third day,
for on the third day
YHWH will come down before the eyes of all the people,
upon Mount Sinai.

12 Fix-boundaries for the people round about, saying:
Be on your watch against going up the mountain or against
touching its border!
Whoever touches the mountain—he is to be put-to-death,
yes, death;

13 no hand is to touch him,
but he is to be stoned, yes, stoned, or shot, yes, shot,
whether beast or man, he is not to live!
When the (sound of the) ram's-horn is drawn out, they may
go up on the mountain.

14 Moshe went down from the mountain to the people,
he made the people holy, and they washed their clothes,

15 then he said to the people:
Be ready for three days; do not approach a woman!

16 Now it was on the third day, when it was morning:
There were thunder-sounds, and lightning,
a heavy cloud on the mountain
and an exceedingly strong trumpet sound.
And all of the people that were in the camp trembled.

17 Moshe brought the people out toward God, from the camp,
and they stationed themselves beneath the mountain.

18 Now Mount Sinai smoked all over,
since YHWH had come down upon it in fire;
its smoke went up like the smoke of a furnace,
and all of the mountain trembled exceedingly.

19 Now the trumpet sound was growing exceedingly stronger
—Moshe kept speaking,
and God kept answering him in the sound (of a voice)—

20 and YHWH came upon Mount Sinai, to the top of the
mountain.
YHWH called Moshe to the top of the mountain,
and Moshe went up.

21 YHWH said to Moshe:
Go down, warn the people
lest they break through to YHWH to see, and many of them
fall;

as a "stammering account"). In any event, the entire description of the fateful meeting between God and the Israelites at Sinai is confined to a mere four verses (19:16–19). This stands in blatant contrast to other ancient Near Eastern traditions, which would have treated such an event with epic length and poetic diction (see, for intance, Deut. 32, or Psalm 78). So here, as in the opening chapter of Genesis, all has been stripped down, focusing attention on the covenant rather than on the mysterious nature of God.

In that vein, it must be observed that the narrative centers around speaking, words, and sounds, keeping the visual to a minimum (in line with the warning in Deut. 4:2: "The sound of words you heard/ a form you did not see/ only a sound-of-a-voice"). It also abounds in terms connoting warning and boundaries/separateness—the text contains three sets of warnings: verses 10–13, 21–22 (introducing the phrase "burst out," which refers to God's potential destructiveness if the boundaries are violated), and 24. This recalls Moshe's own experience at Sinai earlier (cf. 3:5). And the number 3 gives the story the same touch of meaning provided by the numbers in Genesis; Israel arrives at the mountain three months after the exodus and meets God on the third day after their preparations.

As Cassuto (1967) points out, the chapter does not begin with "Now it was . . ." (Heb. *va-yehi*), a normal marker for continuing a previous narrative. The Sinai material thus presents itself in utter newness. To use the previously cited wedding analogy: this text betokens a new relation-

13 **no hand is to touch him:** As if his contact with holiness would somehow contaminate him—a common idea in much of ancient society, and put forth with particular force throughout Leviticus. **shot:** With bow and arrows.

15 **do not approach a woman:** The need for the people to be in a state of ritual purity precludes sexual contact.

16 **morning:** Perhaps to convey that there was nothing deceptive or dream-like about this event, which was to be seen as a large-scale group experience (and hence a large-scale group commitment). **trumpet:** Perhaps, as part of an ancient Near Eastern convention, heralding the approach of YHWH as a warring storm-god (see the Commentary, above). **trembled:** Note how both people and mountain (v. 18) seem to be in synchrony with one another (yet some scholars emend the text!).

18 **like the smoke of furnace:** A standard biblical way of describing extensive smoke (see Gen. 19:28, which uses "dense-smoke").

19 **sound (of a voice):** Some interpret as "thunder," which is often described biblically as the "voice of God" (in Psalm 18:14 and in Ugaritic literature as well). But the emphasis in the revelation of these chapters seems to be on God's voice and the clarity of his words.

21 **fall:** That is, die, because of too-close contact with the divine.

22 even the priests who approach YHWH must make themselves holy,
   lest YHWH burst out against them.
23 But Moshe said to YHWH:
   The people are not able to go up to Mount Sinai,
   for you yourself warned us, saying: Fix boundaries for the
      mountain and make it holy!
24 YHWH said to him:
   Go, get down,
   and then come up, you and Aharon with you,
   but the priests and the people must not break through to go
      up to YHWH, lest he burst out against them.
25 Moshe went down to the people and said to them

20:1 God spoke all these words,
   saying:

2 I am YHWH your God,
   who brought you out
   from the land of Egypt, from a house of serfs.

3 You are not to have
   any other gods
   before me.
4 You are not to make yourself a hewn-image
   or any figure
   that is in the heavens above, that is on the earth beneath,
      that is in the waters beneath the earth;
5 you are not to bow down to them,
   you are not to serve them,
   for I, YHWH your God,
   am a jealous God,
   calling-to-account the iniquity of the fathers upon the sons,
      to the third and the fourth (generation)
   of those that hate me,
6 but showing loyalty to the thousandth
   of those that love me,
   of those that keep my commandments.

ship between God and Israel, however well they have known one another previously.

Also notable in Chapter 19 is the emphasis on movement: going up (Heb. *'aloh*) and down (*yarod*) (see also 24:15–18). This movement serves to bridge the gap, usually great, between heaven and earth; but note that it is Moshe, and not the people, who does the ascending and descending.

Structurally, verses 20–25 appear to have been added, to emphasize the warning theme. They also delay the pronouncement of the "Ten Commandments," creating thereby a more dramatic effect with the appearance of the latter. But it seems clear that considerable editing has taken place.

The Ten Words (The Decalogue) (20:1–14): This section, among the most famous and important in all of religious literature, is set in dramatic tone. Its rhetoric could hardly be more striking. In a form relatively rare in ancient Near Eastern legal documents, a god sets forth demands, with no punishments listed. This "apodictic" form seems to indicate that the Ten Words function as a preamble to the actual laws of Chapters 21–23, by laying forth the major principles on which Israel's relationship to God is to be based (as is to be expected, the secondary literature on Chapter 20 is enormous; see Childs 1974 for a bibliography).

The numbering of the ten differs slightly in the Jewish and Christian traditions, with the main divergences coming in the split of verses 2–3 (or 3–4, as here); see Cassuto (1967). There are also different opinions on the overall structure of the "Commandments." Jewish tradition separates out those that treat the relationship between God and human beings (vv.2–11, numbers 1–5) and those that involve human society alone (vv.12–14, numbers 6–10), although it should be kept in mind that all offenses in

---

22 **lest YHWH burst out:** Lest God slay them with fire or plague. One recalls the demonic character of God portrayed in 4:24ff. The phrase is repeated in verse 24 for emphasis.

25 **and said to them:** The Hebrew is ambiguous; did Moshe report God's previous speech to them, or the following (Decalogue)? I have left this verse without final punctuation to express the unresolved nature of the question.

20:3 **before me:** Or "besides me." "Before" may connote "to affront," as in literally "in my face."

4 **figure . . .:** A representation of an animal or person.

5 **jealous:** The Hebrew word (*kanna*) has a cognate meaning in Arabic, "red (with dye)," so an interesting English analogy, expressing facial color changes, would be "livid" (from the Latin "color of lead"). **the third and the fourth (generation):** A long time (Plaut 1981).

6 **the thousandth:** That is, forever (Plaut 1981).

7 You are not to take up
  the name of YHWH your God
  to a delusion,
  for YHWH will not clear him
  that takes up his name to a delusion.

8 Remember
  the Sabbath day, to hallow it.
9 For six days, you are to serve, and are to make all your
    work,
10 but the seventh day
  is Sabbath for YHWH your God:
  you are not to make any kind of work,
  (not) you, nor your son, nor your daughter,
  (not) your servant, nor your maid, nor your beast,
  nor your sojourner that is within your gates.
11 For in six days
  YHWH made
  the heavens and the earth,
  the sea and all that is in it,
  and he rested on the seventh day;
  therefore YHWH gave the seventh day his blessing, and he
    hallowed it.

12 Honor
  your father and your mother,
  in order that your days may be long
  on the soil that YHWH your God is giving you.

13 You are not to murder.

  You are not to adulter.

  You are not to steal.

  You are not to testify
  against your fellow as a false witness.

14 You are not to desire
  the house of your fellow,
  you are not to desire the wife of your fellow,
  or his servant, or his maid, or his ox, or his ass,
  or anything that is your fellow's.

15 Now all of the people were seeing
   the thunder-sounds,
   the flashing-torches,
   the trumpet sound,
   and the mountain smoking;

ancient Israel were seen as affronts to God. This division might be borne out by stylistic considerations, for the last five, of course, begin "You are not to . . ." and numbers 2–4 all use the Hebrew word *ki* ("for") to express reasons or results of the initial stipulations (vv.5, 7, 11, with the substitution of "in order that" in verse 12).

Other notable stylistic aspects here include the fact that "you" is always singular, and that numbers 2–4 and 6–10 are all put in the negative.

Several other features of the "Decalogue" are unique: the prohibition against worshipping images, which would have had a strange ring in the ancient world; the Sabbath as a holy day on which not even servants, farm animals, or noncitizens are to work, equally unprecedented in its time and place; and, strangest of all, the final prohibition against desiring (another person's property).

The language and the content of the Decalogue, then, cooperate to create a lofty and challenging ethical code, which both the people of Israel and the Western world in general have struggled with ever since. The reader may wish to consult Buber's stimulating essays (1968, 1948) "The Words on the Tablets" and "What Are We to Do about the Ten Commandments?"

Aftermath (20:15–23): The verses that follow the Decalogue highlight an important aspect of the Sinai tradition: its occurrence in a public setting.

7 **take up . . . to a delusion:** Use for a false purpose. The traditional translation, "take in vain," limits its scope unnecessarily.   **clear:** To acquit or hold innocent.

13 **You are not to . . .:** Closer to the Hebrew rhythmically would be a sequence like "No murder!/ No adultery!" etc., or "Murder not!/ Adulter not!" etc.   **murder:** Some interpreters view this as "killing" in general, while others restrict it, as I have done here.   **steal:** Ancient Jewish tradition understood this as a reference to kidnapping (see Lauterbach 1976).   **adulter:** The English has been tailored to fit the Hebrew rhythm of the last five "commandments," all of which begin with *lo* ("no") and a two-syllable command.

14 **desire:** Trad. "covet." Another possibility is "yearn for."

15 **were seeing:** Others, "perceived." The use of the Hebrew participle again emphasizes immediacy.   **flashing-torches:** Perhaps a poetic description of lightning.

when the people saw,
they faltered
and stood far off.

16 They said to Moshe:
You speak with us, and we will hearken,
but let not God speak with us, lest we die!

17 Moshe said to the people:
Do not be afraid!
For it is to test you that God has come,
to have his fear be upon you,
so that you do not sin.

18 The people stood far off,
and Moshe approached the stormy-darkness where God
was.

19 YHWH said to Moshe:
Say thus to the Children of Israel:
You yourselves have seen
that it was from the heavens that I spoke with you.

20 You are not to make beside me
gods of silver, gods of gold you are not to make for yourselves!

21 An altar of soil, you are to make for me,
you are to slaughter upon it
your offerings-up, your well-being-sacrifices,
your sheep and your oxen!
At every place
where I cause my name to be recalled
I will come to you
and bless you.

22 But if an altar of stones you make for me,
you are not to build it smooth-hewn,
for if you hold-high your iron-tool over it, you will have
profaned it.

23 And you are not to ascend my altar by ascending-steps,
that your nakedness not be laid-bare upon it.

21:1 Now these are the judgments that you are to set before
them:

2 When you acquire a Hebrew serf,
   he is to serve for six years,
   but in the seventh he is to go out at liberty, for nothing.

Verses 15–18 could fit nicely after 19:20a; the Decalogue would then follow 20:18. Yet it seems to have been important for the narrator to stress (v.19) that God spoke to the people as a whole, not merely secretly in a revelation to a visionary or priest. To emphasize this point, the verb *ra'oh*, "see/perceive," occurs seven times in verses 15–19. Verse 19 also serves as a framework for the entire Revelation episode, recalling as it does the language of 19:4. Israel now has two reasons for obeying God: he brought them out of Egyptian bondage and he talked to them "from the heavens" (v.19).

The rest of the chapter functions as an introduction to the general body of the legislation that begins in the next chapter. Like Israel's other law collections in Leviticus and Deuteronomy, it starts with rules pertaining to worship.

On the Laws: The reader should bear in mind again that the section headings used in the Commentary are for reference only. This is especially true for Chapters 21–24, where the final form of the Hebrew text discourages distinguishing between different types of offenses (see p. 105, "On Biblical Law").

Laws Regarding Israelite Serfdom (21:1–11): Given the importance of the root "serve" in the book of Exodus, it is fitting that the Covenant Code

18 **stormy-darkness:** Heb. *'arafel*, frequently used in conjunction with *'anan*, "cloud."
21 **of soil:** Cf. verse 22. The altar was to be made of natural materials.
     well-being–sacrifices: Others, "peace-offerings"; but see Orlinsky (1970). **you:** Here, second personal singular, as well as through verse 23.
22 **profaned:** In folklore, iron was said to drive out the soul of the stone—that is, rob it of its essence (Driver 1911).
23 **that your nakedness:** To make sure that the priests' genitals not be uncovered during the rites; the Egyptians wore rather short skirts (Plaut 1981). Note again the desexualizing of religion.
21:1 **judgments:** Others, "judicial decisions," "rules." See Daube (1947).
   2 **you:** Singular, to stress the perspective of the buyer. **Hebrew:** Cassuto (1967) suggests that the term here has a wide meaning: a member of a bondman class (Akkadian *Hapiru*) found all over the ancient Near East.
     for nothing: Without paying redemption money (Cassuto 1967).

3 If he came by himself, he is to go out by himself;
   if he was the spouse of a wife, his wife is to go out with him.
4 If his lord gives him a wife, and she bore him sons or
      daughters,
   the wife and those she bore are to remain her lord's, and he
      is to go out by himself.
5 But if the serf should say, yes, say:
   I love my lord, my wife and my children, I will not go out at
      liberty!,
6 his lord is to have him approach God's-oracle,
   and then he is to have him approach the door or the post;
   his lord is to pierce his ear with a piercer,
   and he is to serve him forever.

7 When a man sells his daughter as a handmaid,
   she is not to go out as serfs go out.
8 If she is displeasing in the eyes of her lord, who designated
      her for himself,
   he is to have her redeemed;
   to a foreign people he has not the power to sell her,
   since he has betrayed her.
9 But if it is for his son that he designates her,
   according to the just-rights of women he is to deal with her.
10 If another he takes for himself,
   (then) her board, her clothing, or her oil he is not to diminish.
11 If these three (things) he does not do for her,
   she is to go out for nothing, with no money.

12 He that strikes a man, so that he dies,
   is to be put-to-death, yes, death.
13 Now should he not have lain in wait (for him), but should
      God have brought him opportunely into his hand:
   I will set aside for you a place where he may flee.

open with this theme. In verses 1–6 the text considers the case of the
native serf, a status rather like that of the indentured servant in early
American history. Immediately, the act of releasing such an individual—
providing for his "going out"—is stipulated. "For they are my servants,
whom I brought forth out of the land of Egypt" (Lev. 25:42). While the
institution of serfdom existed of necessity in ancient Israel, it could not be

tolerated as a permanent and fully dehumanizing one (on the other hand, these regulations deal with natives, not with foreigners). Note the use of seven here, as the number of perfection and limit—the servant goes free after seven years, just as the land rests every seven years (23:10–11).

The second case (vv.7–11) deals with a woman whose poverty-stricken father sells her as a servant. Here, too, there is an attempt to soften the conditions and to humanize what appears as essentially a property situation in the ancient world.

Capital Crimes of Violence (21:12–17): Four situations involving grave crimes are cited in this section, each ending with the pronouncement of the death penalty in rhetorical form (Heb. *mot yumat,* "He is to be put-to-death, yes, death"): murder, striking one's parents, kidnapping, and denigrating one's parents. Our society has in general supported the first and third of these; but the regulations concerning father and mother do not accord with twentieth-century Western practice, and point up well the enormous importance of the parent–child relationship in ancient Israel (already suggested by "Honor your father and your mother" in the Ten Words). That relationship was often used to describe the one between God and Israel, and thus obedience is an important theme in the covenant as a whole.

3   **by himself:** I.e., as an unmarried man.
4   **and she bore him . . .:** The birth of children changes the situation, and the wife must now remain behind, in bondage, with the children.
5   **say, yes, say:** Or "declare."
6   **God's-oracle:** Others, "God," "the judges."   **door . . . post:** It is not clear whether the sanctuary or the master's house is meant.   **pierce his ear:** The symbolism of this act is not clear. Gaster (1969) theorizes that it establishes the serf's permanent bond to his master's house, through the blood on the doorpost.
7   **handmaid:** In this instance, a free woman is bound over to be a slave.   **as serfs go forth:** As we saw above. In Cassuto's (1967) view, now that she has a new status (that of wife), she may not be so easily disposed of.
8   **he has betrayed her:** He has not married her off, as was intended in the sale.
10 **her board:** "Her" refers to the first woman, mentioned in verse 8.   **her oil:** So Paul (1970), on the basis of Mesopotamian parallels. Others, "marital-relations."
11 **with no money:** Again, without having to pay redemption money.
12 **put-to-death:** Stronger than simply saying "die."
13 **opportunely:** Accidentally.   **a place where he may flee:** The so-called cities of refuge (see Num. 35:9–34, Deut. 19:1–12).

14 But when a man schemes against his fellow, to kill him with
      cunning,
   from my very altar you are to take him away, to die!

15 And he that strikes his father or his mother,
   is to be put-to-death, yes, death.

16 And he that steals a man,
   whether he sells him or whether he is found in his hand,
   is to be put-to-death, yes, death.

17 And he that reviles his father or his mother,
   is to be put-to-death, yes, death.

18 When men quarrel, and a man strikes his fellow with a stone
      or with (his) fist, yet he does not die, but rather takes to
      his bed:
19 If he can rise and walk about outside upon his crutch,
   he that struck (him) is to go clear,
   only: he is to make good for his resting-time, and provide-
      that-he-be-healed, yes, healed.

20 When a man strikes his serf or his handmaid with a rod, so
      that he dies under his hand,
   it is to be avenged, yes, avenged;
21 nonetheless, if for a day or two-days he endures,
   it is not to be avenged, for he is his own "money."

22 When two men fight and deal a blow to a pregnant woman,
      so that her children abort-forth, but (other) harm does not
      happen,
   he is to be fined, yes, fined, as the woman's spouse imposes
      for him,
   but he is to give it (only) according to assessment.
23 But if harm should happen,
   then you are to give life in place of life—
24 eye in place of eye, tooth in place of tooth, hand in place of
25   hand, foot in place of foot,/burnt-scar in place of burnt-
      scar, wound in place of wound, bruise in place of bruise.

26 When a man strikes the eye of his serf or the eye of his
    handmaid, and ruins it,
  he is to send him free at liberty for (the sake of) his eye;
27 if the tooth of his serf or the tooth of his handmaid he breaks
    off,
  he is to send him free at liberty on account of his tooth.

Injuries (21:18–32): The vocabulary of verbs in these verses outlines the
subject at hand: "quarrel," "strike," "contend," "harm," "strike,"
"break-off," "give." The text treats a number of extenuating circumstances, imposing penalties of varying degrees. The case of a caused abor-
tion is especially highlighted (vv.22–25), and in a famous verse (25), the
law-giver breaks into rhetoric in order to stress that punishments be scru-
pulously fair. Also notable is the regulation concerning the goring ox
(vv.28–32), where an *animal* is made to pay the death penalty, since it has
destroyed the most sacred thing of all—life itself. Both of the latter cases
have received exhaustive treatment in the scholarly literature (see Sarna
1986).

14 **from my very altar:** Even the traditional concept of sanctuary will not aid
    such a man.
15 **strikes:** Some interpret this as "strikes dead." But the wording does not
    warrant this here (cf. 21:12), and such a society would in any case be
    supportive of this kind of severe penalty in reference to not "honoring"
    (see 20:12) parents. This is further supported by verse 17, below.
17 **reviles:** Others, "belittles," "insults."
18 **fist:** Some ancient versions read "club" or "spade."
19 **to make good . . . healed:** But he is not liable for criminal action.
20 **avenged:** The exact punishment is not specified, but it sounds like death.
21 **it is not . . . "money":** "He has human rights, but not those of a free
    man" (Plaut 1981). Alternatively, Cassuto (1967) suggests that the master
    has lost his own money thereby.
22 **assessment:** As agreed by the judges.
23 **you:** Singular. **life in place of life:** This has historically been taken to
    indicate a kind of strict Hebrew vengeance, as in the current expression
    "an eye for an eye." But the passage (note, by the way, its length) may
    have been meant as a contrast to the Babylonian system, where the rich
    could in essence pay to get out of such situations. In Israel this could not
    be done, and thus we are dealing not with strict justice but with strict
    fairness.

28 When an ox gores a man or a woman, so that one dies,
   the ox is to be stoned, yes, stoned, and its flesh is not to be
      eaten,
   and the owner of the ox is to be clear.
29 But if the ox was (known as) a gorer, from yesterday and the
      day-before, and it was so designated to its owner,
   and he did not guard it,
   and it causes the death of a man or of a woman,
   the ox is to be stoned, and its owner as well is to be put-
      to-death.
30 If a purging-ransom is established for him,
   he is to give it as a redemption for his life, all that is imposed
      for him.
31 Whether it is a son it gores or a daughter it gores,
   according to this (same) judgment it is to be done to him.
32 If (it is) a serf the ox gores, or a handmaid,
   silver—thirty *shekels*—he is to give to his lord, and the ox is
      to be stoned.

33 When a man opens up a pit, or when a man digs a pit, and
      does not cover it up, and an ox or an ass falls into it,
34 the owner of the pit is to pay, the worth-in-silver he is to
      restore to its owner, and the dead-animal is to remain his.
35 When a man's ox deals-a-blow to his fellow's ox, so that it
      dies,
   they are to sell the live ox and split its worth-in-silver, and
      the dead-animal they are also to split.
36 Yet if it was known that it was a goring ox from yesterday
      and the day-before, and its owner did not guard it,
   he is to pay, yes, pay, an ox in place of the ox, and the
      dead-animal is to remain his.

37 (Now) when a man steals an ox or a lamb, and slaughters it
      or sells it,
   five cattle he is to pay in place of the ox, and four sheep in
      place of the lamb;
22:1 if in (the act of) digging through, the stealer is caught and is
      struck down, so that he dies,
   there is to be on his account no bloodguilt;

2 (but) if the sun shone upon him,
  bloodguilt there is on his account;
  he is to pay, yes, pay—if he has nothing, he is to be sold
    because of his stealing.
3 (Now) if what was stolen is found, yes, found in his hand,
    whether ox, or ass, or lamb, (still) alive,
  twofold he is to pay.

4 When a man has a field or a vineyard grazed in,
  and sends his grazing-flock free, so that it grazes in another's
    field,
  the best-part of his field, the best-part of his vineyard is he
    to pay.

Property (21:33–22:14): These regulations cover various damages to property, commonly through negligence. The key word here is "pay" (Heb. *shallem*, denoting restitution); also repeated are "fellow" and "God's-oracle."

28 **When an ox gores . . . :** The ox may be taken here as the paradigm of the domestic animal. The secondary literature on this law and its parallels is enormous. **its flesh is not to be eaten:** Since the ox has not been properly slaughtered for eating or sacrificial purposes, and possibly also because it is connected with the taking of another life (carnivores are forbidden food in the Bible).

30 **purging-ransom:** Others, "expiation payment." This functions as a way out of his being put to death (as in the case of the firstborn son, in Chap. 12).

37 **(Now) . . . lamb:** In most English translations, this verse is labeled 22:1, and hence 22:1 here appears as 22:2 elsewhere. **five cattle . . . four sheep:** In contradistinction to the case of a stolen animal that is found alive (v.3, above), where the payment is only twofold.

22:1 **digging through:** Secretly, at night; the owner presumably has neither the time nor the light to examine the situation rationally. This issue is still a matter of considerable debate in many state legislatures in America. **no bloodguilt:** He is not considered a murderer.

2 **if the sun shone:** Then the owner could have restrained himself from killing the man.

4–5 **grazed . . . blaze:** The Hebrew is perhaps a pun on *b'r*, which is used for both verbs. Some take the entire case to refer to burning.

5 When fire breaks out and reaches thorn-hedges, and a
   sheaf-stack or the standing-grain or the (entire) field is
   consumed,
   he is to pay, yes, pay, he that caused the blaze to blaze up.

6 When a man gives silver or goods to his fellow for safekeeping, and it is stolen from the man's house;
   if the stealer is found, he is to pay twofold;
7 if the stealer is not found, the owner of the house is to
   come-near God's-oracle,
   (to inquire) if he did not send out his hand against his fellow's property.
8 Regarding every matter of misappropriation,
   regarding oxen, regarding asses, regarding sheep, regarding
   garments, regarding any kind of loss about which one can
   say: That is it!—
   before God's-oracle is the matter of the two of them to come;
   whomever God's-oracle declares guilty, is to pay twofold to
   his fellow.
9 When a man gives his fellow an ass or an ox or a lamb, or any
   kind of beast, for safekeeping,
   and it dies, or is crippled or captured, no one seeing (it
   happen),
10 the oath of YHWH is to be between the two of them,
   (to inquire) if he did not send out his hand against his fellow's property;
   the owner is to accept it, and he does not have to pay.
11 But if it was stolen, yes, stolen away from him,
   he is to pay it back to its owner.
12 If it was torn, torn-to-pieces,
   he is to bring it as evidence; what was torn, he does not have
   to pay back.
13 When a man borrows it from his fellow, and it is crippled or
   it dies:
   (if) its owner was not with it, he is to pay, yes, pay;
14 if its owner was with it, he does not have to pay.
   If it was hired, its hiring-price is received.

15 When a man seduces a virgin who has not been spoken-for
   and lies with her,
   (for) the marrying-price he is to marry her, as his wife.

16 If her father refuses, yes, refuses to give her to him,
   silver he is to weigh out, according to the marriage-price of
   virgins.

17 A sorceress you are not to let live.

Laws Concerning Social Relations and Religious Matters (22:15–23:19): A
great variety of offenses is covered in this section: rape, oppression, tale-
bearing, unjust sentencing, and bribery, among others. Yet the category is
not so neatly drawn; interspersed with these are laws concerning what we
would consider religious affairs: sorcery, idolatry, blasphemy, and the
sacred calendar. Once again the implication seems to be that all of these
areas are of immediate concern to God, regardless of how they are labeled
or pigeonholed.

Stylistically there is also great variety, as categorical prohibitions (22:18)
alternate with pleas (23:5–6) and positive commands (23:10–12). A number of times the justification for the law is given in the text itself (e.g.
22:20, 26; 23:7, 8, 9, 11, 12), with the operative word being "for." (Such a

5 **pay:** Yet not necessarily the "best-part," as in verse 4.
6 **stealer:** The Hebrew form (*ganav*) indicates a professional thief, not a
   casual one.
7 **the owner of the house:** That is, the temporary guardian of the goods.
8 **say:** Others, "allege."
9 **crippled or captured:** Heb. *nishbar o nishbe*.
10 **oath of YHWH:** It functions like a lie-detector test. **he does not:** The
    guardian, as above.
12 **torn-to-pieces:** A technical term for "devoured by a wild animal" (Daube
    1947); cf. Gen. 37:33. **he does not have to pay:** Since this could happen
    to anyone.
14 **he does not have to pay:** It is assumed that he did his best to protect his
    charge. **its hiring-price is received:** The rental price covers the loss.
15 **spoken-for:** Lit., "paid for." Others, "betrothed," but it is not clear that
    there was such an institution as betrothal in biblical Israel (Orlinsky
    1970).
16 **marriage-price of virgins:** As in many cultures, biblical society prized a
    virgin as a bride.
17 **sorceress:** The specifying of women here seems to indicate their involve-
    ment in this practice in ancient Israel. Magic as such was forbidden (see
    the famous story of the "witch of Endor" in I Sam. 28) all over the Bible,
    as an attempt to manipulate God's world behind his back, as it were.
    you: Singular, and so basically through verse 29. The exceptions, verse 21
    and the end of verse 24, may simply be stylistic variations. **not to let
    live:** An unusual Hebrew phrase, perhaps for emphasis.

18 Anyone who lies with a beast,
    is to be put-to-death, yes, death.

19 He that slaughter-offers to (other) gods is to be made-taboo.
    Only to YHWH alone!

20 Now a sojourner, you are not to maltreat, you are not to
        oppress him,
    for sojourners were you in the land of Egypt.

21 Any widow or orphan you are not to afflict.
22 Oh, if you afflict, afflict them . . . !
    For (then) they will cry, cry out to me,
    I will hearken, yes, hearken to their cry,
23 my anger will rage
    and I will kill you with the sword,
    so that your wives become widows, and your children,
        orphans!

24 If you lend money to my people, to the afflicted-one (who
        lives) beside you,
    you are not to be to him like a creditor,
    you are not to place on him excessive-interest.

25 If you take-in-pledge, yes, pledge, the cloak of your fellow,
    before the sun comes in, return it to him,
26 for it is his only clothing,
    it is the cloak for his skin,
    in what (else) shall he lie down?
    Now it will be that when he cries out to me,
    I will hearken,
    for a Compassionate-One am I!

27 God you are not to revile,
    one exalted among your people you are not to curse.

28 Your full fruit of your trickling-grapes, you are not to delay.

    The firstborn of your sons, give to me.

29 Do thus with your ox, with your sheep:
    for seven days let it be with its mother, (and) on the eighth
        day, give it to me!

30 Men of holiness are you to be to me!
    Flesh that is torn-to-pieces in the field, you are not to eat;
    to the dogs you are to throw it.

23:1 You are not to take up a delusive rumor.
    Do not put your hand (in) with a guilty person, to become a
        witness for wrongdoing.

verse is called a "motive clause," and is characteristically although not
exclusively biblical; see Sonsino 1980.)
  Most notable about this section is the full use that it makes of rhetoric.
Several key laws are accompanied by an emotional appeal—e.g., "Oh, if
you afflict, afflict them. . . !" (22:22); "for it is his only clothing . . . in
what (else) shall he lie down?" (v.26); "for a Compassionate-One am I"

18 **lies with a beast:** Interestingly, Hittite law distinguishes between some
    animals in this regard, while Israelite law does not. Just as the Bible has
    essentially excised mythology concerning half-gods and half-humans, or
    half-humans/animals such as the Sphinx, so the spheres are not to mix in
    real life.
27 **God . . . one exalted:** Here God and ruler are equated, as later in the
    story of Naboth's vineyard in I Kings 21:10 ("You cursed God and the
    king").
28 **Your full fruit . . .:** Heb. difficult. Cassuto (1967) cites a parallel Hittite
    law. **give to me:** Paralleling 13:13 (Cassuto 1967).
29 **eighth day:** Circumcision also takes place on the eighth day, reflecting
    either a belief that the young are more viable by then, or a symbolic
    number (7 + 1). Others suggest that it takes seven days for the impurity of
    birth to be expunged (cf. Lev. 12:2).
30 **Men of holiness:** The idea is continued in Leviticus, where Chapters
    19ff. have come to be known as the "Holiness Code," a collection of
    varied laws dealing with different aspects of human conduct. **Flesh that
    is torn-to-pieces:** Leviticus 17:15 and 22:8 forbid the eating of an animal
    that has been slain by another. **to the dogs:** The force of the idea is
    similar in both Hebrew and English.
23:1 **You:** Singular through verse 12, except for the second and third lines of
    verse 9. **delusive:** Insubstantial, not based on fact. **Do not put your
    hand in:** That is, do not throw your weight toward, side with.

2 You are not to go after many (people) to do evil.

And you are not to testify in a quarrel so as to turn aside
toward many—(and thus) turn away.

3 Even a poor-man you are not to respect as regards his quarrel.

4 (Now) when you encounter your enemy's ox or his ass stray-
ing, return it, return it to him.

5 (And) when you see the ass of one who hates you crouching
under its burden, restrain from abandoning it to him—
unbind, yes, unbind it together with him.

6 You are not to turn aside the rights of your needy as regards
his quarrel.

7 From a false matter, you are to keep far!
And (one) clear and innocent, do not kill,
for I do not acquit a guilty-person.

8 A bribe you are not to take,
for a bribe blinds the open-eyed,
and twists the words of the just.

9 A sojourner, you are not to oppress:
you yourselves know (well) the feelings of the sojourner,
for sojourners were you in the land of Egypt.

10 For six years you are to sow your land and to gather in its
produce,

11 but in the seventh, you are to let it go and to let it be,
that the needy of your people may eat,
and what they (allow to) remain, the wildlife of the field may
eat.
Do thus with your vineyard, with your olive-grove.

12 For six days you are to make your labor,
but on the seventh day, you are to cease,
in order that your ox and your ass may rest
and the son of your handmaid and the sojourner may
pause-for-breath.

13 In all that I say to you, keep watch!
   The name of other gods, you are not to mention,
   it is not to be heard in your mouth.

14 At three points you are to hold-festival for me, every year.
15 The Festival of *matzot* you are to keep:
   for seven days you are to eat *matzot,* as I commanded you,
   at the appointed-time of the New-Moon of Ripe-Grain—
   for in it you went out of Egypt,
   and no one is to be seen in my presence empty-handed;
16 and the Festival of the Cutting, of the firstlings of your
   labor, of what you sow in the field;
   and the Festival of Ingathering, at the going-out of the year,

(v.26); and "you yourselves know (well) the feelings of the sojourner"
(23:9).

No passage in these chapters, and indeed throughout the entire Torah,
can easily surpass vv. 21–23 (as I have mentioned above), with their
appeal to language and emotions alike. So at the core of the legal concerns
here is the protection of the powerless.

2 **quarrel:** Legal dispute. **many:** Or "the majority." **turn away:** Referring to either turning the judgment in favor of the wicked, or else the
"turning" of justice itself.
3 **respect:** Others, "prefer." Contrast this idea with verse 6.
5 **abandoning . . . unbind:** That same Hebrew root, *'azov,* is used for both.
It is also possible that the text is the result of a scribal error, and some read
the second verb as *'azor,* "help."
8 **open-eyed:** Here, the equivalent of "wise."
9 **oppress:** Recalling the oppression suffered at the hands of the Egyptians
in 3:9.
12 **pause-for-breath:** Later (31:17), God himself is portrayed as having
needed to rest after his work of creation.
13 **you:** Plural. **name . . . it:** Understood as plural.
14 **you:** Singular.
15 **in my presence empty-handed:** No one is to make a religious pilgrimage
on these occasions without bringing "gifts" (sacrifices).
16 **Festival of the Cutting:** The wheat harvest and that of first-fruits, occurring in the third month, usually in early June (also known as Shavu'ot,
"Weeks"). **Festival of Ingathering:** The final (grape) harvest, in the
seventh month in late September or early October (also known as Sukkot,
"Booths").

when you gather in your labor's (harvest) from the field.

17 Three times in the year
    are all your males to be seen
    in the presence of the Lord, YHWH.

18 You are not to slaughter-offer with anything fermented my
        blood offering.

    The fat of my festive-offering is not to remain overnight,
        until morning.

19 The choicest firstlings of your soil, you are to bring to the
        house of YHWH your God.

    You are not to boil a kid in the milk of its mother.

20 Here, I am sending a messenger before you
    to watch over you on the way,
    to bring you to the place that I have prepared.
21 Be on your watch in his presence,
    and hearken to his voice,
    do not be rebellious against him,
    for he is not able to bear your transgressing,
    for my name is with him.
22 So then, hearken, hearken to his voice,
    and do all that I speak,
    and I will be-an-enemy to your enemies,
    and I will be-an-adversary to your adversaries.
23 When my messenger goes before you
    and brings you
    to the Amorite, the Hittite, the Perizzite, and the Canaanite,
        the Hivvite and the Yevusite,
    and I cause them to vanish:
24 you are not to bow down to their gods,
    you are not to serve them,
    you are not to do according to what they do,
    but: you are to tear, yes, tear them down,
    and are to smash, yes, smash their standing-stones.
25 You are to serve YHWH your God!

Toward the end (23:10–19), emphasis shifts to the festivals of Israel, with a special focus on the agricultural setting. As a result the general scholarly consensus is that these laws could not be wilderness regulations, but refer instead to life after the conquest of Canaan. Be that as it may, the fact that this section ends with ritual concerns provides a rounding-out of the entire body of Exodus legislation, which, as I noted above, began with worship as its subject (20:20ff.).

Finally, the ending passage is notable for its numerical layout—two sets of seven (years and days) and one of three (times a year).

Epilogue: The Future Conquest (23:20–33): It would not be suitable, given the grave nature of the covenant, to end the legal passages merely with a particular law, and so our narrator appends a long speech, in the style of Deuteronomy, warning the Israelites, first, to follow God's messenger, and second, not to assimilate with the nations they are about to conquer. The Deuteronomic themes are classic: "being on your watch," smashing Canaanite idols, God's removing disease from the faithful Israelites, and the spelling-out of Israel's future borders.

17 **be seen in the presence of . . . YHWH:** A technical expression for one's appearing at the sanctuary (Plaut 1981). **the Lord, YHWH:** Some see this title as a polemic against the Canaanite Baal, whose name means "master" or "lord."

18 **with anything leavened:** Excluding bread and honey (cf. Lev. 2:11) from the offering, possibly since these were included by the Canaanites (Cassuto 1967), or because the sacrifice was to be kept as "natural" as possible.

19 **You are not to boil . . .:** This law occurs three times in the Torah, and so must have been of particular importance. Despite this, interpreters disagree as to its origins and meaning. Some see it as directly opposing a Canaanite practice; others, as parallel to the law in Deuteronomy (22:6–7) against taking the mother bird along with her young. It also keeps the separation between milk (life-giving) and blood (life-taking); it was thus understood in Jewish mystical tradition of the Middle Ages. The phrase is also cited by Talmudic sages as a basis for the separation of milk and meat in postbiblical Jewish dietary laws (*kashrut*).

20 **a messenger:** As sometimes occurs with this word, it is not entirely clear what the distinction is between God and messenger. Here, however, the context seems to require a separate being, whether an angel or Moshe himself.

21 **my name is with him:** Or "in him"; "my authority rests with him" (Clements 1972).

22 **be-an-enemy:** The Hebrew expresses this idea with one verb, without auxiliary.

23 **to the Amorite . . .:** To their land, Canaan.

24 **standing-stones:** Possibly, phallic representations of Canaanite gods.

and he will give-blessing to your food and your water;
I will remove sickness from amongst you,

26 there will be no miscarrier or barren-one in your land,
(and) the number of your days I will make full.

27 My terror I will send on before you,
I will stir up all the peoples among whom you come,
I will give all your enemies to you by the neck.

28 I will send Despair on before you
so that it drives out the Hivvite, the Canaanite and the Hittite from before you.

29 I will not drive them out from before you in one year,
lest the land become desolate
and the wildlife of the field become-many against you.

30 Little by little will I drive them out from before you,
until you have borne-fruit and possessed the land.

31 And I will make your territory
from the Sea of Reeds to the Sea of the Philistines,
from the Wilderness to the River.
For I give into your hand the settled-folk of the land, that
you may drive them out from before you.

32 You are not to cut with them or with their gods any covenant,

33 they are not to stay in your land, lest they cause you to sin
against me,
indeed, you would serve their gods—
indeed, that would be a snare to you.

24:1 Now to Moshe he said:
Go up to YHWH,
you and Aharon, Nadav and Avihu, and seventy of the
elders of Israel,
and bow down from afar;

2 Moshe alone is to approach YHWH,
but they, they are not to approach,
and as for the people—they are not to go up with him
(either).

3 So Moshe came
and recounted to the people all the words of YHWH and all
the judgments.

And all the people answered in one voice, and said:
All the words that YHWH has spoken, we will do.
4 Now Moshe wrote down all the words of YHWH.
He (arose) early in the morning,
he built an altar beneath the mountain
and twelve standing-stones for the twelve tribes of Israel.

Also to be remarked are the sevenfold repetition of "before you" as a stylistic unifying device, and the ending theme of serving YHWH as opposed to "their gods."

Sealing the Covenant (24:1–11): To close out the account of covenant-making which began back in Chapter 19, the text recounts a formalized ceremony which has many points of contact with what was generally done throughout the ancient Near East when a covenant was "cut." Twice Moshe reads God's words to the people, and twice (vv.3 , 7) they give their assent. This is no imposing of laws by a dictator, but a freely accepted, "signed, sealed, and delivered" agreement cemented by blood, the signifier of life itself.

26 **no miscarrier:** No distinction is made here between human and animal, and presumably both would share in the blessing.
27 **terror . . . stir up:** Heb. *'emati . . . hammati.* **stir up:** As in 14:24, above, describing God's routing of the Egyptians. **give all your enemies to you by the neck:** I.e., they will be routed by you, their backs turned.
28 **Despair:** Others, "hornet"; the Hebrew implies both.
29 **I will not drive them out . . . in one year:** This is the situation at the beginning of the book of Judges (after the Conquest); apparently Yehoshua did not finish the job, and so various (later) biblical texts attempt to explain the reason for this.
31 **Sea of the Philistines:** The Mediteranean. **Wilderness:** The southland or Negev. **the River:** The Euphrates, in the north. **drive them out:** Heb. *gerashtemo* is an archaic form (such as we find in 15:17—*tevi'emo ve-titta'emo*), used perhaps for reasons of rhythm.
32 **cut . . . any covenant:** A common Semitic idiom for concluding a treaty (see Gen. 15), perhaps stemming from a ritual. The parties would pass between the halves of sacrificed animals, perhaps implying that such would be the penalty for any party that would break the agreement.
24:1 **Nadav and Avihu:** Aharon's first two sons. **seventy:** The "perfect" number with which the book of Exodus began.
4 **standing-stones:** As distinct from the phallic stones mentioned in 23:24, these functioned as boundary markers and memorials.

5 Then he sent the (serving-) lads of the Children of Israel,
   that they should offer-up offerings-up, slaughter slaughter-
      meals, well-being-offerings for YHWH—bulls.
6 Moshe took half of the blood and put it in basins,
   and half of the blood he tossed against the altar.
7 Then he took the account of the covenant
   and read it in the hearing of the people.
   They said:
   All that YHWH has spoken, we will do and we will hearken!
8 Moshe took the blood, he tossed it on the people
   and said:
   Here is the blood of the covenant
   that YHWH has cut with you
   by means of all these words.

9 Then went up
   Moshe and Aharon, Nadav and Avihu, and seventy of the
      elders of Israel.
10 And they saw
   the God of Israel: beneath his feet
   (something) like work of sapphire tiles,
   (something) like the substance of the heavens in purity.
11 Yet against the Pillars of the Children of Israel, he did not
      send forth his hand—
   they beheld Godhood
   and ate and drank.

12 Now YHWH said to Moshe:
   Go up to me on the mountain
   and remain there,
   that I may give you tablets of stone:
   the Instruction and the Command
   that I have written down, to instruct them.
13 Moshe arose, and Yehoshua his attendant,
   and Moshe went up to the mountain of God.
14 Now to the elders he said:
   Stay here for us, until we return to you;
   here, Aharon and Hur are with you—
   whoever has a legal-matter is to approach them.

15 So Moshe went up the mountain,
   and the cloud covered the mountain;
16 the Glory of YHWH took up dwelling on Mount Sinai.
   The cloud covered it for six days,
   and he called to Moshe on the seventh day from admidst the
     cloud.
17 And the sight of the Glory of YHWH
   (was) like a consuming fire
   on top of the mountain
   in the eyes of the Children of Israel.

As representatives of the people, Moshe, Aharon, Aharon's sons, and
seventy elders ascend Mount Sinai, and, most remarkably, "see" God in
some sort of vision—without, as one might expect, their being destroyed.
They also eat and drink, as was customary in the sealing of the agreement
(and often done in business to this day; see Gen. 31:44–54).

Moshe Ascends Alone (24:12–18): Finally, Moshe leaves the people, in
order to receive the laws in permanent (stone) form. He "goes up" the
mountain four times (or, most likely, is on his way up). In order to give his
absence the weight it needs—so that the people will grow restless, setting
up the situation that produces the Golden Calf in Chapter 32—the text will
now turn to a completely different matter for fully seven chapters.
   The ending of this section anticipates the ending of the book of Exodus,
with its mention of God's "glory," "dwelling," "fire," and "day/night."

5 **lads:** Or "youths"; the Hebrew term (*na'ar*) is analogous to "apprentice."
7 **hearing:** Lit., "ears." **and we will hearken:** this is an addition to the
  "we will do" of 19:8. In Deuteronomy "hearken" is often found connoting "obey."
10 **work of sapphire tiles:** Others, "pavement." Childs (1974) notes parallel
   Ugaritic texts to this description. **purity:** In Ugaritic, this word has an
   association of clarity or brightness, especially as regards precious stones
   (see "pure gold" in the Tabernacle account: 24:11, 17, 24, 31, 39, below).
11 **Pillars:** Apparently a technical term for the representatives of the people
   (Buber 1958: "corner-joints"). **send forth his hand:** Kill them. **beheld:** Heb. *hazoh*, often used in connection with prophetic vision (see
   Isaiah 1:1).
12 **them:** The Children of Israel.
17 **like a consuming fire:** In contrast to Moshe's striking positive experience
   of God in Chapter 3, where the bush burned but was not consumed, the
   Israelites experience him through fear.

18 Moshe came into the midst of the cloud
   when he went up the mountain.
   And Moshe was on the mountain
   for forty days and forty nights.

18 **forty:** Another meaningful number, reminiscent of the Flood. It is echoed
   in Elijah's later experience on the same summit (I Kings 19:8).

PART IV The Instructions for the Dwelling and the Cult (25–31)

DESPITE THE IMPORTANCE of all that has preceded, the section of Exodus we now encounter occupies a significant amount of text, and therefore commands our attention, in the overall scheme of the book. It may seem puzzling to modern readers that a book that purports to be about a people's origins should choose to fill a third of its pages with a detailed description of a sanctuary, down to the last piece of tapestry and the last ritual vessel. Yet it is an indication of the "Tabernacle's" centrality in Israel's idea system that the story of its construction dominates the last half of Exodus.

Several factors may help to explain. First, the system of animal and grain sacrifices, or cult, was as important in ancient Israel as it was elsewhere in antiquity, as the chief means of formally expressing religious feeling. Indeed, the Bible traces this institution back to the beginning of human history, to Cain and Abel (Gen. 4:3–4). The cult's centrality survived the railings of the Prophets and the destruction of Solomon's Temple, and was still strong enough in late antiquity to provoke a severe crisis when its chief site, the Second Temple, fell to the Romans in the year 70 C.E. The latter event was a crux upon which the creation of classical Judaism took place, and the process was a painful one. So the opinion that many moderns have, that animal sacrifice was a barbaric custom, is quite beside the point as far as ancient Israel was concerned.

Second, there is the great theme of the book of Exodus, "Is YHWH in our midst or not?" (17:7), to which our account gives a resounding positive answer. The book of Exodus traces not only the journey of the people of Israel from Egypt to Sinai, but also the journey of God to rescue the people and to dwell ("tabernacle") among them (Greenberg 1972). A detailed presentation of God's "residence," as it were, is meant to convey the assurance that the people are led by God himself. This further supports the biblical image of the divine king, who dwells among his subjects and "goes before" them.

Third, the Israelites shared with their neighbors the idea that a victorious God, following his triumph, was to be honored by his enthronement in a human-built structure (see Hallo, in Plaut 1981). Thus the last half of Exodus, far from trailing off into obscure priestly details, fits a well-known mold in its contemporary environment.

A final explanation of the prominence of the Tabernacle sections may be found in their intimate connection with the idea of the Sabbath. The "blueprint" chapters, 25–31, end with an extended passage on observing the Sabbath; the construction chapters, 35–40, begin with a brief passage on the prohibition of work on the holy day. These structural aspects suggest (as the ancient rabbis also saw) that cessation from work here means precisely from the tasks of construction, and that once a week human beings must step back from their own creating to acknowledge the true "work" of creation. Chapters 25–40, including the Golden Calf narrative, bring out these ideas through their use of refrainlike phrases, especially the repetition of one key word: "make" (Heb. *'asoh*). The entire section is an object lesson in what the Bible deems it proper for human beings to make, and is a vehicle of contrast between God's creation and human attempts to reach the divine. Israel is engaged in the making of the Tabernacle (notice how "build," which would make more sense, is not used); when the time comes for the work to be put aside temporarily, they are to "make" the Sabbath. To these observations may be added the long-observed fact that the vocabulary of the Tabernacle's completion ("finished," "work," "blessed") recalls the completion of Creation in Gen. 2:1–4. Thus we are taught that Israel, through its religious life as typified by Sabbath and cult, becomes a partner in the process of Creation, either by imitating the divine act or by celebrating it.

Other peoples, to be sure, recall the beginning of the world in ritual and story, so it is important to make an anthropological observation. The purpose of all sanctuaries is to build a bridge to the divine, to link up with the forces that transcend human beings. It is perceived that certain places are particularly appropriate for this (folklore terms such places "the navel of the earth"), and, by extension, sanctuaries firmly anchor that inherent holiness. What the Tabernacle account initially accomplishes, most notably in its closing chapter (40), is to transfer a topographic "bridge" to a human-made and portable one. With the completion of this Dwelling, we find God resident neither on Sinai nor in the later Jerusalem, but rather accompanying the people "upon all their travels" (40:38). The sacred center here thus moves; it is a portable anchor that establishes stability wherever it goes. The vitality that surrounded this idea is still to be seen in the successors of the Hebrew Bible, classical Judaism and Christianity, for whom, respectively, Torah and Cross provide a center that is at once movable and stabilizing.

But the sacred center, for biblical religion, finds equal expression in *time*. While the Dwelling account seems obsessed with matters of space, its setting among the Sabbath passages stresses more the concept of time. Such an aspect already begins to make itself felt in 24:16, where Moshe, on Sinai to receive the laws, waits for six days while the "cloud" covers the mountain, and is able to ascend only on the seventh day, at God's summons. We are thus left, paradoxically, with a structure (Dwelling) which at first glance uses many well-known art forms and religious motifs common to the ancient Near East, but which is a total departure from them via its connection with the Sabbath—an institution with no known equivalent in the ancient world. The Dwelling account presents us with a people for whom sacred time takes precedence over sacred space (for more on these themes, see Sarna 1986).

There have been many attempts, textually and artistically, to reconstruct the Tabernacle on the basis of our text here, the rationale being that surely so much detail as we find here will serve as the guidelines for an an actual structure. Rabbinic and medieval Jewish commentators, as well as modern scholars, have expended considerable energy to that end. But in fact none of the reconstructions has succeeded, for, as with narrative, the text is as much message as description. The text's main concern, it seems, is for the Dwelling to reflect holiness, in its choice of measurements and materials (see Haran 1985). The layout of the Dwelling expresses aesthetic ideas of perfection, through various symmetrical proportions (see Appendix A); the materials are graded such that the closer one gets to God (in the "Holiest Holy-Place"), the more precious the metal. In addition, both the colors used and the types of workmanship employed are similarly graded. In a general way, the intent of the narrator seems to have been close to the intent of the great cathedral builders of the Middle Ages: to reflect divine perfection and order in the perfection and order of a sacred structure.

The Dwelling, as described in Exodus, resembles other ancient Near Eastern sanctuaries in many particulars (for which, see the Commentary below), as well as strongly reflecting aspects of the later Temple of Solomon (I Kings 6–7). Some scholars have also likened it to a Bedouin tent (Heb. *shakhen* seems to be an archaic verb for "to tent"), appropriate to

desert conditions. It is perhaps all three, a coalescing of Israel's ideas of
the cult from a variety of historical and religious settings. That the
Dwelling was viewed as historical is clear from biblical tradition itself (see
II Sam. 7:6, for instance). But one should keep in mind that it is also a
paradigmatic model, that helps to round out the overall scheme of Exodus.
The book traces the progress of the people of Israel from servitude (to
Pharaoh) to service (of God), and uses the human activity of building to do
so. Thus, as Exodus opens, the Israelites are forcibly made to build royal
storage cities; as the book ends, the people complete a structure through
which they may serve the divine king.

Finally, there is the sequence of description in these chapters: the text
begins with the blueprint for the holiest object, the "coffer" (ark), and
proceeds through the structure in descending order of holiness. After the
building instructions themselves are given, a number of related matters
are treated, chief among them the attire of the priests and the ceremony
consecrating the priests. The establishment of the cult, like that of the
system of justice, is thus viewed as the command of God rather than the
result of the need or request of human beings (contrast this with the
"requested" monarchy in I Samuel 8).

25:1 Now YHWH spoke to Moshe, saying:
    2 Speak to the Children of Israel,
         that they may take me a raised-contribution;
         from every man whose heart makes-him-willing, you are to
            take my contribution.
    3 And this is the contribution that you are to take from them:
         gold, silver, and bronze,
    4 violet, purple, worm-scarlet, byssus, and goats'-hair,
    5 rams' skins dyed-red, dugongs' skins,
         acacia wood,
    6 oil for lighting,
         spices for oil of anointing and for fragrant smoking-incense,
    7 onyx stones, stones for setting
         for the *efod* and for the breastpiece.
    8 Let them make me a Holy-Place
         that I may dwell amidst them.

9 According to all that I grant you to see,
  the building-pattern of the Dwelling and the building-
  pattern of all its implements,
thus are you to make it.

The "Contribution" (25:1–9): In the first seven verses of this opening
section dealing with the Dwelling, the Israelites' contribution toward the
structure is described in detail; but only in verse 8 is the purpose of this
activity made clear. Despite the concreteness of the description, however,
the actual blueprints, as it were, are shown to Moshe by God, and are not
recorded in the text. Architects in the creative sense are superfluous here.

Moderns want to know where the Israelites procured such materials as
gold and silver in quantity (see Chapter 38), or how they acquired the
skills necessary for the fine artisanry involved (e.g., weaving, dyeing,
manufacture of incense, and the setting of jewels). These questions, while
logical in a historical setting, do not take the Bible on its own terms. The
text appears to present the awed report of the Dwelling and its construction without leaving room for totally practical issues (just as Genesis 4
deals with Cain and his descendants without being concerned with the
origins of Cain's wife).

25:2 **raised-contribution:** A collective noun (Plaut 1981). The image is a common one, as in English "raise money."

4 **violet:** The exact color is not certain; others, "blue." What does seem
clear is that this was precious, probably because the dye was difficult to
extract from its natural setting, and was the color of royalty (viz., "royal
purple") (Milgrom 1983). The same color was used on the fringes commanded as a memorial garment in Num. 15:37–38. **worm-scarlet:**
Others, "crimson." The dye was produced by crushing the shell of a
certain insect, and hence the two-word Hebrew name. **byssus:** Fine
linen (Heb. *shesh*, a loan word from Egyptian), as opposed to the plain *bad*
(linen) of 28:42.

5 **dugongs':** The identification of *tahash* with this walruslike animal is not
certain, but the skin is known to be suitable for purposes such as the one
in this passage, as opposed, for instance, to dolphin skin. **acacia:** This
particular tree, well suited for construction, is found most often in the
Bible in reference to the Tabernacle.

6 **anointing:** For consecrating priests (e.g., 29:7) and kings (e.g., I Sam.
10:1). **fragrant smoking-incense:** See 30:34–38, below.

7 **for setting:** In the high priest's breastpiece (see 28:17–21, below). **efod:**
An important garment of the high priest (see 28:6ff., below). **breastpiece:** Hung on the *efod* (see 28:15ff., below).

8 **Holy-Place:** Others, "sanctuary."

10 They are to make
    a coffer of acacia wood,
    two cubits and a half its length,
    a cubit and a half its width,
    and a cubit and a half its height.
11 You are to overlay it with pure gold,
    inside and outside you are to overlay it,
    and are to make upon it a rim of gold all around.
12 You are to cast for it four rings of gold
    and are to put them upon its four feet,
    with two rings on its one flank
    and two rings on its second flank.
13 You are to make poles of acacia wood
    and are to overlay them with gold
14 and are to bring the poles into the rings on the flanks of the
        coffer,
    to carry the coffer by (means of) them.
15 In the rings of the coffer are the poles to remain,
    they are not to be removed from it.
16 And you are to put in the coffer
    the Testimony that I give you.

17 You are to make a purgation-cover of pure gold,
    two cubits and a half its length
    and a cubit and a half its width.

The Coffer (25:10–16). The coffer or ark was a cult object of major importance in premonarchic and early monarchic Israel. In our text it contains
the "Testimony" (i.e., the tablets with the Ten Words); in Josh. 3:14–15
it precedes the people into the Promised Land; in I Sam. 4:11–5:12 it is
captured in battle but mysteriously wreaks havoc among the enemy (hence
its cinematic offspring *Raiders of the Lost Ark*). Finally, David's transporting of it to Jerusalem (II Sam. 6) marks the formal establishment of that
city as a holy one and as the capital of Israel.

In Exodus the coffer literally plays a central role. It stands in the inner-most recesses of the Tabernacle, at the sacred center. Considering what the coffer contained—tablets with God's words on them rather than stat-ues of gods—it addresses the primacy of divine word over divine represen-tation in ancient Israelite thought.

The Purgation-Cover (25:17–22): *Kapporet* here could indicate simply "cover," yet its function goes beyond mere protection. The name of this central part of the above-cited central cult object may be a play on words. The Hebrew verb *kapper,* which occurs again later in these texts (see 29:33–37), often means "purge" or "purify"; earlier translators rendered it as "expiate" or even "propitiate," and the *kapporet* as "mercy-seat" or "propitiatory." The *kapporet* was apparently the holiest spot in the Israel-ite cult system, and it was there that God was said to speak his will to the people. This idea represents a remarkable shrinking and intimatizing pro-cess: the God who spoke to the assembled people, amid thunder, fire, and trembling earth at Sinai, now communicates with them from an area roughly the size of a small desk or table. In addition, there is a shift from a one-time event (Sinai) to the permanent fact of a sanctuary—a develop-ment which will later be repeated in Solomon's Temple.

10 **coffer:** Others, "ark." The Hebrew word *aron,* like "ark," means a chest or box, and is also used of Yosef's "coffin" in Gen. 50:20. I have used a different word here so as not to confuse it with Noah's ark (Heb. *teva*).
   cubits: The cubit was a common measure in the ancient world, conceived of as the length of a man's forearm. The biblical cubit existed in two versions, measuring between 17½ and 20½ inches. **two cubits and a half . . . :** Thus the proportions of the coffer are 5:3:3.
11 **a rim of gold all around:** Heb. *zer zahav saviv.*
16 **testimony:** B-R, seeking to connect *'edut* ("Testimony") with the sound of *mo'ed* ("appointment"), translate these two terms as "representation" and "presence." The tablets bear the name "testimony" because they "testify" or bear witness to God's relationship with the Israelites. It should also be noted that Akkadian *'adu,* cognate with our *'edut,* means "treaty," somewhat like the Hebrew *berit* ("covenant"), which is often found parallel to *'edut* in the Bible (DeVaux 1965).
17 **purgation-cover:** Heb. *kapporet.* There are two long-held traditions of translating this word: "expiation" or "mercy-seat" and plain "cover." I have kept both ideas in the present rendering. The *kapporet* was used for the purpose of obtaining forgiveness from God (see Lev. 16:13–15), and also served symbolically as God's "footstool" to the throne represented by the coffer. Such symbolism is in line with ancient Near Eastern practice, as is the keeping of the covenant documents within the footstool.

18 You are to make two winged-sphinxes of gold,
of hammered-work are you to make them,
at the two ends of the purgation-cover.

19 Make one sphinx at the end here
and one sphinx at the end there;
from the purgation-cover are you to make the two sphinxes,
at its two ends.

20 And the sphinxes are to be spreading (their) wings upward
with their wings sheltering the purgation-cover,
their faces, each-one toward the other;
toward the purgation-cover are the sphinxes' faces to be.

21 You are to put the purgation-cover on the coffer, above it,
and in the coffer you are to put
the Testimony that I give you.

22 I will appoint-meeting with you there
and I will speak with you
from above the purgation-cover,
from between the sphinxes that are on the coffer of Testi-
    mony—
all that I command you
concerning the Children of Israel.

23 You are to make a table of acacia wood,
two cubits its length,
a cubit its width,
and a cubit and a half its height;

24 you are to overlay it with pure gold.
You are to make a rim of gold for it, all around,

25 you are to make for it a border, a handbreadth all around,
thus you are to make a rim of gold for its border, all around.

26 You are to make for it four rings of gold
and are to put the rings at the four edges, where its four legs
    (are).

27 Parallel to the border are the rings to be,
as holders for the poles, to carry the table.

28 You are to make the poles of acacia wood, and are to overlay
    them with gold,
that the table may be carried by (means of) them.

29 You are to make its plates and its cups,

its jars and its bowls, from which (libations) are poured;
of pure gold are you to make them.
30 And you are to put on the table
the Bread of the Presence, in my presence, regularly.

The Table (25:23–30): The table and its implements, like some of the other features of the Tabernacle, are holdovers from a more blatantly pagan model, where the gods were seen to be in need of nourishment. By thus using conventions of worship common throughout the ancient Near East, Israel expressed its desire to serve God, even while it was aware that he was not the sort of deity who requires food and drink. It might also be mentioned that another common object found in ancient sanctuaries, a bed, has intentionally been omitted from our structure.

18 **winged-sphinxes:** Others, "cherubim," which, however, is too reminiscent of chubby-cheeked baby angels in Western art. In Mesopotamian temples, these mythical figures in sculpture served as guardians; so too at the end of the Garden of Eden story in Gen. 3:24. See Albright (1961).
19 **here . . . there:** Or "on one side . . . on the other side"; at either end.
    from: Or "out of"; others, "of one piece with." This one-piece construction is a frequent feature of the objects associated with the Tabernacle.
20 **toward the purgation-cover:** Facing downward, as if to avoid the direct presence of God.
22 **appoint-meeting:** The Hebrew verb refers to fixing a time, and is not the same as the earlier "meeting" (5:3). Exodus speaks of the "Tent of Appointment" from Chapter 27 on; it is unclear as to whether the Tabernacle itself or a separate structure is meant. **from above the purgation-cover,/ from between the sphinxes:** So this was seen as the precise spot of God's presence in the Tabernacle.
27 **as holders for the poles:** Heb. *le-vatim le-vaddim. Batim* are literally "housings."
29 **plates . . . cups . . . jars . . . bowls:** Translations vary considerably on these terms. Haran (1985) cites several (e.g., "plates, bowls, dishes, cups," "ladles, jars, saucers, beakers").
30 **Bread of the Presence:** Trad. English "shewbread." **regularly:** Not "perpetually," as earlier interpreters understood.

31 You are to make a lampstand of pure gold;
    of hammered-work is the lampstand to be made, its shaft
        and its stem;
    its goblets, its knobs and its blossoms are to be from it.
32 Six stems issue from its sides,
    three lamp-stems from the one side,
    and three lamp-stems from the second side:
33 three almond-shaped goblets on the one stem, with knobs
        and blossoms,
    and three almond-shaped goblets on the other stem, with
        knobs and blossoms—
    thus for the six stems that issue from the lampstand;
34 and on the lampstand (itself) four almond-shaped goblets,
        with their knobs and their blossoms,
35 a knob beneath two stems, from it,
    a knob beneath two stems, from it,
    and a knob beneath two stems, from it,
    for the six stems that issue from the lampstand.
36 Their knobs and their stems are to be from it,
    all of it hammered-work, of pure gold.
37 You are to make its lamps, seven (of them),
    you are to set up its lamps so that they light up (the space)
        across from it.
38 And its tongs and its trays (shall be) of pure gold.
39 (From) an ingot of pure gold they are to make it, together
        with all these implements.
40 Now see
    and make,
    according to their building-pattern which you are granted to
        see upon the mountain.

26:1 Now the dwelling you are to make
      from ten tapestries
      of twisted byssus, violet, purple and worm-scarlet (yarn),
      with sphinxes, of designer's making, you are to make it.
   2 The length of each one tapestry (shall be) twenty-eight by
         the cubit,
      and the width, four by the cubit
      of each one tapestry,
      one measure for all of the tapestries.

The Lampstand (25:31–40): Despite the wealth of detail lavished on this striking symbol, its exact construction, like that of the Dwelling in general, remains unclear. The vocabulary used for its constituent parts comes from the realm of plants: shaft, stems, blossoms, almond shapes, etc. Indeed, the major latent symbol behind the lampstand is the tree—which appears in many forms and in almost all religions (Meyers 1976). The tree as a symbol is to be found throughout human culture, in such diverse settings as Native American stories and Norse myths; in the ancient Near East it specifically connoted permanence, growth, and majesty—in other words, a reflection of the divine. If one adds to this range of meanings the function of the lampstand—illumination (which often implies not only the giving of physical light but also, as the English phrase has it, enlightenment)—the lampstand will be seen to emerge as an object with considerable evocative power. All these meanings may not have been immediately obvious and conscious to the ancient pilgrim or worshipper, but they periodically surfaced; the lampstand was ancient Judaism's symbol of preference (judging from synagogue ruins) and not the "Star of David," which, as Gershom Scholem (1972) has shown, was a medieval mystical addition.

The importance of the lampstand in our text is indicated by verse 40, where the motif of God's revealing the structure of a sacred object on the mountain is resumed. Its significance is also attested by its major material of construction: pure gold.

The Dwelling Proper (26:1–14): The text describes the network of tapestries or curtains that comprise the structure itself, in two layers (vv.1–6 and 7–12), with two additional layers mentioned (v.14). The outer layers function to protect the inner ones from the elements, while the inner ones, true to the gradations of holiness previously mentioned, are more elaborate.

31 **shaft . . . stem:** Meyers (1976) interprets this as a hendiadys (two Hebrew words that yield a composite meaning), "thickened shaft." **knobs . . . blossoms:** Others, "calyxes . . . petals."
33 **almond-shaped:** Like the shape of the almond flower.
35 **from it:** See the note to verse 19, above.
38 **tongs:** Others, "snuffers."
26:1 **the dwelling:** In this context it signifies the inside portion of the Tabernacle; lowercase is used here to distinguish it from the entire structure. **tapestries:** Others, "curtains," "cloths." **designer's making:** According to the designer's craft.

3 Five of the tapestries are to be joined, each-one to the other,
   and five tapestries joined, each-one to the other.

4 You are to make loops of violet
   on the edge of one tapestry, at the end of the one joint;
   and thus you are to make at the edge of the end tapestry, at
      the second joint.

5 Fifty loops are you to make on the first tapestry,
   and fifty loops are you to make at the end of the tapestry that
      is at the second joint,
   the loops opposite, each-one from the other.

6 You are to make fifty clasps of gold
   and you are to join the tapestries, each-one to the other, with
      the clasps,
   so that the dwelling may be one-piece.

7 You are to make the tapestries of goats'-hair for a tent over
      the dwelling,
   eleven tapestries you are to make them.

8 The length of each one tapestry (shall be) thirty by the cubit,
   and the width, four by the cubit,
   for each one tapestry,
   one measure for the eleven tapestries.

9 You are to join five of the tapestries separately
   and six of the tapestries separately,
   but you are to double over the sixth tapestry, facing the tent.

10 You are to make fifty loops at the edge of the one tapestry,
      the end-one, at the joint,
   and fifty loops at the end of the second joining tapestry.

11 You are to make clasps of bronze, fifty,
   and you are to bring the clasps into the loops, so that you
      join the tent together,
   that it may become one-piece.

12 And as for the extension that overlaps in the tapestries of the
      tent,
   half of the overlapping tapestry you are to extend over the
   back of the dwelling.

13 The cubit over here and the cubit over there of the overlap,
      in the long-part of the tapestries of the tent,
   is to be extended over the sides of the tent over here and over
      there, in order to cover it.

14 You are to make a covering for the tent of rams' skins dyed-
    red,
    and a covering of dugongs' skins, above it.

15 You are to make boards for the Dwelling
    of acacia wood, standing-upright;
16 ten cubits, the length of a board,
    and a cubit and a half, the width of each one board;
17 with two pegs for each one board, parallel one to the other,
    thus are you to make for all the boards of the Dwelling.
18 And you are to make the boards for the Dwelling:
    twenty as boardwork on the Negev border, southward,
19 and forty sockets of silver are you to make beneath twenty of
    the boards,
    two sockets beneath each one board for its two pegs
    and two sockets beneath each other board for its two pegs;
20 and for the second flank of the Dwelling, on the northern
    border, twenty as boardwork,
21 with their forty sockets of silver,
    two sockets beneath each one board,
    and two sockets beneath each other board.
22 And for the rear of the Dwelling, toward the sea, you are to
    make six boards,

The Framework (26:15–30): The rigid part of the Tabernacle structure, while described in some detail, leaves room for many questions about specifics (e.g., how exactly did the boards fit together? was there one corner board or two? is the text perhaps describing planks or frames?) What is most important, as mentioned above, is the sense of proportion and approach to the divine implied by symmetrical numbers.

  9 **double over:** Since it overlaps (see vv. 12–13).

  4 **covering:** A different Hebrew verb (*kasse*) from the one translated by "purgation-cover" (*kapper*).

15 **boards:** Some interpret as "beams" or "frames." See the discussion of the possibilities in Haran (1965).

17 **pegs:** Others, "tenons," a more technical architectural term. **parallel:** Heb. obscure.

18 **Negev:** The desert southland of Israel.

22 **the sea:** The Mediterranean, and hence the west, from the perspective of one living in the land of Israel.

23 and two boards you are to make for the corners of the
     Dwelling, at the rear,
24 so that they may be of twin-use, (seen) from the lower-end,
     and together may be a whole-piece, at the top, toward the
       first ring;
     thus shall it be for the two of them,
     for the two corners shall they be.
25 Then there are to be eight boards with their sockets of silver,
       sixteen sockets,
     two sockets beneath each one board,
     and two sockets beneath each other board.
26 You are to make running-bars of acacia wood,
     five for the boards of Dwelling's one flank
27 and five bars for the boards of the Dwelling's second flank,
     and five bars for the Dwelling's flank at the rear, toward the
       sea.
28 And the middle bar (shall be) amidst the boards, running
       from end to end.
29 Now the boards you are to overlay with gold,
     their rings you are to make of gold, as holders for the bars,
     and are to overlay the bars with gold.
30 So erect the Dwelling, according to its plan,
     as you have been granted to see upon the mountain.

31 You are to make a curtain
     of violet, purple, worm-scarlet and twisted byssus;
     of designer's making, they are to make it, with winged-
       sphinxes.
32 You are to put it on four columns of acacia,
     overlaid with gold, their hooks of gold,
     upon four sockets of silver;
33 and you are to put the curtain beneath the clasps.
     You are to bring there, inside the curtain,
     the coffer of Testimony;
     the curtain shall separate for you
     the Holy-Place from the Holiest Holy-Place.
34 You are to put the purgation-cover
     on the coffer of Testimony;
     in the Holiest Holy-Place.

35 You are to place the table outside the curtain,
   and the lampstand opposite the table on the south flank of
      the Dwelling,
   but the table you are to put on the north flank.
36 You are to make a screen for the entrance to the tent,
   of violet, purple, worm-scarlet and twisted byssus,
   of embroiderer's making;
37 you are to make for the screen five columns of acacia,
   you are to overlay them with gold, their hooks of gold,
   and are to cast for them five sockets of bronze.

27:1 You are to make the altar of acacia wood,
   five cubits in length
   and five cubits in width;
   square is the altar to be,
   and three cubits its height.
2 You are to make its horns on its four points,

The Curtain and the Screen (26:31–37): Two hangings separate different parts of the Tabernacle: the curtain, which closes off the inner sanctum; and the screen, which separates tent and courtyard.

The Altar (27:1–8): As Cassuto (1967) points out, Israelite worship, like that in surrounding cultures, would have been unthinkable without an altar for animal sacrifices. The one described here is a compromise between permanence and portability: it was hollow for transporting, to be filled in with earth at each encampment.

As with the lampstand, the exact construction of the object is to proceed along lines given to Moshe by God at Sinai.

24 **of twin-use:** Used for two purposes? The exact meaning here has been long debated, with many sketches as to what the corners of the Tabernacle might have looked like.   **toward the first ring:** Heb. obscure.
26 **running-bars:** Horizontal bars designed to hold the structure together.
33 **Holiest Holy-Place:** Trad. "Holy of Holies."
27:2 **horns:** Many altars have been dug up in the area, both Israelite and non-Israelite in origin, fitting this description. The origin and purpose of the "horns" is not clear. We do know that when an Israelite wanted to be granted asylum, for instance, he could grasp the horns of the altar (see I Kings 1:50ff.).

from it are its horns to be;
and you are to overlay it with bronze.

3 You are to make its pails for removing-its-ashes,
its scrapers, its bowls, its forks and its pans—
all of its implements, you are to make of bronze.

4 You are to make for it a lattice,
as a netting of bronze is made,
and are to make on the netting four rings of bronze
on its four ends;

5 you are to put it beneath the ledge of the altar, below,
so that the netting (reaches) to the halfway-point of the altar.

6 You are to make poles for the altar,
poles of acacia wood,
and are to overlay them with bronze.

7 Its poles are to be brought through the rings,
so that the poles are on the two flanks of the altar when they
carry it.

8 Hollow, of planks, are you to make it;
as he has granted you to see it on the mountain, thus are they
to make it.

9 You are to make the courtyard of the Dwelling:
on the Negev border, southward,
hangings for the courtyard, of twisted byssus,
a hundred by the cubit, the length on one border;

10 with its columns, twenty, their sockets, twenty, of bronze,
the hooks of the columns and their binders, of silver.

11 And thus on the northern border, lengthwise,
hangings a hundred (cubits) in length,
with its columns, twenty, their sockets, twenty, of bronze,
the hooks of the columns and their binders, of silver.

12 And (along) the width of the courtyard on the sea border
hangings of fifty cubits,
with its columns, ten, their sockets, ten.

13 And (along) the width of the courtyard on the eastern
border, toward sunrise,
fifty cubits,

14 namely: fifteen cubits of hangings for the shoulder-piece,
their columns, three, their sockets, three,

15 and for the second shoulder-piece, fifteen (cubits) of hang-
     ings,
   their columns, three, their sockets, three,
16 and for the gate of the courtyard, a screen of twenty cubits,
   of violet, purple, worm-scarlet and twisted byssus, of em-
     broiderer's making,
   their columns, four, their sockets, four.
17 All the columns of the courtyard all around are attached
     with silver, their hooks of silver,
   their sockets of bronze,
18 —the length of the courtyard, a hundred by the cubit, the
     width, fifty by fifty, the height, five cubits of twisted
     byssus,
   their sockets of bronze.
19 All the implements of the Dwelling for all its service (of
     construction),
   and all its pins, and all the pins of the courtyard,
   —bronze.

The Courtyard (27:9–19): Returning to the Tabernacle structure, the outer
courtyard is laid out, composed of hangings and columns. Again, the
numbers fit meaningfully together. Since we are dealing with the extrem-
ity of the Dwelling, the material used is the least precious: bronze.

3 **scrapers . . . bowls . . . forks . . . pans:** As in 25:29, above, the exact
   identification of these objects is not known.
4 **lattice . . . netting:** To let air through and facilitate burning (Cassuto
   1967).
7 **poles:** In contrast to those of the coffer, these were apparently removable.
   The altar was of lesser sanctity than the coffer, and it was not deemed as
   crucial that no human hand touch it.
8 **Hollow:** And thus easily transportable, to be filled with dirt every time it
   was set up.
9 **twisted byssus:** Heb. *shesh moshzar.*
10 **binders:** Others, "rods."
14 **shoulder-piece:** That is the literal Hebrew; "side" would be acceptable
   idiomatically.
19 **service (of construction):** Not worship (divine service), but rather a term
   referring to the Levites' setting up and dismantling of the Tabernacle
   (Milgrom 1983).   **pins:** Others, "pegs."

20 Now you,
   command the Children of Israel,
   that they may take you
   oil of olives, clear, beaten,
   for the light,
   to set up for a lamp, regularly.
21 In the Tent of Appointment,
   outside the curtain that is over the Testimony,
   Aharon and his sons are to arrange it,
   from evening until morning
   in the presence of YHWH—
   a law for the ages, into your generations,
   on the part of the Children of Israel.

28:1 Now you, have come-near to you
   Aharon your brother and his sons with him,
   from amidst the Children of Israel,
   to be-priests for me;
   Aharon,
   Nadav and Avihu, Elazar and Itamar, the sons of Aharon.
 2 You are to make garments of holiness for Aharon your
      brother,
   for glory and for splendor.
 3 So you, speak to each who is wise of mind
   whom I have filled with the spirit of practical-wisdom,
   that they may make Aharon's garments,
   to hallow him, to be-priest for me.
 4 And these are the garments that they are to make:
   breastpiece and *efod* and tunic,
   braided coat,
   wound-turban and sash.
   So they are to make garments of holiness
   for Aharon your brother and for his sons,
   to be-priests for me.
 5 And they, they are to take gold, violet, purple, worm-scarlet
      and byssus.

 6 They are to make the *efod*
   of gold, of violet and of purple, of worm-scarlet and of
      twisted byssus,
   of designer's making.

The Oil (27:20–21): The transition from structure to human institution (the priesthood) is accomplished by both the opening formula here, "Now you. . . ," and by the oil itself, which is here used for light but which will soon be spoken of (Chap. 29) as a major agent in the anointing of the priests.

The Priestly Garments (28:1–5): As in the opening section on the Tabernacle itself (25:1–9), we are now given a listing of what is to come, the clothing in which the priests will perform their sacred functions. The purpose of the objects is mentioned again, this time at both the beginning and the end of the section.

In virtually all traditional religions such garments are of great importance, often signalling the status of the wearer as representative of the community (hence Aharon's breastpiece in this chapter). An additional function, stressed in our account, is that the garments somehow reflect God himself, through the use of certain colors and/or materials. That the term "glory" is used to indicate their function—a key term in the book, and always applied to God, never to Moshe, for instance—signals what is at stake.

The Efod (28:6–12, 13–14): This garment, which here seems to be a kind of apron worn only by the high priest, is mentioned elsewhere in the Bible in connection with worship (e.g., Judges 8:27), but with unclear meaning. Even here, the exact nature of the *efod* is not entirely certain; but what *is* cited is its function as the setting for the stones that symbolize the twelve tribes of Israel in God's presence. This is followed by a description of chains, whose use is mentioned immediately thereafter.

20 **beaten:** Crushed until the substance is pure.
21 **Tent of Appointment:** See the note to 25:22, above. DeVaux (1965) translates as "Tent of Rendezvous," and Moffatt (in his 1926 Bible translation) as "Trysting Tent," but these are too romantic in English, even in view of what I have said about the relationship between God and Israel. **arrange:** Or "set up."
28:1 **be-priests:** One translation possibility was to coin an English verb, "to priest."
2 **glory . . . splendor:** Others, "dignity and magnificence," but retaining "glory" for *kavod* enables one to see in the priest's garb a reflection of the divine splendor.
3 **wise of mind:** Idiomatically, "skilled" or "talented." **practical-wisdom:** Wisdom in biblical literature most often denotes worldly wisdom or artisanry, not abstract intellectual prowess.

7 Two shoulder-pieces, joined, it is to have, at its two ends,
and it is to be joined.

8 The designed-band of its *efod*, which is on it,
according to its making, is to be from it,
of gold, of violet, of purple, of worm-scarlet and of twisted
byssus.

9 You are to take two onyx stones
and are to engrave on them the names of the Children of
Israel,

10 six of their names on the one stone,
and the names of the six remaining-ones on the second
stone,
corresponding to their begettings.

11 Of stone-cutter's making, with seal engravings,
you are to engrave the two stones,
with the names of the Children of Israel;
surrounded by braids of gold are you to make them.

12 You are to place the two stones on the shoulder-pieces of the
efod,
as stones of remembrance for the Children of Israel.
Aharon is to bear their names in the presence of YHWH
on his two shoulders,
for remembrance.

13 You are to make braids of gold

14 and two chains of pure gold,
(like) lacings are you to make them, of rope-making,
and are to put the rope chains on the braids.

15 You are to make the breastpiece of Judgment
of designer's making,
like the making of the *efod* are you to make it,
of gold, of purple, of worm-scarlet and of twisted byssus are
you to make it.

16 Square it is to be, doubled-over,
a span its length and a span its width.

17 You are to set-it-full with a setting of stones,
four rows of stones—
a row of carnelian, topaz and sparkling-emerald, the first
row,

18 the second row: ruby, sapphire, and hard-onyx,
19 the third row: jacinth, agate, and amethyst,
20 the fourth row: beryl, onyx, and jasper.
   Braided with gold are they to be in their settings.
21 And the stones are to be with the names of the Children of
      Israel,
   twelve with their names,
   (with) signet engravings, each-one with its name, are they to
      be,
   for the twelve tribes.
22 You are to make, on the breastpiece, laced chains, of rope
      making, of pure gold;
23 and you are to make, on the breastpiece, two rings of gold;
   you are to put the two rings on the two ends of the breast-
      piece.

The Breastpiece (28:15–30): The central garment in this section is the
breastpiece, which seems to be some sort of woven pouch or bag. On the
outside it displays precious stones, each one engraved with the name of an
Israelite tribe; inside, it holds the oracular objects known as *Urim* and
Tummin (see the note to verse 30, below). In this passage, which is cast in
poetic form, the narrator appears to be drawing our attention to the specific function of the garments. Verses 29 and 30 repeat the phrase "over
his/Aharon's heart" (three times), "in the presence of YHWH" (three
times), and "regularly" (twice) to make clear their importance: Aharon
represents the people whenever he officiates in the sanctuary, and bears
the emblem of this office upon his very heart.

 8 **designed-band:** Perhaps resembling a belt.
10 **begettings:** Birth order.
11 **braids:** Others, "mesh," "checkered-work."
12 **for remembrance:** For a visible symbol.
16 **a span:** A measure taken to be the distance between the outstretched
      thumb and the little finger, half a cubit or about nine inches.
17–20 **carnelian . . . jasper:** The exact identification of many of these stones is
      uncertain. The reader will find a different list in virtually every Bible
      translation.

24 And you are to put the two ropes of gold on the two rings
   at the ends of the breastpiece;
25 and the two ends of the two ropes, you are to put on the two
     braids
   and you are to put them on the shoulder-piece of the *efod*,
     facing frontward.
26 You are to make two rings of gold,
   and are to place them on the two ends of the breastpiece, on
     its edge, which is across from the *efod*, inward,
27 and you are to make two rings of gold,
   and are to put them on the two shoulder-pieces of the *efod*,
     below, facing frontward, parallel to its joint, above the
     designed-band of the *efod*.
28 They are to tie the breastpiece from its rings to the rings of
     the *efod*
   with a thread of violet,
   to be (fixed) on the designed-band of the *efod;*
   the breastpiece is not to slip from the *efod*.
29 So Aharon is to bear
   the names of the Children of Israel
   on the breastpiece of Judgment
   over his heart,
   whenever he comes into the Holy-Place
   for remembrance, in the presence of YHWH,
   regularly.
30 And you are to put
   in the breastpiece of Judgment
   the *Urim* and the *Tummim*,
   that they may be over Aharon's heart,
   whenever he comes into the presence of YHWH.
   So Aharon is to bear
   the breastpiece of Judgment for the Children of Israel
   over his heart
   in the presence of YHWH,
   regularly.

31 You are to make the tunic for the *efod*
   all of violet.
32 Its head-opening is to be in its middle;

there shall be a seam for its opening, all around, of weaver's
making,
like the opening for armor is it to be for him, it is not to be
split.
33 You are to make on its skirts
pomegranates of violet, purple, and worm-scarlet,
on its skirts, all around,
and bells of gold amidst them, all around:
34 bell of gold and pomegranate,
bell of gold and pomegranate,
on the skirts of the tunic, all around.

The Tunic (28:31–35): Aharon's tunic or shirt is notable for its design of
bells and pomegranates, but even more for its protective function, sup-
plied by actual bells, of maintaining the proper distance between Aharon
and God in the sanctuary.

29 **over his heart:** Or "upon his heart," three times here. A similar idea
occurs in later Judaism, which interpreted Deut. 6:8 ("you shall bind
them as a sign upon your hand, and they shall serve as bands between your
eyes") literally. The resulting *tefillin* ("phylacteries"), leather straps with
small boxes containing the relevant Deuteronomy passages, worn during
weekdays morning prayers, include a text that is worn on the arm in such
a way as to point to the heart.

30 **Urim . . . Tummim:** Oracular objects, used for divining God's plans (e.g.
learning if it was the right time to go into battle). Their exact shape and
mode of operation are the subject of much scholarly debate (see Cassuto
1967, for instance). In I Sam. 28:6, *Urim* are equated with dreams and
prophets as a means of answering human queries. B-R, following Luther,
translate the terms as "Lichtende und Schlichtende" ("lights and perfec-
tions"), a possible literal but unclear translation. It is also worth noting
that *Urim* begins with the first letter of the Hebrew alphabet, and *Tummim*
the last, giving rise to the possibility that the names themselves are
symbolic.

31 **tunic:** Others, "robe."

32 **armor:** Or "coat of mail." **split:** Or "splittable."

33 **pomegranates:** Cassuto (1967) notes that these were a common ornamen-
tal device in the ancient world, and a symbol of fertility (as in Song of
Songs 6:7, 11; 8:2). **bells:** Their use is explained in verse 35, "so that he
[Aharon] does not die." Bells serve to drive away demons or to warn of
human approach in many cultures; see Gaster (1969) for parallels.

34 **bell of gold and promegranate:** In alternating design.

35 It is to be (put) on Aharon, for attending,
that its sound may be heard
whenever he comes into the Holy-Place in the presence of
    YHWH, and whenever he goes out,
so that he does not die.

36 You are to make a plate of pure gold
and are to engrave on it signet engravings:
Holiness for YHWH.

37 You are to place it on a thread of violet,
that it may be on the turban;
on the forefront of the turban is it to be.

38 It is to be on Aharon's brow.
So Aharon is to bear
the iniquity of the holy-offerings that the Children of Israel
    offer-as-holy,
all their gifts of holiness;
it is to be on his brow
regularly,
for (receiving) favor for them, in the presence of YHWH.

39 You are to braid the coat with byssus;
you are to make a turban of byssus,
and a sash you are to make, of embroiderer's making.

40 And for the sons of Aharon, you are to make coats,
you are to make them sashes
and caps you are to make for them,
for glory and for splendor.

41 You are to clothe in them Aharon your brother, and his sons
    with him,
you are to anoint them,
you are to give-mandate to them,
and you are to hallow them,
that they may be-priests for me.

42 You are to make them breeches of linen
to cover the flesh of nakedness;
from the hips to the thighs are they to extend.

43 They are to be on Aharon and on his sons,
whenever they come into the Tent of Appointment
or whenever they approach the altar

> to attend at the Holy-Place,
> that they do not bear iniquity and die
> —a law for the ages, for him and for his seed after him.

29:1 Now this is the ceremony
       that you are to make for them:

The Head-Plate (28:36–38): Foremost among the symbols on Aharon's garments is what he bears on his brow: a band with the words "Holiness for YHWH." It serves as a symbol of his efforts to obtain forgiveness on behalf of the Israelite people, one of his primary functions as priest. This function extends to cover even unintentional transgressions, such as accidents in the handling of sacred cultic objects.

Other Priestly Garments (28:39–43): These include remaining vestments for Aharon and his sons, to the end that "they do not bear iniquity and die" (v.43)—a major concern of the priesthood, which viewed all impurities as ritually dangerous before God. Note the solemn ending of this passage:"—a law for the ages, for him and for his seed after him."

The Investiture Ceremony (29:1–45): Although the text still has a number of Tabernacle items to discuss, viz., the incense and its altar, other objects, and the commissioning of the artisans for the construction work, it natur-

36 **plate:** Lit., "flower" or "gleamer," perhaps alluding to its shining quality, or to its shape of some kind.
38 **to bear/ the iniquity of the holy-offerings:** To atone for accidental violations of purity concerning sacrifices brought by the people. This is a classic concern of priests.
40 **caps:** Of less splendor than Aharon's turban, but constructed along the same lines (wound cloth).
41 **give-mandate:** Lit., "fill the hand." The term indicates induction into office; possibly something was put into the inductee's hand symbolizing their new status. *Mandatus* in Roman law is similar, and hence the present translation. Plaut (1981) also points out that this expression in Akkadian means "to appoint." **anoint . . . give mandate . . . hallow:** "A rising trilogy of near synonyms" (Plaut 1981).
42 **breeches . . . to cover . . . nakedness:** As previously (20:23), any hint of sexuality is separated from the cult.
29:1 **ceremony:** Lit., "matter." The actual implementation of the ceremony is recounted in Lev. 8:13ff. So unlike the rest of the Tabernacle material, (Chaps. 35–40), this ritual is delayed.

to hallow them, to be-priests for me:
Take a steer, a young-one of the herd, and rams, two, hale,

2 and bread of *matza* and flat cakes of *matza*, mixed with oil,
   and wafers of *matza*, dipped in oil,
   of fine-ground wheat are you to make them.

3 You are to put them in one basket
   and are to bring-them-near in the basket,
   along with the steer and along with two rams.

4 And Aharon and his two sons
   you are to bring-near to the entrance of the Tent of Appoint-
      ment
   and are to wash them with water.

5 You are to take the garments
   and are to clothe Aharon—
   in the coat, in the tunic of the *efod*, in the *efod* and in the
      breastpiece;
   you are to robe him in the designed-band of the *efod*,

6 you are to place the turban on his head,
   and are to put the sacred-diadem of holiness on the turban.

7 You are to take the oil for anointing
   and are to pour it on his head, anointing him.

8 And his sons, you are to bring-near
   and are to clothe them in coats;

9 you are to gird them with a sash, Aharon and his sons,
   and are to wind caps for them.
   It shall be for them as priestly-right,
   a law for the ages.
   So you are to give-mandate to Aharon and to his sons:

10 You are to bring-near the steer, before the Tent of Appoint-
       ment.
    and Aharon and his sons are to lay their hands on the head of
       the steer.

11 You are to slay the steer in the presence of YHWH,
    at the entrance of the Tent of Appointment,

12 and are to take some of the blood of the steer
    and are to put it on the horns of the altar with your finger,
    but all the rest of the blood, you are to throw against the
       foundation of the altar.

13 You are to take all the fat that covers the innards,

with what hangs over the liver, the two kidneys and the fat
   that is on them,
and turn-them-into-smoke on the altar.

14 And the flesh of the steer, its skin and its dung,
   you are to burn with fire, outside the camp;
   it is removal-of-sin.

15 And the first ram, you are to take,
   and Aharon and his sons are to lay their hands on the head of
      the ram.

16 You are to slay the ram,
   you are to take its blood
   and you are to toss it on the altar, all around.

17 And the ram you are to chop up into carcass-choppings,
   you are to wash its innards and its legs
   and you are to put (them) on its choppings and on its head

18 and are to turn-into-smoke the entire ram, on the altar;
   it is an offering-up for YHWH,
   Soothing Savor,
   a fire-gift for YHWH is it.

ally moves from describing the priestly garb to the ritual through which
the priests are installed in their sacred office. First, sacrifical animals and
bread are brought and prepared; then the priests are systematically
clothed in their sacred vestments. After the first animal is slaughtered, its
blood is dashed against the altar and the innards are burned as an offering;
then the second ram is slain, and its blood is placed on the priests' extremi-

2 **matza:** See 12:8 and the accompanying note.

6 **sacred-diadem:** See 28:36 above; the diadem was apparently in the shape
   of a flower, and was a "sign of consecration" (DeVaux 1965).

9 **to wind caps:** Like small turbans: see the note to 28:40, above.

14 **removal-of-sin:** Another major concern of the cult: the purity of the
   sanctuary. This is also reflected in the Levitical description of the Day of
   Purgation (Yom Kippur) in Lev. 16.

18 **Soothing Savor:** Heb. *re'ah niho'ah*. The original signification of this
   concept must have been the common ancient one of feeding the gods, and
   hence the idea of an attractive smell. Already in Gen. 9:21 (after the
   Flood), however, it has been severed from that context, and the smell only
   pleases God and induces him to be more merciful with human beings.

19 And you are to take the second ram
    and Aharon and his sons are to lay their hands on the head of
        the ram.
20 You are to slay the ram,
    you are to take (some) of its blood
    and you are to put (it)
    on the ear lobe of Aharon and on the right ear lobe of Aha-
        ron's sons,
    and on the thumb of their right hands and on the thumb-toe
        of their right feet,
    then you are to toss the blood on the altar, all around.
21 You are to take some of the blood that is on the altar, and
        some of the oil for anointing,
    and you are to toss it on Aharon and on his garments, on his
        sons and on his sons' garments with him,
    that he and his garments may be hallowed, and his sons and
        his sons' garments with him.
22 You are to take the fat from the ram,
    the tail, the fat that covers the innards and what hangs over
        the liver, the two kidneys and the fat that is on them,
    and the right thigh,
    for it is the ram for giving-mandate;
23 and one loaf of bread and one cake of oil-bread and one
        wafer from the basket of *matza* that is in the presence of
        YHWH;
24 you are to place them all
    on the palms of Aharon and on the palms of his sons,
    and you are to hold them high as a high-offering, in the
        presence of YHWH.
25 You are to take them from their hand
    and you are to turn-them-into-smoke on the altar, beside the
        offering-up,
    for a Soothing Savor in the presence of YHWH,
    it is a fire-gift for YHWH.
26 You are to take the breast from the ram of giving-mandate
        that is Aharon's,
    and you are to hold it high as a high-offering, in the presence
        of YHWH,
    that it may be an allotment for you.

27 So you are to hallow the breast for the high-offering, and the
     thigh of the raised-contribution,
   that is held-high, that is raised
   from the ram of giving-mandate,
   from what is Aharon's and from what is his sons'.
28 It is to be Aharon's and his sons',
     a fixed-allocation for the ages, on the part of the Children of
       Israel,
   for it is a raised-contribution,
   and a raised-contribution is it to be on the part of the Chil-
     dren of Israel,
   from their well-being–offering meals,
   their raised-contribution for YHWH.
29 Now the garments of holiness that are Aharon's
   are to belong to his sons after him,
   to anoint them in them and to give-them-mandate in them.
30 For seven days is the one of his sons that acts-as-priest in his
     stead to be clothed in them,
   the one who comes into the Tent of Appointment to attend
     at the Holy-Place.

ties. Blood is sprinkled on the priests' garments; then they hold up the
fat-parts and breast of the ram, and follow by offering it up. Then the
priests eat the cooked flesh of a special ram, the remains of which are to be
burnt. Finally, the altar is purified.

After the regular sacrifice is specified (vv.38–41), the section ends with
a powerful meditation on the purpose of the Tabernacle: "hallow" occurs
three times, and "dwell" twice. In a word: by "meeting" with the Children of Israel at the Tent, God's glory makes tent, altar, priests, and most
important, the people of Israel, holy. Indeed, the root *kaddesh*, "holy,"
occurs numerous times in the chapter, presaging its multiple use in the
next book, Leviticus.

20 **ear lobe . . . thumb . . . thumb-toe:** These comprise the extremities of
   the body, and thus are a way of including the entire body symbolically.
24 **high-offering:** The earlier translation of "wave-offering" has been shown
   to be incorrect by Milgrom (1983).
26 **allotment:** For the priests.
27 **that is held-high, that is raised:** Heb. *asher hunaf va-asher huram.*

31 And the ram for giving-mandate you are to take
   and are to boil its flesh in the Holy-Place.
32 Aharon and his sons are to eat the flesh of the ram, along
       with the bread that is in the basket,
   at the entrance of the Tent of Appointment.
33 They are to eat them—those who are purged by them,
   to give-them-mandate, to hallow them;
   an outsider is not to eat (them), for they are holiness.
34 Now if there be anything left over of the flesh of giving-
       mandate or of the bread, by morning,
   you are to burn what is left by fire,
   it is not to be eaten, for it is holiness.
35 You are to make (thus) for Aharon and for his sons,
   according to all that I have commanded you,
   for seven days, you are to give-them-mandate.
36 A steer for removing-sin, you are to make-ready for each
       day, concerning the purging,
   that you may remove-sin from the altar, by your purging it,
   and you are to anoint it, to hallow it.
37 For seven days you are to purge the altar, that you may
       hallow it.
   Thus the altar will become
   holiest holiness;
   whoever touches the altar shall become-holy.

38 And this is what you are to make-ready on the altar:
   year-old lambs, two for each day, regularly.
39 The first lamb you are to make-ready for the morning,
   and the second lamb you are to make-ready at twilight.
40 A tenth-measure of fine-meal, mixed with beaten oil, a
       quarter of a *hin*,
   and (as) libation, a quarter of a *hin* of wine—for the first
       lamb.
41 And the second lamb you are to make-ready at twilight,
   like the leading-donation of the morning, and like its liba-
       tion, (that) you make-ready for it,
   for a Soothing Savor,
   a fire-gift for YHWH;
42 a regular offering-up, throughout your generations,

at the entrance to the Tent of Appointment, in the presence
of YHWH;
for I will appoint-meeting with you there,
to speak to you there.
43 So I will appoint-meeting there
with the Children of Israel,
and it will be hallowed
by my Glory.
44 I will hallow the Tent of Appointment and the altar,
and Aharon and his sons I will hallow,
to be-priests for me.
45 And I will dwell amidst the Children of Israel
and I will be a God for them,
46 that they may know
that I am YHWH their God
who brought them out of the land of Egypt
to dwell, myself, in their midst,
I, YHWH their God.

31 **boil:** This clearly indicates that the food in question is meant for the priests' consumption, since sacrifices were normally completely burned.

33 **purged:** Purified.   **outsider:** Not in the sense of "foreigner," but of "one unauthorized" for the purpose, a layman (Clements 1972).

36 **purging it:** Or "purging in regard to it."

37 **whoever:** Others, "whatever."   **become-holy:** When a person came in contact with holy objects, he became temporarily removed from the everyday, in a state resembling what we, in a sense more negative than the Bible means it, would call contamination (as in radioactivity).

38 **make-ready:** Others, "offer."   **year-old:** That is, newly mature and hence in a state of perfection.

40 **hin:** About a gallon.

41 **leading-donation:** As part of the terminology of sacrifice, the *minha* was to "lead to" God (just as *'ola* bears the sound of "ascend," and *korban* "bring-near") (Buber and Rosenzweig 1936).

46 **that they may know:** This pervasive theme of Exodus finds its true resolution through the Tabernacle texts—not only will the Israelites experience ("know") God through the "wonders" wrought on their behalf in Egypt, but also through their communication with him in ritual.

30:1 You are to make an altar, a smoking-site for smoking-incense,
     of acacia wood are you to make it,
   2 a cubit its length and a cubit its width;
     square is it to be, and two cubits its height,
     its horns from it.
   3 You are to overlay it with pure gold—
     its roof, its walls all around, and its horns,
     and you are to make a rim of gold all around.
   4 And two rings of gold you are to make for it, beneath its rim,
     on its two flanks, you are to make (them) on its two sides,
     that they may be for holders for poles, to carry it by (means
       of) them.
   5 You are to make the poles of acacia wood
     and you are to overlay them with gold.
   6 And you are to put it in front of the curtain that is over the
       coffer of Testimony,
     in front of the purgation-cover that is over the Testimony,
     where I will appoint-meeting with you.
   7 And Aharon is to send-up-in-smoke, fragrant smoking-
       incense on it,
     morning by morning;
     when he polishes the lamps, he is to send-it-up-in-smoke.
   8 And when Aharon sets up the lamps,
     at twilight,
     he is to send-it-up-in-smoke,
     regular smoke-offering in the presence of YHWH, through-
       out your generations.
   9 You are not to offer-up upon it any outsider's smoking-in-
       cense,
     either as offering-up or as leading-donation,
     nor are you to pour out any libation upon it.
  10 Aharon is to do-the-purging upon its horns,
     once a year,
     with the sin-removing blood of purgation;
     once a year
     he is to do-the-purging upon it,
     throughout your generations,
     holiest holiness is it for YHWH.

  11 Now YHWH spoke to Moshe, saying:

12 When you lift up the heads of the Children of Israel, in
    counting them,
   they are to give, each-man, a purgation-payment for his life,
    for YHWH,
   when they count them,
   that there be no plague on them, when they count them.
13 This (is what) they are to give, everyone that goes through
    the counting:
   half a *shekel* of the Holy-Place *shekel*—twenty grains to the
    skekel—
   half a *shekel*, a contribution for YHWH.

The Incense Altar (30:1–10): This altar, which is not mentioned again, is
seen by some as a later interpolation (DeVaux 1965): here it links up with
what has gone before through the theme of purging (purification), in verse
10. For more on the incense itself, see verses 22ff., below.

Census and Ransom (30:11–16): Continuing the theme of purgation, divine
command provides for a ransom to be given to the priests, in order to
remove ("purge away") sin incurred by census-taking.

The idea that numbering the people could bring down the wrath of God
is portrayed in most striking fashion in II Sam. 24:1–9, where David
usurps God's prerogative in numbering the men for military purposes,
leading to a plague among the people. It seems that a census was viewed as
a dangerous undertaking, perhaps analogous to the taking of photographs
among certain peoples (which is felt to be threatening to one's essence).
One who can number, can control (Gaster 1969).

30:6 **in front of . . . :** Some ancient versions and manuscripts omit this entire
      line as a redundancy.
   7 **fragrances:** Incense.   **when he polishes:** Others, "when he dresses" or
      "trims."
   9 **outsider's smoke:** This prohibition is violated by Aharon's sons in Lev.
      10:1 ("offering outsider's fire"), resulting in their death by "fire from
      before YHWH."
  10 **do-the-purging:** On the day of Yom Kippur, when the ancient sanctuary
      was, as it were, detoxified (of sins).
  12 **lift up the heads:** In idiomatic English we would say "count heads."
      purgation-payment: Others, "ransom."
  13 **shekel:** Literally, a "weight" of silver. Coins as such are not documented
      in the land of Israel until centuries after the events documented in Exodus
      took place. For a full discussion of biblical currency, see Sellers (1962).

14 Everyone that goes through the counting, from the age of
       twenty years and upward,
     is to give the contribution of YHWH.
15 The rich are not to pay-more and the poor are not to pay-less
       than half a *shekel*
     when giving the contribution of YHWH,
     to do-purgation for your lives.
16 You are to take the silver for doing-purgation
     from the Children of Israel
     and are to give it over for the construction-service of the
       Tent of Appointment,
     that it may be for the Children of Israel
     as a remembrance in the presence of YHWH,
     to do-purgation for your lives.

17 Now YHWH spoke to Moshe, saying:
18 You are to make a basin of bronze,
     its pedestal of bronze,
     for washing,
     and you are to put it between the Tent of Appointment and
       the altar;
     you are to put water therein,
19 that Aharon and his sons may wash with it
     their hands and their feet.
20 When they come into the Tent of Appointment
     they are to wash with water
     so that they do not die,
     or when they approach the altar, to be-in-attendance,
     to send up fire-offering in smoke for YHWH,
21 they are to wash their hands and their feet,
     so that they do not die.
     It is to be for them a law for the ages,
     for him and for his sons, throughout their generations.

22 Now YHWH spoke to Moshe, saying:
23 And as for you, take you fragrant-spices, essence,
     streaming-myrrh, five hundred,
     cinnamon-spice, half as much—fifty and two hundred,
     fragrant-cane, fifty and two hundred,

24 and cassia, five hundred
   by the *shekel*-weight of the Holy-Place,
   as well as olive oil, a *hin*,
25 and you are to make (from) it anointing oil of holiness,
   perfume from the perfume-mixture, of perfumer's making;
   anointing oil of holiness is it to be.
26 You are to anoint with it
   the Tent of Appointment
   and the coffer of Testimony
27 and the table and all its implements
   and the lampstand and all its implements
   and the altar for smoke-offerings
28 and the altar for offering-up and all its implements
   and the basin and its pedestal.
29 You are to hallow them
   that they may become holiest holiness,
   whoever touches them is to become-holy.

The Basin (30:17–21): Returning to the familiar stylistic pattern of the Tabernacle account, "You are to make. . . ," we are told of the basin in which the priests washed. Yet this brief aside links up with the motif of protection from death that was encountered earlier (see 28:35).

The Anointing Oil (30:22–33): "Holy" is once again heard as a key word, both in the sense of making something sacred and in the sense of being reserved for special use only. Oil was used in many ancient cultures for positive purposes; elsewhere in the Bible, of course, it played its role in the anointing of kings and prophets, as well as the courteous treatment of guests and after bathing. Oil, then, carried with it connotations of brightness (see Psalm 104:15) and life itself.

14 **twenty years:** The age for military service (and so referring to males).
18 **basin:** Others, "laver." The Hebrew denotes something round.
20 **so that they do not die:** Twice here, underscoring the power of water to do away with ritual impurity.
23 **essence:** Lit., "head." **five hundred:** The measure here is "by the *shekel*-weight," as clarified in the next verse.
25 **perfume . . . perfume-mixture . . . perfumer's:** Heb. *rokah mirkhahat . . . roke'ah.* The verb seems to mean "to mix."
26 **to anoint with it/ the tent . . . :** Oil is thus used to anoint not only people but also objects.

30 And Aharon and his sons you are to anoint,
   you are to hallow them
   to be-priests for me.
31 And to the Children of Israel you are to speak, saying:
   Anointing oil of holiness
   this is to be for me
   throughout your generations.
32 On any (other) human body it is not to be poured out;
   in its (exact) proportion, you are not to make any like it—
   holiness it is,
   holiness shall it remain for you.
33 Any man who mixes perfumes like it
   or who puts any of it on an outsider
   is to be cut off from his kinspeople.

34 Now YHWH said to Moshe:
   Take you fragrant-spices,
   drop-gum, onycha, and galbanum,
   (these) fragrances and clear incense;
   part equalling part are they to be.
35 You are to make (with) it smoking-incense,
   perfume, of perfumer's making,
   salted, pure—holy.
36 You are to beat some of it into fine-powder
   and are to put some of it
   in front of the Testimony
   in the Tent of Appointment,
   where I will appoint-meeting with you;
   holiest holiness is it to be for you.
37 As for the smoking-incense that you make,
   you are not to make any for yourselves in its (exact) propor-
      tion;
   holiness shall it be for you, for YHWH.
38 Any man that makes any like it
   to savor it
   is to be cut off from his kinspeople.

31:1 Now YHWH spoke to Moshe, saying:
   2 See,
     I have called by name

Betzalel son of Uri, son of Hur, of the tribe of Yehuda.

3 I have filled him with the spirit of God
   in practical-wisdom, discernment and knowledge
   in all kinds of workmanship,
4 to design designs,
   to make them in gold, in silver and in bronze,
5 in the carving of stones for setting and in the carving of
   wood,
   to make them through all kinds of workmanship.
6 And I, here I give (to be) with him
   Oholiav son of Ahisamakh, of the tribe of Dan;

The Incense (30:34–38): This particular incense, warns the text, was to be used only for the sanctuary and not for everyday purposes.

The offering-up of incense was a feature common to worship all over the ancient Near East. At least two reasons have been advanced for its use: purification, and a fragrance pleasing to the deity. It is also curious how our text speaks of God's being with the Israelites as a column of cloud and of fire; the incense smoke might also then be reminiscent of this divine manifestation.

Craftsmen (31:1–11): As the Tabernacle account opened with a summary description of what was to be constructed, so it ends, with some names added. The craftsmen for the task, Betzalel and Oholiav, are depicted as "wise" (Heb. *hakham*), that is, skilled; they will make what Moshe has been given to see.

32 **according to its proportion:** That is, according to an exact "recipe."
33 **cut off:** The exact meaning of this is not clarified anywhere, but it seems to indicate the death penalty. It is often mentioned in connection with violations of the cult (see 12:15, for example).
34 **drop-gum . . .:** The identification of some of these substances is debated.
35 **salted:** Salt was employed in sacrifices perhaps originally to ward off demons; it has taken on importance in both worship and folklore (viz., the practice of throwing salt over one's shoulder). Some suggest that salt was used simply to improve the taste of the food, or to absorb the blood.
31:2 **called by name:** Or "chosen/singled out."
3 **spirit of God:** Or "breath of God," the transfer of which to human beings in the Bible results in great strength, leadership qualities, or, especially, prophetic inspiration.
6 **Oholiav:** Trad. English "Oholiab"; the name means "Tent of Father/ God," rather appropriate here.

in the mind of all those wise of mind I place wisdom,
that they may make all that I have commanded you:

7 the Tent of Appointment
and the coffer of Testimony
and the purgation-cover that is over it
and all the implements of the Tent

8 and the table and all its implements
and the pure lampstand and all its implements
and the altar for smoke-offering

9 and the altar for offering-up and all its implements
and the basin and its pedestal,

10 and the officiating garments
and the garments of holiness for Aharon the priest and the
garments of his sons for being-priests

11 and oil for anointing
and fragrant smoke for the holy-offerings—
according to all that I have commanded you, they are to
make.

12 Now YHWH said to Moshe:

13 And you, speak to the Children of Israel, saying:
However: my Sabbaths you are to keep!
For it is a sign
between me and you, throughout your generations,
to know that I, YHWH, hallow you.

14 You are to keep the Sabbath,
for holiness is it for you,
whoever profanes it is to be put-to-death, yes, death!
For whoever makes work on it—
that person is to be cut off from amongst his kinspeople.

15 Six days is work to be made,
but on the seventh day
(is) Sabbath, Sabbath-Ceasing, holiness for YHWH,
whoever makes work on the Sabbath day is to be put-to-
death, yes, death.

16 The Children of Israel are to keep the Sabbath,
to make the Sabbath-observance throughout their generations
as a covenant for the ages;

17 between me and the Children of Israel
  a sign is it, for the ages,
  for in six days
  YHWH made the heavens and the earth,
  and on the seventh day
  he ceased and paused-for-breath.

18 Now he gave to Moshe
  when he had finished speaking with him on Mount Sinai
  the two tablets of Testimony,
  tablets of stone,
  written by the finger of God.

The Sabbath (31:12–17): *The Tablets* (31:18): As a reminder of the Sabbath's importance amid all the anticipated construction activity, the Israelites are now commanded to observe the holy day. The section is also a prelude to the Golden Calf story, which will be concerned with improper "making"; and "make" appears in a variety of different contexts.

A second prelude draws the initial Tabernacle section to a close. Moshe receives God's word engraved in stone, by God himself; this will presumably be deposited in the "coffer" of which the text spoke in its opening chapter (25). But the section is forward-looking as well, in that the tablets will play a dramatic role in the story immediately following this passage.

10 **officiating:** The Hebrew (*serad*) is not entirely clear, but may be related to *sharet*, "attending" (in the sanctuary).

13 **However:** In contrast to all the previous activity, the Israelites are not to forget about the Sabbath, the "ceasing" from work (so too Rashi). *Akh* may also be taken as a positive term, "above all."

17 **paused-for-breath:** A rather daring anthropomorphism which, by describing God's resting, encourages humans and animals to do the same (see 23:12).

18 **he gave:** God gave. **the finger of God:** Just as in Egypt (8:15), God intervenes in human affairs here as well.

PART V The Covenant
Broken and Restored

(32–34)

WITHOUT THE STORY that follows, the book of Exodus would be incomplete—or at least hopelessly idealistic and idealized. Thanks to the inclusion of the Golden Calf episode, we recognize the people of Israel so familiar from the bulk of the wilderness narrative—stubborn, untrusting, and utterly unable to comprehend what has just occurred at Sinai (note the parallel between this section and 15:22ff.: after witnessing the awesome displays of God, the people fall prey to typical human anxieties about their own survival). We are also given a classic biblical description of God in this story—that he is demanding but also compassionate.

There is no doubt that the narrative wishes to portray the breaking of the recently made covenant, and also to focus once again on the anxiety about God's presence that pervades the whole book. Some see it as a political polemic, given that a similar story is found in I Kings 12:28ff., about Jeroboam's split from the Solomonic monarchy; according to this theory, the Exodus account is a projection backward of the sin of the Northern Kingdom. Jeroboam, leading a secessionist movement, intended to set up a sanctuary to rival Jerusalem. At the same time, the Exodus story does appear first, and thereby helps to explain why Jeroboam's deed was considered so terrible by later generations.

But surely the Golden Calf story plays such an important role in the present book of Exodus as to sidestep the question of which version came first. It puts into sharp relief the nature of the people, its leader, and its God, and provides some insights into the complex relationships between these parties; it focuses particular aspects of the Tabernacle idea (see above); and it makes clear the difficulties of the emerging faith community.

The story also contributes some welcome dramatic scenes at this point. It is as if the reader has awakened from a dream: major characters, including God himself, reemerge as real personalities, while secondary characters (Aharon and Yehoshua) are fleshed out. Everywhere there are fierce emotions: doubt, anger, panic, pleading for mercy, courage, fear. And, indeed, the entire enterprise of Exodus hangs in the balance, as God wishes only to destroy the faithless people (a rough parallel exists in Genesis 22, where all that has previously been promised to Avraham is threatened). Only after the stark emotions just mentioned have been cathartically absorbed, and the covenant restored, can there be a return to the task at hand—the building of an abode for the divine amid the very human community of Israel. As to the stylistic aspects of the story, we should note the repeated use of the verbs "see" and "know," among others. Their transformation at different points of the story signals a return to these earlier Exodus themes, this time with a new urgency and a new enterprise at stake: the continuity of the fledgling people.

32:1 Now when the people saw that Moshe was shamefully-late in
          coming down from the mountain,
       the people assembled against Aharon
       and said to him:
       Arise, make us a god who will go before us,
       for this Moshe, the man who brought us up from the land of
          Egypt,
       we do not know that has become of him!
  2   Aharon said to them:
       Break off the gold rings that are in the ears of your wives,
          your sons and your daughters,
       and bring (them) to me.
  3   All the people broke off the gold rings that were in their
          ears,
       and brought (them) to Aharon.
  4   He took (them) from their hand,
       fashioned it with a graving-tool,
       and made it into a molten calf.
       Then they said:
       This is your God, O Israel,
       who brought you up from the land of Egypt!
  5   When Aharon saw (this), he built an altar before it,
       and Aharon called out and said:
       Tomorrow is a festival to YHWH!

6 They (arose) early on the morrow,
   offered offerings-up
   and brought well-being-offerings;
   the people sat down to eat and drink
   and proceeded to revel.

The Sin of the Molten Calf (32:1–6): We have spent twelve chapters—a major portion of the book of Exodus—dwelling on the heights of Sinai; we have witnessed revelation, law-giving, the command to build a shelter for the presence of God, and the establishment of a priestly cult. But now, as Moshe prepares to descend from the mountain, we are reminded of the other side of the coin: the real world of human frailty. This has occurred before, at the very same site: in Chapters 19 and 20 we observed a fearfulness on the part of the people toward getting too close to the divine, as a power too awesome to deal with. Now the fear goes the other way, and, with the disappearance of Moshe, the intermediary, turns to despair. The very thing that had been warned against in the Decalogue (and hence, the first of the terms of the covenant)—the making of a "hewn-image/ or any figure/ that is . . . on the earth beneath" (20:4), and bowing down to it (20:5)—takes place here, requested by the people in their hour of need. It is abetted by, of all people, their divine spokesman and priest, Aharon.

Some scholars have sought to soften the sin of the calf by claiming that the Israelites did not view it as an idol but rather merely as a representation of the divine. This does not seem to be borne out by the text, either in the Decalogue or later in the Jeroboam incident, which is often equated with the most heinous crimes (see I Kings 16:26).

32:1   **saw:** Ironically, after all the "seeing" of revelation in Chapters 19–24, what now impresses the people most is Moshe's absence, leading to a need to make a god that can be "seen." **was shamefully-late:** Others, "delayed," but the Hebrew verb (*boshesh*) carries the connotation of "causing-shame/embarrassment." **a god:** Others, "gods"; but there is one calf and one god that it represents. **go before us:** As in 23:23 the meaning is to lead, especially in battle.
2   **break off:** Or simply "remove."
4   **fashioned it with a graving-tool:** Others, "cast it in a mold" or even "tied it in a bag" (see Plaut 1981). **calf:** Or young bull, symbol of fertility in Canaan. **this is your God . . .:** Cf. 20:2 above, "I am YHWH your God, who brought you out. . . ."
5   **called out:** Or "proclaimed."
6   **proceeded:** Or the Hebrew *kum* can be understood as "arose," as opposed to "sat down" in the phrase to follow. **revel:** There seems to be a sexual connotation here (as in Gen. 26:8; 39:14, 17) which would support the use of the calf as the divine symbol.

7 YHWH said to Moshe:
Go, down!
for your people
whom you brought up from the land of Egypt
has wrought ruin!

8 They have been quick to turn aside from the way that I
   commanded them,
they have made themselves a molten calf,
they have bowed to it, they have slaughter-offered to it,
and they have said: This is your God, O Israel, who brought
   you up from the land of Egypt!

9 And YHWH said to Moshe:
I see this people—
and here, it is a hard-necked people!

10 So now,
let me be,
that my anger may rage against them
and I may destroy them—
but you I will make into a great nation!

11 Moshe soothed the face of YHWH his God,
he said:
For-what-reason,
O YHWH,
should your anger rage against your people
whom you brought out of the land of Egypt
with great might,
with a strong hand?

12 For-what-reason
should the Egyptians (be able to) say, yes, say:
With evil intent he brought them out,
to kill them in the mountains,
to destroy them from the face of the soil?
Turn away from your raging anger,
be sorry for the evil (intended) against your people!

13 Recall Avraham, Yitzhak and Yisrael your servants,
to whom you swore by yourself
when you spoke to them:
I will make your seed many
as the stars of the heavens,

Response: God's Anger (32:7–14): Now that the people have committed what amounts to a capital crime, the issue at stake is what the punishment shall be. After informing the unsuspecting Moshe of what has taken place down below, with the words "*your* people [italics mine] . . . has wrought ruin" (v.7), God indicates his intent to destroy Israel, and to found a new nation beginning with Moshe. However, early Jewish tradition already sensed that something deeper might be happening here. The phrase "let me be" (Heb. *hanikhoti*), it has been observed, suggests that God actually wishes Moshe to argue with him, and this is supported by his acquiescence in record time (v.14). Indeed, the text never says "God's anger raged," reserving that key verb for Moshe (v.19). What we learn from this section is not only God's forgiving nature but something significant about Moshe: faced with a dictator's dream—the cloning of an entire nation from himself—he opts for staunchly defending the very people who have already caused him grief through their rebelling, and who will continually do so in the ensuing wanderings. And he does not even eschew blackmail to attain his goal. His argument in verse 12, that the Egyptians will jeer at this God who liberated a people only to kill them in the wilderness, rings truer in a pagan context than in the Bible. But the next verse reveals Moshe's vision: he knows that his task is to continue the foundation established by the Patriarchs and to assure the continuity that has been imperiled so many times before.

7 **your people:** God not so subtly renounces his kingship of Israel.
   wrought ruin: The verb *shahet* is often used to describe moral decay (see Gen. 6:11–12).
8 **turn aside from the way:** In the Bible, as in many religious systems, the correct mode of behavior is often called "the way" or "path." Here it is probably elliptical for "the way of God." Postbiblical Judaism calls its system of laws *Halakhah*, from the Hebrew *halokh*, "to go/walk."
9 **hard-necked:** Others, "stiff-necked." The usage of "hard" ironically recalls the earlier hard-hearted character, Pharaoh.
11 **soothed:** Lit., "softened."
12 **be sorry:** Others, "repent" or "change your mind." **the evil:** Destruction. The biblical use of "evil" (*ra'*) corresponds more closely to our idea of "ill" as in "ill-fortune"; it includes not only immorality but also disasters that befall people.
13 **recall:** This particular form of the verb *zakhor* (with the preposition *le-*) means "to remember to one's credit" (Childs 1974). **I will make . . .:** Recalling the promise to Avraham and Yitzhak in Gen. 15:5 and 22:17, also 26:4.

and all this land which I have promised,
I will give to your seed,
that they may inherit (it) for the ages!
14 And YHWH let himself be sorry concerning the evil
that he had spoken of doing to his people.

15 Now Moshe faced about to come down from the mountain,
the two tablets of the Testimony in his hand,
tablets written on both their sides,
on this-one, on that-one they were written;
16 and the tablets were God's making,
and the writing was God's writing,
engraved upon the tablets.
17 Now when Yehoshua heard the sound of the people as it
shouted, he said to Moshe:
The sound of war is in the camp!
18 But he said:
No sound of the song of prevailing,
no sound of the song of failing,
sound of choral-song is what I hear!
19 And it was,
when he neared the camp
and saw the calf and the dancing,
Moshe's anger raged,
he threw the tablets from his hands
and smashed them beneath the mountain.
20 He took the calf that they had made,
burned it with fire,
ground it up until it was thin-powder,
strewed it on the surface of the water
and made the Children of Israel drink it.
21 Then Moshe said to Aharon:
What did this people do to you
that you have brought upon it (such) a great sin!
22 Aharon said:
Let not my lord's anger rage!
You yourself know this people, how set-on-evil it is.
23 They said to me: Make us a god who will go before us,
for this Moshe, the man who brought us up from the land of
Egypt,

Response: Moshe's Anger (32:15–29): In a sense, the text backtracks chronologically here, to focus solely on Moshe. The first four verses are prefatory but important. Possibly to set the drama of the scene to follow, Moshe is described as carrying the "tablets of the Testimony," which are dubbed the work of God. Yet another point is being made: the work of God is contrasted with the imperfect work of human beings, the law with its hope versus the idol with its underlying despair.

Sounds of revelry, implied as being worse than sounds of war, reach Moshe, and upon his descent into the Israelite camp he loses control. But smashing the tablets has implications beyond the emotional: it is a legal voiding of the covenant (as in the English "breaking an agreement"). Moshe deals with all concerned in swift succession: the calf is destroyed, Aharon is confronted, and the people are brutally purged.

It is possible that there are historical considerations behind this section. Some see the portrayal of Aharon, who certainly comes across as weak, as part of a strain in the political thinking of a later period. According to this view, the later decline of Aharon's priestly line is reflected in his behavior here. Others see the "mandating" of the Levites (v.29) as a reflection of a later power struggle among the priestly classes in Israel. Childs (1974)

16 **God's making . . . God's writing:** In contrast to the "making" of the Calf.

17 **as it shouted:** Heb. *be-re'o*, possibly a pun on *ve-ra* ("set-on-evil") in verse 22.

18 **song:** Heb. *'anot*, as distinct from *shira* in 15:1. **prevailing . . . failing:** Heb. *gevura . . . halusha*, meaning "victory" and "defeat." **choral-song:** Or "antiphonal (alternating) song." The Hebrew is *'annot* as opposed to *'anot*. But some interpreters view it as identical to the two previous uses, and find something missing here (as in "the sound of ——— is what I hear.").

19 **the calf and the dancing:** Apparently both angered Moshe. **beneath the mountain:** The very same place where the covenant was concluded! (Cassuto 1967).

20 **burned . . . ground . . . strewed . . . made . . . drink:** The first three of these verbs also occur together in a Canaanite (Ugaritic) text, describing the goddess Anat's destruction of the god Mot; our text perhaps plays off that literature (Childs 1974). At any rate, Moshe's action is the equivalent of making the Israelites "eat their words." As has long been noted, this echoes the treatment of the suspected adulteress in Num. 5:11–31; the connection appears intentional, in light of the constant "marriage" imagery used of God and Israel in the Bible (Sarna 1986 discusses the parallels at length).

we do not know what has become of him!

24 So I said to them: Who has gold?
They broke it off and gave it to me,
I threw it into the fire, and out came this calf.

25 Now when Moshe saw the people: that it had gotten-loose,
for Aharon had let-it-loose for whispering among their foes,

26 Moshe took-up-a-stand at the gate of the camp
and said:
Whoever is for YHWH—to me!
And there gathered to him all the Sons of Levi.

27 He said to them:
Thus says YHWH, the God of Israel:
Put every-man his sword on his thigh,
proceed and go back-and-forth from gate to gate in the
camp,
and kill
every-man his brother, every-man his fellow, every-man his
neighbor!

28 The Sons of Levi did according to Moshe's words.
And there fell of the people on that day some three thousand
men.

29 Moshe said:
Be-mandated to YHWH today,
even though it be every-man at the cost of his son, at the cost
of his brother,
to bestow blessing upon you today.

30 It was on the morrow,
Moshe said to the people:
You, you have sinned a great sin!
So now, I will go up to YHWH,
perhaps I may be able to purge away your sin.

31 Moshe returned to YHWH and said:
Ah now,
this people has sinned a great sin,
they have made themselves gods of gold!

32 So now,
if you would only bear with their sin— !
But if not,
pray blot me out of the record that you have written!

33 YHWH said to Moshe:
　　Whoever sins against me,
　　I blot him (alone) out of my record.
34 So now,
　　go,
　　lead the people to where I have spoken to you.
　　Here, my messenger will go before you,
　　but on the day of my calling-to-account,
　　I will call-them-to-account for their sin.

finds Aharon's role in the story to be a literary one: he is a foil for Moshe. Aharon is willing to capitulate to the people, seeing them (perhaps realistically) as "set-on-evil" (v.22). Moshe holds fast to his dream of a "kingdom of priests" (19:6) and thus demands of himself a type of leadership that cannot compromise. The Calf story, then, focuses not only on the great crime of idolatry but also on the nature of Moshe as leader. It is the resumption of the biblical portrait of Moshe, which will return again with greatest force throughout the book of Numbers.

After the Purge (32:30–33:6): Although blood has been spilled to punish the guilty, Moshe must still expiate Israel's sin. In this vein, he offers to be erased from God's "record" if the people are not forgiven. Then commences God's reply, couched in terms of who will lead the people to the Promised Land. He will not do it himself, as previously (see the glorious image of 13:21–22), but through the agency of a "messenger." He will fulfill his promise to the Patriarchs, but not himself among his "hard-

24 **out came this calf:** Aharon's reply sounds like that of a child who has been caught in the act.
25 **gotten-loose:** The same verb (*paro'a*) was used in 5:4, where Pharaoh complained about the Israelites. **for whispering:** A derisive kind of whispering.
27 **every-man . . . :** the repetition stresses the horror of the situation.
28 **three thousand:** Another stereotyped number (e.g., Samson kills 3,000 Philistines in Judges 16:27).
32 **blot . . . out:** Erase, as in writing. **record:** Heb. *sefer*, earlier (17:14) rendered as "account."
34 **my messenger will go before you:** Apparently restoring the state of affairs promised in 23:20ff. **calling-to-account:** In Gen. 50:24, *pakod* meant "taking account of," that is, remembering the Israelites in their Egyptian bondage.

35 And YHWH plagued the people
because they made the calf that Aharon made.

33:1 YHWH said to Moshe:
Go, up from here,
you and the people that you brought up from the land of
    Egypt,
to the land of which I swore to Avraham, to Yitzhak and to
    Yaakov, saying:
I will give it to your seed.
2 I will send a messenger before you
and will drive out the Canaanite, the Amorite and the Hittite
    and the Perizzite, the Hivvite and the Yevusite—,
3 to a land flowing with milk and honey.
But: I will not go up in your midst,
for a hard-necked people are you,
lest I destroy you on the way!
4 When the people heard this evil word
they mourned,
no man put on his ornaments (again).
5 Now YHWH said to Moshe:
Say to the Children of Israel:
You are a hard-necked people—
if for one moment I were to go up in your midst,
I would destroy you!
So now, take down your ornaments from yourselves,
that I may know what I am to do with you.
6 So the Children of Israel stripped themselves of their orna-
    ments from Mount Sinai on.

7 Now Moshe would take the Tent
and pitch it for himself outside the camp, going-far from the
    camp.
He called it the Tent of Appointment.
And it was,
whoever besought YHWH
would go out to the Tent of Appointment that was outside
    the camp.
8 And it was:
whenever Moshe would go out to the Tent,

all the people would rise,
they would station themselves, each-man, at the entrance to
   his tent,
and would gaze after Moshe
until he had come into the Tent.
9 And it was:
whenever Moshe would come into the Tent
that the column of cloud would come down
and stand at the entrance to the Tent,
and he would speak with Moshe.

necked" people. Their "sin" (the word occurs eight times in verses 30–34) has destroyed that possibility.

An interesting chord is struck at the end. Israel must strip themselves of their ornaments, the spoils of battle, as it were, from the Egyptians. Those ornaments had been used to build the Calf. The final note is ominous: God is yet to decide "what to do with you," reminiscent perhaps of another scene with identical wording—2:4, where Moshe's sister had followed the little-ark downstream, "to know what would be done to him." In both cases, the people of Israel stand on the brink of disaster, saved only by divine intervention.

Moshe at the Tent (33:7–11): This brief digression seems to function as support for Moshe's role, so important in the book as a whole and in this story in particular. Only one who is accustomed to speaking to God face to face (see also Deut. 34:17) can effect forgiveness for Israel's crime.

35 **they made . . . Aharon made:** Heb. ambiguous; possibly a scribal error. Or the ambiguity may serve to shift the blame from the perpetrator to the act itself (Edward Greenstein, personal communication).

33:1 **the people that you brought up:** The use of "you" (Moshe) suggests that God still has not fully reaccepted them.

3 **I will not:** Myself, in person, as it were.

6 **stripped themselves:** This feels analogous to having one's battle ribbons stripped off, or having one's spoils taken away.

7 **outside the camp:** Already in early Jewish tradition it was pointed out that this phrase often has negative connotations (that is, one was sent outside the camp because of ritual impurity), and it has been suggested that our passage shows Moshe separating himself from the sinning people. On the other hand, it is usually the carrier/causer of impurity who goes outside!

9 **he:** God.

10 And all the people would see
   the column of cloud
   standing at the entrance to the Tent,
   and all the people would rise,
   they would bow down,
   each-man at the entrance to his tent.
11 And YHWH would speak to Moshe
   face to face,
   as a man speaks to his fellow.
   Now when he would return to the camp,
   his attendant, the lad Yehoshua,
   would not depart from within the Tent.

12 Moshe said to YHWH:
   See,
   you,
   you say to me:
   Bring this people up!
   But you,
   you have not let us know
   whom you will send with me!
   And you,
   you said:
   I have known you by name,
   and you have found favor in my eyes!
13 So now—
   if I have, pray, found favor in your eyes,
   pray let me know your ways,
   that I may (truly) know you,
   in order that I may find favor in your eyes:
   See,
   this nation is indeed your people!
14 He said:
   If my presence were to go (with you), would I cause you to
      rest-easy?
15 He said to him:
   If your presence does not go,
   do not bring us up from here!
16 For wherein, after all, is it to be known
   that I have found favor in your eyes,

I and your people?
Is it not (precisely) in that you go with us,
and that we are distinct,
I and your people,
from every people that is on the face of the soil?
17 YHWH said to Moshe:
Also this word that you have spoken, I will do,
for you have found favor in my eyes,
and I have known you by name.
18 Then he said:
Pray let me see your Glory!

Moshe's Plea and God's Answer (33:12–34:3): Continuing the dialogue with God from 32:34f., Moshe now pleads that what is necessary is nothing less than the personal assurance that God will lead the people. Six times the verb "know" echoes, along with repetitions of "pray" and "favor"—and so the issue at hand is intimacy and the bonded relationship of covenant. Significantly, also, Moshe refers to Israel three times as "your people," trying to force God to acknowledge them as his own once more. Answering Moshe's request for intimacy, God agrees to let him get close, but with limits, and we are reminded of Sinai once more (see the boundary-setting in 19:12–13, 21ff.). The earlier revelation scene is about to be replayed, in altered form—most notably, without the people themselves present.

11 **face to face:** See Gen. 32:31, where Jacob is amazed at still being alive after an encounter with a manifestation of God. In the ancient world in general, direct contact with the gods is often portrayed as leading to madness or death (see the Greek story of Semele, the mortal mother of the god Dionysus). Cf. verse 20, below.   **Yehoshua/ would not depart:** Once again, he appears in a fragmentary way, but importantly, as Moshe's attendant (and so he will be not only a military leader, as in 17:9ff., but also a spritual one).

13 **know:** Intimately.   **indeed your people:** And not only Moshe's, as God suggests in verse 1.

16 **that we are distinct:** The text returns to a motif important in the Plague Narrative.

18 **your Glory:** In the Greek story, Semele desires to see Zeus in full battle dress; the Hebrew narrative is understandably more vague.

19 He said:
    I myself will cause all my Goodliness to pass
    in front of your face,
    I will call out the name of YHWH
    before your face:
    that I show-favor to whom I show-favor,
    that I show-mercy to whom I show-mercy.

20 But he said:
    You cannot see my face,
    for no human can see me and live.

21 YHWH said:
    Here is a place
    next to me;
    station yourself on the rock,

22 and it shall be:
    when my Glory passes by,
    I will place you in the cleft of the rock
    and screen you with my hand
    until I have passed by.

23 Then I will remove my hand;
    you shall see my back,
    but my face shall not be seen.

34:1 Then YHWH said to Moshe:
      Hew yourself two tablets of stone
      like the first-ones,
      and I will write on the tablets the words
      that were on the first tablets
      which you smashed.

2   And be ready by the morning:
    go up in the morning to Mount Sinai,
    station yourself for me there, on top of the mountain.

3   No man is to go up with you,
    neither is any man to be seen on all the mountain,
    neither are sheep or oxen to graze in front of this mountain.

4   So he hewed two tablets of stone like the first-ones.
    Moshe (arose) early in the morning
    and went up to Mount Sinai,
    as YHWH had commanded him,
    and he took in his hand the two tablets of stone.

5   YHWH came down in the cloud,

he stationed himself beside him there
and called out the name of YHWH.

6 And YHWH passed before his face
and called out:
YHWH YHWH
God,
showing-mercy, showing-favor,
long-suffering in anger,
abundant in loyalty and faithfulness,
7 keeping loyalty to the thousandth (generation),
bearing iniquity, rebellion and sin,
yet not clearing, clearing (the guilty),
calling-to-account the iniquity of the fathers upon the sons
and upon sons' sons, to the third and fourth (generation)!
8 Quickly Moshe did-homage, on the ground, bowing low,
9 and said:
Pray if I have found favor in your eyes,
O my Lord,

God Reveals Himself (34:4–9): This passage is another one of the climaxes of the book, of which I spoke in "On the Book of Exodus and Its Structure," above. In contrast to the scenes given in other ancient literatures, where, for instance, the texts speak of a physical brightness too great to bear, or of epic descriptions of the gods, our passage is remarkably brief and devoid of physical description. All that is ventured here is a statement

19   **that I show-favor . . .**: Recalling the earlier answer to Moshe in 4:13. The meaning here is "I choose to whom to reveal myself."
23   **my back:** That is, hiding the actual appearance of God.
34:2   **in the morning:** As at Sinai, there is no question of a night vision/illusion.
6–7   **YHWH YHWH . . .**: These two verses became an important part of later Jewish liturgy, and are known as the "Thirteen Attributes of God." **showing-mercy, showing-favor:** Heb. *rahum ve-hanun.*
7   **third and fourth (generation):** This may mean an entire household, that is, generally the largest number of generations alive at one time (Clements 1972).
8   **Quickly:** This, as perhaps the greatest moment of divine–human intimacy in the Bible, is the one most ripe for forgiveness, and Moshe seizes the opportunity.

pray let my Lord go among us!
Indeed, a hard-necked people is it—
so forgive our iniquity and our sin,
and make-us-your-inheritance!

10 He said:
Here,
I cut a covenant:
before all your people I will do wonders
such as have not been created
in all the earth, among all the nations.
Then shall all the people among whom you are, see
the work of YHWH, how awesome it is,
which I do with you.

11 Be-you-watchful
of what I command you today!
Here, I am driving out before you
the Amorite, the Canaanite, the Hittite, the Perizzite, the
    Hivvite and the Yevusite,—

12 keep-you-watch,
lest you cut a covenant
with the settled-folk of the land against which you are coming,
lest they become a snare among you.

13 Rather:
their altars you are to pull down,
their standing-pillars you are to smash,
their tree-poles you are to cut down.

14 For: You are not to bow down to any other god!
For YHWH—
Jealous-One is his name,
a jealous God is he!

15 —Lest you cut a covenant with the settled-folk of the land:
when they go whoring after their gods
and slaughter-offer to their gods,
they will call to you to eat of their slaughter-offering;

16 should you take of their women (in marriage) for your sons,
their women will go whoring after their gods,
and they will cause your sons to go whoring after their gods.

17 Molten gods you are not to make for yourselves!

18 The Festival of *Matzot* you are to keep;
   for seven days you are to eat *matzot*, as I commanded you,
   at the appointed-time, in the New-Moon of Ripe-Grain,
   for in the New-Moon of Ripe-Grain you went out of Egypt.
19 Every breacher of a womb is mine,
   and every one that your herd drops-as-male, breacher
       among oxen and sheep;
20 the breacher among asses you are to redeem with a sheep,
   and if you do not redeem it, you are to break-its-neck.
   Every firstborn among your sons you are to redeem.

of God's essence, or, more precisely, of his essence for human beings:
merciful but just. This image, which had such a great influence on the
development of Christianity and Islam as well as Judaism, is of the highest
importance in the understanding of the biblical God; it is almost as if the
text is saying "This is all that can be known, intimately, of this God, and
this is all one needs to know." There is no shape, no natural manifestation
(in contrast to the thunder and lightning approach at Sinai—but one
should bear in mind what has just happened with the Calf): only words,
which describe God's relationship to human beings.

Moshe hastens, at the climactic moment, to plead on behalf of the
people. Most curious is the fact that God does not seem to agree to "go in
their midst," nor does he ever give in and reinstate Israel with the term
"my people" (see v.10). Nevertheless, it appears that the rift between
deity and people has been satisfactorily repaired, given what comes next.

The New Covenant (34:10–28): A preamble (vv. 10–16) promises God's
continued "wonders" and warns emphatically against Israel's mixing with
the Canaanites upon its future possession of the land. Once the actual

10 **Here . . .:** Does God ever really answer Moshe's request to "let my Lord
   go among us!"? We can only tell by the ending of the entire book, when all
   seems right again (40:34–38). **Then shall all . . . see:** The Hebrew
   word order is "Then shall see . . ."
13 **standing-pillars:** These stood near Canaanite altars (Plaut 1981). **tree-
   poles:** Phallic idols.
14 **jealous:** Cf. 20:5, above.
15 **whoring:** A common biblical metaphor for faithlessness to God.
16 **their women:** They are singled out as the ones enticing the Israelite men
   into idolatry, perhaps based on the prominence of goodesses and sacred
   prostitutes in Canaanite worship.
19 **drops-as-male:** Others, "every male."

No one is to be seen in my presence empty-handed.

21 For six days you are to serve,
   but on the seventh day, you are to cease,
   at plowing, at grain-cutting, you are to cease.
22 The Festival-observance of Weeks you are to make for
      yourselves,
   of the first-fruits of the wheat cutting,
   as well as the Festival-observance of Ingathering
   at the turning of the year.
23 At three points in the year
   are all your male-folk to be seen
   in the presence of the Lord, YHWH,
   the God of Israel.
24 For I will dispossess nations before you, and widen your
      territory,
   so that no man will desire your land,
   when you go up to be seen in the presence of YHWH your
      God,
   at three points in the year.

25 You are not to slay with anything fermented my blood offer-
      ing.

   You are not to leave-overnight the festival-offering of
      Passover.

26 The beginning of the first-fruits of your soil you are to bring
      into the house of YHWH your God.

   You are not to boil a kid in the milk of its mother.

27 YHWH said to Moshe:
   Write you down these words,
   for in accordance with these words
   I cut with you a covenant, and with Israel.

28 Now he was there beside YHWH
   for forty days and forty nights;
   bread he did not eat

and water he did not drink,
but he wrote down on the tablets the words of the covenant,
the Ten Words.

legislative content of the passage begins in verse 17, one notes the continuation of the stylistic pattern which began with verse 10: Deuteronomic
language. The laws bespeak an agricultural society, not a nomadic one,
and suggest that the warning against blending with Canaanite society may
be from the perspctive of a later period—an Israel long settled in the land.
Although some scholars see Egypt as the origin of the Calf symbol, it also
has a well-known existence in Canaanite mythology, as a symbol of Baal,
god of fertility. Therefore the connection between our text and that of
Kings may be close indeed, and the Calf story may have had a very
contemporary ring to later audiences.

As is typical of the Calf narrative, our passage concludes, not only with
wider issues—the formal writing-down of the covenant—but also with
Moshe: that he neither ate nor drank during the encounter with God. We
see the story both from its inception and its end concerned with the man
whose task it must be to bring the divine word to the Israelite people.

Moshe Radiant (34:29–35): As if to underscore the point just made, and
like the Tent section in Chapter 33, the Calf account ends with a focus on
Moshe's leadership. Gone is any reference to the molten image; the central
concern is the effect of God's communication upon Moshe. Indeed,
"speak" occurs seven times here, and the formula "the skin of Moshe's
face was radiating" three times. Putting this section at the end of the
narrative leaves the reader with the sense that Moshe's prayer for God's
closeness in Chapter 33 has at last been answered, and that his very body
now bears the sign of divine favor (note the use of the rich symbol of
light). Communication between God and Moshe, with Israel witnessing

21 **serve:** Here perhaps connoting farm work, as in Gen. 2:5, 4:12. See also
   Ex. 20:9.
21 **plowing . . . grain-cutting:** For once, the Bible specifies the work that is
   not to be done on the Sabbath.
22 **turning of the year:** When the last harvest occurs (September-October),
   and hence connected to a solar calendar model.
23 **points:** Lit., "beats."   **Lord:** Cf. the note to 23:17.
24 **no man will desire your land:** Not even desire it, much less take it away.
28 **Ten Words:** These are known in the Bible as such, not as the "Ten
   Commandments."

29 Now it was
   when Moshe came down from Mount Sinai
   with the two tablets of Testimony in Moshe's hand,
   when he came down from the mountain
   —(now) Moshe did not know that the skin of his face was
      radiating because of his having-spoken with him,—
30 Aharon and all the Children of Israel saw Moshe:
   and here, the skin of his face was radiating!
   So they were afraid to approach him.
31 Moshe called to them,
   and then Aharon and all those exalted in the community
      came back to him,
   and Moshe spoke to them.
32 Afterward all the Children of Israel approached,
   and he commanded them
   all that YHWH had spoken with him on Mount Sinai.
33 Now when Moshe had finished speaking with them,
   he put a veil upon his face.
   Now whenever Moshe would come into the presence of
      YHWH, to speak with him,
   he would remove the veil, until he had gone out;
34 and whenever he would come out and speak to the children
      of Israel that which he had been commanded,
35 the Children of Israel would see Moshe's face,
   that the skin of Moshe's face was radiating;
   but then Moshe would put back the veil on his face,
   until he came in to speak with him.

and therefore involved again (in contrast to its removal from this activity at the beginning of Chapter 32), may now proceed again without interruption, and it will now be possible and appropriate to resume construction of the structure whose purpose it is to embody God's presence in the world of human beings.

29 **radiating:** Or "radiant." As is well known, Michelangelo created his famous horned status of Moses (in the Roman church of San Pietro in Vincoli) on the basis of the Latin translation of the Bible, the Vulgate, which rendered the Hebrew *karan* as "horned." There have now been found other ancient Near Eastern texts that support this reading, although the present context and comparative religion seem also to throw weight to "radiating."

PART VI The Building of the Dwelling (35–40)

A S IF NOTHING had gone awry, the narrative now returns to describe how the Dwelling was built. This time, as was noted by the sages of the Talmud, the order follows the natural logic of construction (i.e., dwelling, tapestries, covering, boards, sockets, bars, etc., and then the ritual objects), rather than the earlier one of sanctity (i.e., coffer, purgation-cover, table, lampstand, etc., and then the structure itself). The most notable omission is the carrying out of priestly ordination; that is reserved for Leviticus 8, perhaps so as not to interfere with the narrative momentum of the construction process, or else to focus more on the Dwelling itself and its divine resident. The only major interruption in this part is 38:21–31, which fits in with one of the important themes of these chapters: the extent of the Israelites' contribution to the sanctuary.

As there is no need to repeat what was said about each part of the Tabernacle in the commentary to Chapters 25–31, the commentary here will be limited to brief remarks on the differences between the two long Tabernacle sections (Parts IV and VI); here Cassuto (1967) has provided most of the necessary material.

35:1 Now Moshe assembled all the community of the Children of
        Israel
     and said to them:
     These are the words that YHWH has commanded, to do
        them:

   2 For six days is work to be made,
     but on the seventh day
     there is to be for you holiness,
     Sabbath, Sabbath-Ceasing for YHWH;
     whoever makes work on it is to be put-to-death.
   3 You are not to let fire burn throughout all your settlements
        on the Sabbath day.

   4 Now Moshe spoke to all the community of the Children of
        Israel,
     saying:
     This is the matter that YHWH has commanded, saying:
   5 Take, from yourselves, a raised-contribution for YHWH,
     whoever is of willing mind is to bring it,
     YHWH's contribution:
     gold, silver, and bronze,
   6 violet, purple, worm-scarlet, byssus and goats'-hair,
   7 rams' skins dyed-red, dugongs' skins,
     acacia wood,
   8 oil for lighting,
     spices for oil of anointing and for fragant smoking-incense,
   9 onyx stones and stones for setting,
     for the *efod* and for the breastpiece.
  10 And everyone wise of mind among you
     is to come and is to make all that YHWH has commanded:
  11 The Dwelling, its tent and its cover,
     its clasps and its boards,
     its running bars, its columns and its sockets;
  12 the coffer and its poles,
     the purgation-cover and the curtain for the screen;
  13 the table and its poles and all its implements,
     and the Bread of the Presence;
  14 and the lampstand for lighting and its implements and its
        lamps,

and the oil for lighting;

15 and the altar for smoke-offering and its poles,
and the oil for anointing,
and the fragrant smoking-incense;
and the entrance screen for the entrace of the Dwelling;

16 the altar for offering-up and the bronze lattice that (belongs)
to it, its poles and all its implements;
the basin and its pedestal;

17 the hangings of the courtyard, its columns and its sockets,
and the screen for the gate of the courtyard;

18 the pins of the Dwelling and the pins of the courtyard, and
their cords,

19 the officiating garments for attending at the Holy-Place;
the garments of holiness for Aharon the priest
and the garments of his sons for acting-as-priest.

20 So everyone in the community of the Children of Israel
went out from Moshe's presence,

The Sabbath Restated (35:1–3): Bracketing the Calf Narrative, we return
to the regulations concerning the Sabbath, which receive here a different
explanation from what was given in 31:12–17. There the stress was on the
symbolic nature of the Sabbath day, but in the present context no reason
for observance is given. Cassuto (1967) understands this as a clarification
of the rules of "making" as the Dwelling is about to be constructed.

The Contribution Restated (35:4–19): The theme returns to that of the
opening of the Tabernacle account in Chapter 25, with a list of what was to
be brought for the "work of the Dwelling."

Preparations for the Construction (35:20–36:7): The account of what the
Israelites brought as contributions for the work, and the description of

35:3 **You are not to let fire burn:** This prohibition perhaps reflects the anthropological use of fire as a transforming force in culture (see Fredman
1983). Since the Shabbat was apparently to be static in nature, or at least
transformative of time alone, fire (which by its nature causes chemical
changes) could not be employed. **throughout all your settlements:** And
not only in the area of building the Dwelling (Cassuto 1967).

21 and then they came, every man whose mind uplifted him,
   and everyone whose spirit made-him-willing brought
      YHWH's contribution
   for the skilled-work on the Tent of Appointment, for all its
      service (of construction), and for the garments of holiness.

22 Then came men and women alike, everyone of willing mind,
      they brought
   brooch and nose-ring and signet-ring and necklace, every
      kind of gold object,
   every man that wished to hold-high a high-offering of gold
      to YHWH;

23 and everyone with whom could be found
   violet, purple, worm-scarlet, byssus and goats'-hair, rams'
      skins dyed-red and dugongs' skins,
   brought it.

24 Everyone that raised a raised-contribution of silver and
      bronze
   brought YHWH's contribution,
   and everyone with whom could be found
   acacia wood for all the work of the service (of construction),
   brought it.

25 And every woman wise of mind,
   with their hands they spun
   and brought their spinning—
   the violet, the purple, the worm-scarlet and the byssus,

26 and every one of the women whose mind uplifted them in
      practical-wisdom
   spun the goats'-hair.

27 And the exalted-ones brought
   the onyx stones and the stones for setting,
   for the *efod* and for the breastpiece,

28 and the fragrant-spice and the oil
   for lighting, for oil of anointing, for fragrant smoking-in-
      cense.

29 Every man and woman
   whose mind made-them-willing to bring (anything) for all
      the workmanship
   that YHWH had commanded (them) to make through
      Moshe, the Children of Israel brought it,
   freewill-offering for YHWH.

30 Now Moshe said to the Children of Israel:
See,
YHWH has called by name
Betzalel son of Uri, son of Hur, of the tribe of Yehuda,
31 he has filled him with the spirit of God
in practical-wisdom, in discernment and in knowledge,
and in all kinds of workmanship
32 to design designs,
to make (them) in gold, in silver and in bronze,
33 in the carving of stones for setting and in the carving of
     wood,
to make all kinds of designed workmanship,
34 and (the ability) to instruct he has put in his mind,
he and Oholiav son of Ahisamakh, of the tribe of Dan;
35 he has filled them with wisdom of mind
to make all kinds of workmanship
of the carver, the designer and the embroiderer,
in violet, in purple, in worm-scarlet and in byssus,
and of the weaver—
makers of all kinds of workmanship
and designers of designs.
36:1 So are Betzalel and Oholiav to make,
and every man wise of mind
in whom YHWH has put wisdom and discernment,

those who were to carry it out, is long and repetitive. This factor, with the addition of a refrainlike pattern of key words (e.g., "mind," "willing," "service," "work," "wise," "design," "brought"), strongly portrays the people's enthusiasm for and participation in the sacred task. Verses 3–7 push the narrative to a crescendo, with the people actually bringing much more than is needed (and may also be a contrast to their briefly stated surrendering of jewels in the Calf episode, 32:3).

22 **necklace:** This is a conjecture, as the meaning of the Hebrew *kumaz* is uncertain.
25 **spun:** The Hebrew verb *tavoh* occurs only here in the Bible.
34 **(the ability) to instruct:** Now that the actual construction is about to take place, it is crucial that the head craftsman be not only skilled himself, but a master instructor as well.

to know (how) to make all the work for the service of (constructing) the Holy-Place,
for all that YHWH has commanded.

2 So Moshe called
for Betzalel, for Oholiav,
and for all men wise of mind into whose mind YHWH had
put wisdom,
all those whose mind uplifted them to come-near for the
work,
to make it.

3 And they took from Moshe all the contributions
that the Children of Israel had brought for the work of the
service of (constructing) the Holy-Place,
to make it.
Now they brought him further, freewill-offering, morning
after morning;

4 and came, all the wise-ones who were making all the skilled-
worked for the Holy-Place,
man after man, from their skilled-work that they were making,

5 and said to Moshe, saying:
The people are bringing much more
than enough for the service of (doing) the work
that YHWH has commanded, to make it!

6 So Moshe commanded and they had a call go throughout the
camp, saying:
Man and woman—let them not make any further work-
material for the contribution of the Holy-Place!
So the people were restrained from bringing;

7 the work-material was enough for them, for all the work, to
make it, and more.

8 Then made all those wise of mind among the makers of the
work,
the dwelling, of ten tapestries
of twisted byssus, violet, purple and worm-scarlet;
with winged-sphinxes, of designer's making, was it made.

9 The length of each one tapestry, twenty-eight by the cubit,
and the width—four by the cubit,
of each one tapestry,
one measure for all of the tapestries.

10 Then were joined five of the tapestries, each-one to each-one,

and five tapestries were joined, each-one to each-one.
11 Then were made loops of violet
   on the edge of the one tapestry, at the end of the one joint;
   thus were made in the edge of the end tapestry at the second
      joint.
12 Fifty loops were made on the one tapestry,
   and fifty loops were made at the end of the tapestry that is at
      the second joint,
   opposite the loops, this-one to that-one.
13 Then were made fifty clasps of gold
   and then were joined the tapestries, this-one to that-one,
      with the clasps,
   so that the dwelling became one-piece.
14 Then were made the tapestries of goats'-hair for a tent over
      the dwelling,
   eleven tapestries were they made.
15 The length of each one tapestry (was) thirty by the cubit,
   and four cubits, the width of each one tapestry,
   one measure for the eleven tapestries.
16 Then were joined five of the tapestries separately
   and six of the tapestries separately.
17 Then were made loops, fifty (of them), at the edge of the end
      tapestry, at the joint,
   and fifty loops were made at the edge of the second joining
      tapestry.
18 Then were made clasps of bronze, fifty (of them),
   to join the tent together,
   to become one-piece.
19 Then was made a covering for the tent, of rams' skins dyed-
      red,
   and a covering of dugongs' skins, above it.

Dwelling II (36:8–19): Missing here (cf. 26:1–14) is the description of how the tapestries were to be joined to the boards; the section pertains to the actual making of the tapestries.

36:10 **each-one to each-one:** In 26:3, the parallel passage, the text reads "each-one to the other." This is one example of the changes that occur between Chapters 25–31 and 35–40; the reader should consult the parallel accounts for the differences in wording.

20 Then were made the boards for the Dwelling,
   of acacia wood, standing-upright;
21 ten cubits the length of the board
   and a cubit and a half the width of each one board,
22 with two pegs for each one board, parallel this-one to that-one,
   thus were made for all the boards of the Dwelling.
23 And then were made the boards for the Dwelling:
   twenty as boardwork on the Negev border, southward,
24 and forty sockets of silver were made beneath twenty of the
       boards,
   two sockets beneath each one board for its two pegs
   and two sockets beneath each other board for its two pegs;
25 and for the second flank of the Dwelling, on the northern
       border, were made twenty as boardwork,
26 with their forty sockets of silver,
   two sockets beneath each one board
   and two sockets beneath each other board.
27 And for the rear of the Dwelling, toward the sea, were made
       six boards,
28 and two boards were made for the corners of the Dwelling,
       at the rear,
29 so that they were of twin-use, (seen) from the lower-end,
   and together formed a whole-piece, toward the top, toward
       the first ring;
   thus were made for the two of them, for the two corners.
30 So there were eight boards with their bases of silver, sixteen
       bases,
   two bases each, two bases beneath each one board.
31 Then were made running-bars of acacia wood,
   five bars for the boards of the Dwelling's one flank
32 and five bars for the boards of the Dwelling's second flank,
   and five bars for the boards of the Dwelling at the rear,
       toward the sea.
33 Then was made the middle running-bar, to run amidst the
       boards,
   from (this) end to (that) end.
34 And the boards were overlaid with gold,
   and their rings were made of gold, as holders for the bars,
   and the bars were overlaid with gold.

35 Then was made the curtain
   of violet, purple, worm-scarlet and twisted byssus;
   of designer's making was it made, with winged-sphinxes.
36 Then were made for it four columns of acacia
   and were overlaid with gold, their hooks of gold,
   and four bases of silver were cast for them.
37 Then was made a screen for the entrance to the Tent
   of violet, purple, worm-scarlet and twisted byssus,
   of embroiderer's making,
38 and their columns, five (of them), and their hooks,
   and their tops and their binders were overlaid with gold—
   and their bases, five, of bronze.

37:1 Then Betzalel made
   the coffer, of acacia wood,
   two cubits and a half its length,
   a cubit and a half its width,
   and a cubit and a half its height.
2 He overlaid it with pure gold, inside and outside,
   and made for it a rim of gold all around.
3 He cast for it four rings of gold
   (to be) upon its four feet,
   with two rings on its one flank
   and two rings on its second flank.
4 He made poles of acacia wood
   and overlaid them with gold,

Boards II (36:20–34): In reference to 26:15–30, the present text has omitted the command to erect the entire strucutre. The passage is limited in a manner similar to the previous section.

Curtain and Screen II (36:35–38): Again (cf. 26:31–37), only the making of the objects themselves is described, not their positioning within the Tabernacle.

Coffer and Purgation-Cover II (37:1–9): Parallel to 25:10–22, this account specifies Betzalel as the artist, otherwise behaving like the other passages in this chapter.

5 he brought the poles into the rings on the flanks of the
        coffer, to carry the coffer.
6 He made a purgation-cover of pure gold,
        two cubits and a half its length
        and a cubit and a half its width.
7 He made two winged-sphinxes of gold,
        of hammered-work did he make them,
        at the two ends of the purgation-cover.
8 One sphinx at the end here
        and one sphinx at the end there,
        from the purgation-cover did he make the sphinxes, at its
            two ends.
9 And the sphinxes were spreading (their) wings upward,
        with their wings sheltering the purgation-cover,
        their faces, each toward the other;
        toward the purgation-cover were the sphinxes' faces.

10 He made the table of acacia wood,
        two cubits its length,
        a cubit its width,
        and a cubit and a half its height.
11 He overlaid it with pure gold.
        And he made a rim of gold for it, all around,
12 and made a border for it, a handbreadth all around,
        thus he made a rim of gold for its border, all around.
13 He cast for it four rings of gold
        and put the rings at the four edges, where its four legs (are).
14 Parallel to the border were the rings,
        holders for the poles, to carry the table.
15 He made the poles of acacia wood, and overlaid them with
            gold,
        to carry the table.
16 He made the implements that are on the table:
        its plates and its cups,
        its bowls and jars, from which (libations) are poured,
        of pure gold.

17 He made the lampstand of pure gold,
        of hammered-work did he make the lampstand, its shaft and
            its stem,

its goblets, its knobs and its blossoms were from it;
18 six stems issuing from its sides,
   three lamp-stems on the one side,
   three lamp-stems on the second side:
19 three almond-shaped goblets on the one stem, with knobs
   and blossoms,
   and three almond-shaped goblets on the other stem, with
   knobs and blossoms—
   thus for the six stems that were issuing from the lampstand.
20 And on the lampstand (itself) four almond-shaped goblets,
   with their knobs and their blossoms,
21 a knob beneath two stems, from it,
   a knob beneath two stems, from it,
   and a knob beneath two stems, from it,
   for the six stems that were issuing from it.
22 Their knobs and their stems were from it,
   all of it one-piece of hammered-work, of pure gold.
23 He made its lamps, seven (of them),
   and its tongs and its trays, of pure gold.
24 From an ingot of pure gold did he make it, with all its
   implements.

25 He made the altar for smoking-incense, of acacia wood,
   a cubit its length and a cubit its width,
   squared, and two cubits its height,
   from it were its two horns.
26 He overlaid it with pure gold—

Table II (37:10–16): This corresponds to 25:23–30, with the omission of the Bread of the Presence.

Lampstand II (37:17–24): The parallel account is 25:31–40, except for details there regarding its placement in the overall structure.

Incense Altar II (37:25–28): This is a case similar to that of the lampstand (cf. 30:1–5).

its roof, its walls all around, and its horns,
and he made a rim of gold for it, all around.
27 Two rings of gold did he make for it, beneath its rim,
on its two flanks, on its two sides,
as holders for poles, to carry it by (means of) them.
28 He made the poles of acacia wood,
and overlaid them with gold.

29 And he made the anointing oil of holiness
and the fragrant smoking-incense, pure, of perfumer's making.

38:1 Then he made the altar of offering-up, of acacia wood,
five cubits its length, five cubits its width, square,
and three cubits its height.
2 He made its horns on its four points,
from it were its horns.
He overlaid it with bronze.
3 He made all the implements for the altar,
the pails, the scrapers, the bowls, the forks and the pans;
all its implements, he made of bronze.
4 He made for the altar a lattice, as a netting of bronze is
made,
beneath its ledge, below, (reaching) to its halfway-point.
5 He cast four rings on the four edges of the netting of bronze,
as holders for the poles.
6 He made the poles of acacia wood
and overlaid them with bronze.
7 He brought the poles through the rings on the flanks of the
altar,
to carry it by (means of) them;
hollow, of planks, did he make it.

8 He made the basin of bronze, its pedestal of bronze,
with the mirrors of the array-of-women that were arrayed-
in-waiting at the entrance of the Tent of Appointment.

9 And he made the courtyard:
on the Negev border, southward,

the hangings of the courtyard, of twisted byssus, a hundred
by the cubit,
10 with their columns, twenty, their sockets, twenty, of
bronze,
the hooks of the columns and their binders, of silver.
11 And on the northern border, a hundred by the cubit,
their columns, twenty, their sockets, twenty, of bronze,
the hooks of the columns and their binders, of silver.
12 And on the sea border, hangings, fifty by the cubit,
their columns, ten, their sockets, ten,
the hooks of the columns and their binders, of silver.
13 And on the eastern border, toward sunrise, fifty by the
cubit,
14 (namely:) hangings of fifteen cubits to the shoulder-piece,
their columns, three, their sockets, three,
15 and for the second shoulder-piece—(over) here and (over)
there for the gate of the courtyard—
hangings of fifteen cubits,
their columns, three, their sockets, three.
16 All the hangings of the courtyard all around, of twisted
byssus,

Anointing Oil and Incense II (37:29): To round out the description of the
incense altar, the text adds mention of these ingredients (cf. 30:25, 35).

Altar II (38:1–7): Parallel to 27:1–8, the major omission is "to receive its
ashes" (27:3), which does not relate to the actual construction.

Basin and Pedestal II (38:8): Only one line is used to record the making of
the basin; the parallel account in 30:17–21 says much more about its
function. There is a brief allusion in this verse about the "mirrors" which
were the raw material for the basin; Cassuto (1967) sees this as a contemporary citing of what must have been a well-known tradition about the
special contribution of the Israelite women, above and beyond the official
contributions listed in Chapter 35.

Courtyard II (38:9–20): Corresponding to 27:9–19, there are a number of
wording divergencies from the earlier passage, but none of these is particularly significant.

17 and the sockets for the columns, of bronze,
   the hooks of the columns and their binders, of silver,
   and the overlay for their tops, of silver, they themselves
      bound with silver,
   all the columns of the courtyard.
18 The screen of the courtyard gate, of embroiderer's making,
   of violet, purple, worm-scarlet and twisted byssus,
   twenty cubits in length,
   their height along the width, five cubits,
   corresponding to the hangings of the courtyard,
19 their columns, four, their sockets, four, of bronze,
   their hooks, of silver,
   and the overlay for their tops and their binders, of silver,
20 and all the pins for the Dwelling and for the courtyard all
      around, of bronze.

21 These are the accountings of the Dwelling,
   the Dwelling of Testimony,
   that were accounted by Moshe
   for the service of the Levites,
   under Itamar, son of Aharon the priest:
22 So Betzalel son of Uri, son of Hur, of the tribe of Yehuda
   had made
   all that YHWH had commanded Moshe,
23 and with him, Oholiav son of Ahisamakh, of the tribe of
      Dan,
   carver, designer, embroiderer in the violet, purple and
      worm-scarlet and byssus.
24 All the gold that was made-use-of in the work, in all the
      work of (building) the Holy-Place,
   all the gold from the high-offering (was)
   twenty-nine ingots and seven hundred thirty *shekels*, by the
      Holy-Place *shekel*.
25 And the silver accounted for by the community (was) a hun-
      dred ingots,
   and a thousand and seven hundred and seventy-five *shekels*
      by the Holy-Place *shekel*,
26 a *beka*/split-piece per capita, the half of a *shekel* by the Holy-
      Place *shekel*,

for every one who went through the counting,
from the age of twenty years and upward,
for the six hundred thousand and three thousand and five
   hundred and fifty.

27 There were a hundred ingots of silver for the casting of the
   bases of the Holy-Place and of the bases of the curtain,
a hundred bases per hundred ingots, an ingot per base.

28 And the thousand, seven hundred and seventy-five they
   made into hooks for the columns,
and overlaid their tops and bound them.

29 And the bronze from the high-offering (was) seventy ingots,
and two thousand and four hundred *shekels*.

30 They made with it the sockets for the entrance of the Tent of
   Appointment,
the altar of bronze, the netting of bronze that belonged to it,
   all the implements of the altar,

31 the sockets of the courtyard all around and the sockets of the
   courtyard gate
and all the pins of the Dwelling and the pins of the courtyard, all around.

Accountings (38:21–31): A new section enters here, continuing to achieve
the effect of impressing the audience. Previously the reader was to be
struck by the Israelites' zeal in piling up contributions for the new sanctuary (36:3–7); now, toward the end of the actual construction work, there is
a full accounting of the considerable material that went into it. The list
follows the standard order of value: gold, silver, and bronze.

38:21 **the accountings:** I.e., the inventory of materials used to construct the
   Dwelling. **Itamar:** Previously mentioned only in the genealogical list of
   6:23 and the enumeration in 28:1.

24 **ingots:** Others, "talents." These were of fairly large weight, perhaps 75
   pounds.

26 **603,550:** A more specific number than the "about 600,000" mentioned in
   12:37, it has been shown by Cassuto (1967) to conform to a patterned
   scheme (600,000 + 7,000/2 + 100/2), and hence may be a number designed more for didactic than for reporting purposes.

39:1 Now from the violet and the purple and the worm-scarlet
they made the officiating garments for attending at the
    Holy-Place
and they made the garments of holiness that are for Aharon,
as YHWH had commanded Moshe.

2 Then was made the *efod*
of gold, violet, purple, worm-scarlet and twisted byssus.

3 Then were beat out sheets of gold
and they were split into threads,
to make-use-of-them amidst the violet, amidst the purple,
    amidst the worm-scarlet and amidst the twisted byssus,
(all) of designer's making.

4 Shoulder-pieces they made for it, (to be) joined together,
on its two ends joined.

5 The designed-band of its *efod* that was on it, was from it, of
    like making,
of gold, violet, purple, worm-scarlet and twisted byssus,
as YHWH had commanded Moshe.

6 They made the onyx stones,
surrounded by braids of gold,
engraved with seal engravings, with the names of the Chil-
    dren of Israel.

7 They placed them on the shoulder-pieces of the *efod*,
as stones of remembrance for the Children of Israel,
as YHWH had commanded Moshe.

8 Then was made the breastpiece
of designer's making, like the making of an *efod*,
of gold, violet, purple, worm-scarlet and twisted byssus.

9 Square it was, doubled they made the breastpiece,
a span its length and a span its width, doubled.

10 They set-it-full with four rows of stones—
a row of carnelian, topaz, and sparkling-emerald, the first
    row,

11 the second row: ruby, sapphire and hard-onyx,

12 the third row: jacinth, agate, and amethyst,

13 the fourth row: beryl, onyx and jasper;
surrounded, braided with gold in their settings.

14 And the stones were with the names of the Children of
Israel,
twelve with their names,
signet engravings, each-one with its name,
for the twelve tribes.

15 They made, on the breastpiece, laced chains, of rope-making,
of pure gold:

16 They made two braids of gold and two rings of gold,
and put the two rings on the two ends of the breastpiece,

17 and put the two ropes of gold on the two rings on the ends of
the breastpiece,

18 and the two ends of the two ropes they put on the two
braids,
and put them on the shoulder-pieces of the *efod*, on its
forefront.

19 They made two rings of gold,
and placed them on the two ends of the breastpiece, on its
edge that is across from the *efod*, inward,

20 and they made two rings of gold and put them on the two
shoulder-pieces of the *efod*, below, facing frontward, parallel to its joint, above the designed-band of the *efod*.

21 They tied the breastpiece from its rings to the rings of the
efod, with a thread of violet,
to be (fixed) on the designed-band of the *efod*;

Garments II (39:1): Although in scribal tradition this verse is connected to
the previous section, it makes sense as the start of a new one, as it concludes with what will now be in one form or another the refrain to the end
of the book: "as YHWH had commanded Moshe" (see also vv.5, 21, 26,
29, 31, 32, 42, 43; then 40:16, 19, 21, 23, 25, 27, 29, and 32).

Efod and Breastpiece II (39:2-21): Corresponding to 28:6-30, the account
of how these garments were constructed conforms to the previous pattern:
their function "for remembrance" and more, so movingly laid out in
Chapter 28, is not mentioned.

39:3 **to make-use-of them amidst:** Or "to work them into."
   6 **surrounded by braids:** Heb. *meshubbot mishbetzot.*
   8 **an efod:** Some ancient versions read "the *efod.*"

the breastpiece was not to be dislodged from the *efod*,
as YHWH had commanded Moshe.

22 Then was made the tunic of the *efod*
   of weaver's making, all of violet.
23 The head-opening of the tunic (was) in its middle, like the
      opening for armor,
   a seam-edge for its opening, all around—it was not to be
      split.
24 They made, on the skirts of the tunic, pomegranates,
   of violet, purple, worm-scarlet and twisted byssus.
25 They made bells of pure gold
   and they put the bells amidst the pomegranates
   on the skirts of the tunic, all around,
   amidst the pomegranates:
26 bell and pomegranate, bell and pomegranate,
   on the skirts of the tunic, all around,
   for attending,
   as YHWH had commanded Moshe.

27 They made the coat of byssus, of weaver's making,
   for Aharon and for his sons,
28 and the turban of byssus,
   the splendid caps of byssus,
   the breeches of linen, of twisted byssus,
29 and the sash of twisted byssus, violet, purple, and worm-
      scarlet, of embroiderer's making,
   as YHWH had commanded Moshe.

30 They made the plate (for) the sacred-diadem of holiness, of
      pure gold,
   and wrote upon it writing of signet engravings:
   Holiness for YHWH.
31 They put on it a thread of violet, to put on the turban from
      above,
   as YHWH had commanded Moshe.

32 Thus was finished all the service (of construction) for the
      Dwelling, the Tent of Appointment.
   The Children of Israel made (it)

according to all that YHWH had commanded Moshe,
thus they made.
33 And they brought the Dwelling to Moshe:
the tent and all its implements,
its clasps, its beams, its bars and its columns and its bases,
34 the covering of rams' skins dyed-red and the covering of
dugongs' skins,
the curtain for the screen,
35 the coffer of Testimony and its poles
and the purgation-cover,
36 the table, all its implements and the Bread of the Presence,
37 the pure lampstand, its lamps—lamps for arranging, and all
its implements,
and the oil for lighting,
38 the altar of gold,
and anointing oil and the fragant smoking-incense
and the screen for the entrance of the Tent;
39 the altar of bronze and the netting of bronze that belongs to
it, its poles and all its implements,
the basin and its pedestal;

Tunic II (39:22–26): Parallel to 28:31–35, this account leaves out the
protective function of the tunic cited in 28:35.

Other Priestly Garments II (39:27–29): The parallel text is 28:39–43. This
passage should come after the section on the head-plate, as was the case in
the earlier passages; Cassuto (1967) explains the inversion as characteristic
of the construction texts—all the weaving is to take place together.

Head-Plate II (39:30–31): Characteristically, the function of the plate is
omitted (cf. 28:36–38).

The Completion of the Parts: Bringing Them to Moshe (39:32–43): The
listing of all the elements of the Dwelling fittingly closes the account of
their construction, with a certain grandeur, and, because of the pace, even
a certain excitement. The key term "service (of construction)" occurs
three times.

32 **made:** More idiomatically, "did" (similarly in 39:42, 43 and 40:16). See
Gen. 6:22, where Noah also follows God's instructions to the letter.
37 **lamps for arranging:** Others, "lamps in due order." **implements:**
Others, "fittings."

40 the hangings of the courtyard,
   its columns and its sockets,
   and the screen for the courtyard gate,
   its cords and its pegs
   and all the implements for the service (of constructing) the
      Dwelling, the Tent of Appointment;
41 the officiating garments for attending at the Holy-Place, the
      garments of holiness for Aharon the priest and the gar-
      ments for his sons, to be-priests—
42 according to all that YHWH had commanded Moshe,
   thus had made the Children of Israel,
   all the service (of construction).
43 Now Moshe saw all the work, and here: they had made it
   as YHWH had commanded,
   thus had they made.
   Then Moshe blessed them.

40:1 Now YHWH spoke to Moshe, saying:
   2 On the day of the first New-Moon, on the first (day) of the
      New-Moon,
      you are to erect the Dwelling, the Tent of Appointment.
   3 You are to place there the coffer of Testimony
      and you are to screen the coffer with the curtain.
   4 You are to bring in the table and arrange its arrangement,
      you are to bring in the lampstand and are to set up its lamps,
   5 you are to put the altar of gold (there), for smoking-incense,
         before the coffer of Testimony,
      and you are to place the screen of the entrance for the
         Dwelling,
   6 you are to put the altar for offering-up before the entrance of
         the Dwelling, the Tent of Appointment,
   7 you are to put the basin between the Tent of Appointment
         and the altar,
      and you are to put water therein.
   8 You are to place the courtyard all around, and you are to put
         the screen for the gate of the courtyard (there).
   9 Then you are to take the anointing oil
      and you are to anoint the Dwelling and all that is in it,
      you are (thus) to hallow it and all its implements, that they
         may become holiness;

10 you are to anoint the altar for offering-up and all its imple-
      ments,
    you are (thus) to hallow the altar, that the altar may become
      holiest holiness;
11 you are to anoint the basin and its pedestal,
    you are (thus) to hallow it.

More significant is what has long been noted: the literal parallels between our section and the initial creation story in Genesis (see, for instance, Leibowitz 1976 and Sarna 1986). The phrases "Thus was finished . . ." (v.32), "And Moshe saw all the work: and here, they had
made it" (v.43), and "Then Moshe blessed them" (v.43), echo "Thus
were finished . . ." (Gen. 2:1), "Now God saw all that he had made,/ and
here: it was exceedingly good" (Gen. 1:31), and "God gave the seventh
day his blessing" (Gen. 2:3). At the end of the passage describing the
erection of the Tabernacle, there is an additional parallel: "So Moshe
finished the work" (40:33); cf. Gen. 2:2: "God had finished . . . his
work." The close parallels suggest what we find in the case of many
cultures: human building, especially (but not exclusively) of sanctuaries,
is to be viewed as an act of imitating God. The Israelites, at the close of the
book chronicling their founding as a people, link up with God's scheme in
creating the world. The Dwelling is therefore a reflection of the perfection
of the world and the divine hand that oversees it. Yet neither the people
nor Moshe pronounces the Genesis words "it was (exceedingly) good"
over the sanctuary; that would be human *hubris*.

Final Instructions: Setting Up (40:1–16): Most prominent in God's commands to erect the Tabernacle are two related verbs: "hallow" and
"anoint," each of which occurs in one form or another eight times here. So
the major theme here is not the actual building, but dedication for a
purpose. Included in this section, as it was in Part IV, is the appointment
of Aharon and his sons to "be-priests."

40:2 **the first New-Moon . . . the first (day):** The date is almost a year after
      Israel's departure from Egypt. The completion of the sanctuary takes
      place on the first day of the month (new moon), whereas the exodus had
      occurred on the fifteenth (full moon), also considered a sacred time.

12 You are to bring-near Aharon and his sons to the entrance of
      the Tent of Appointment,
    you are to wash them with water,
13 and you are to clothe Aharon in the garments of holiness;
    you are to anoint him,
    you are (thus) to hallow him, to be-priest to me,
14 and his sons you are to bring-near,
    you are to clothe them in coats,
15 and are to anoint them as you anointed their father, that they
      may be-priests for me;
    that shall become for them—their being-anointed—priest-
    hood for the ages, throughout their generations.
16 Moshe made (it)
    according to all that YHWH had commanded him,
    thus he made.

17 And so it was on the first New-Moon in the second year, on
      the first (day) of the New-Moon,
    the Dwelling was erected.
18 Moshe erected the Dwelling:
    he put up its sockets,
    he placed its boards,
    he put up its bars,
    he erected its columns,
19 he spread out the tent over the Dwelling,
    he placed the cover of the tent over it, above,
    as YHWH had commanded Moshe.

20 He took and put the Testimony in the coffer,
    he placed the poles of the coffer,
    he put the purgation-cover of the coffer, above,
21 he brought the coffer into the Dwelling,
    he placed (there) the curtain of the screen and screened the
      coffer of Testimony,
    as YHWH had commanded Moshe.

22 He put the table in the Tent of Appointment,
    on the flank of the Dwelling, northward, outside the
      curtain,

23 he arranged on it the arrangement of the Bread of the Presence, in the presence of YHWH,
   as YHWH had commanded Moshe.

24 He placed the lampstand in the Tent of Appointment,
   opposite the table, on the flank of the Dwelling, southward,
25 he set up the lamps in the presence of YHWH,
   as YHWH had commanded Moshe.

26 He placed the altar of gold in the Tent of Appointment,
   before the curtain,
27 and sent-up-in-smoke on it fragrant smoking-incense,
   as YHWH had commanded Moshe.

28 He placed (there) the screen for the entrance of the
   Dwelling,
29 the altar for offering-up he placed at the entrance of the
   Dwelling, of the Tent of Appointment,
   and offered-up on it the offerings-up and the leading-dona-
   tions,
   as YHWH had commanded Moshe.

30 He placed the basin between the Tent of Appointment and
   the altar,
   and put water therein, for washing,
31 that Moshe and Aharon and his sons might wash from it
   their hands and their feet,

The completion of the sanctuary takes place, appropriately, on the first day of what was the month of the exodus a year earlier; it is also ten months after the people reached Sinai. The dedication thus combines the ideas of sacred space and sacred time.

The Implementation (40:17–33): Meaningfully, the formula "as YHWH had commanded Moshe" ends each of the seven paragraphs that describe the erection of the Dwelling.

32 (that) whenever they came into the Tent of Appointment
       and whenever they came-near the altar, they might wash,
    as YHWH had commanded Moshe.

33 He erected the courtyard all around the Dwelling and the
       altar,
    and put up the screen for the courtyard gate.

    So Moshe finished the work.

34 Now the cloud covered the Tent of Appointment,
    and the Glory of YHWH filled the Dwelling.
35 Moshe was not able to come into the Tent of Appointment,
       for the cloud took-up-dwelling on it, and the Glory of
       YHWH filled the Dwelling.
36 Whenever the cloud goes up from the Dwelling,
    the Children of Israel travel on, upon all their travels;
37 if the cloud does not go up,
    they do not travel on, until such time as it does go up.
38 For the cloud of YHWH (is) over the Dwelling by day,
    and fire is by night in it,
    before the eyes of all the House of Israel
    upon all their travels.

נשלם ספר ואלה שמות
שבח לאלהי המילדות

The End: God's Glory (40:34–38): The book ends, not with a paean to the
completed structure or its builders, but with a description of how its
purpose was fulfilled. Central is the "cloud," basically synonymous with
God's "Glory," which now dwells among the people of Israel. At the end
of the book of Exodus, which began with a people in servitude to an
earthly god-king, we find a people that has completed one aspect of service
to a divine king, ready to set forth on their journey to a Promised Land in
the company of the king's inextinguishable presence.

APPENDIX A

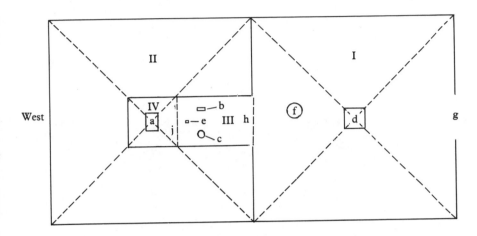

SCHEMATIC FLOOR PLAN OF THE DWELLING

I	Outer Court	a	Coffer	e	Altar for Incense
II	Inner Court	b	Table	f	Basin
III	Holy-Place	c	Lampstand	g	Entrance
IV	Holiest Holy-Place	d	Altar	h	Screen
				j	Curtain

According to the measurements given in Chapters 25–30, the proportions are as follows:

Perfect Squares (1:1) are the Outer Court, the Inner Court, the Holiest Holy-Place, the Altar, and the Altar for Incense.

Perfect Rectangles (2:1) are the Whole Structure, the Holy-Place, and the Table.

The relationship of the whole structure to each court is 2:1, as is that of the Holy-Place to the Holiest Holy-Place.

The relationship of the entrances (Entrance, Screen, and Curtain) is 2:1:1.

The Coffer and the Altar appear to stand at the exact centers of their respective squares. They share proportions different from those above: their length/width/height ratios are 5:3:3 (Coffer) and 5:5:3 (Altar). The departure from the standard 2:1 ratio may be an attempt to draw attention to these two holy objects, which functioned as the spiritual as well as geographical centers of the Israelite encampment in the wilderness.

SUGGESTIONS
FOR FURTHER READING

As a work that is of central importance to both Judaism and Christianity, Exodus has spawned an immense secondary literature. Tradition-minded Jews and Christians will as a matter of course make use of ancient exegetes and their medieval successors to get a fuller understanding of Exodus; much of this material is available in English translation (e.g., through the work of M. M. Kasher listed below, translations of the Midrashim, and of the Church Fathers and Luther). As far as modern commentaries are concerned, here too the amount of material is vast. The reader would be well advised to consult the solid and extensive bibliographies found in Childs (1974) and Sarna (1986).

The list below, which cites only two works not in English, is intended to supplement *Now These Are the Names* in four areas: interpretation of the Exodus text, ancient Near Eastern background, biblical history, and a literary approach to the Bible. It is a rather eclectic list which, it is hoped, will stimulate further interest in specific areas or specific texts. Also included here is material referred to in the Commentary and Notes (cited there by author and date).

Medieval Hebrew Commentaries

Abravanel	Isaac Abravanel, fifteenth-century Spain
Bekhor Shor	Joseph ben Isaac Bekhor Shor, twelfth-century France
Ibn Ezra	Abraham Ibn Ezra, twelfth-century Spain
Kimhi	David Kimhi, twelfth- to thirteenth-century France
Ramban	Moses ben Nahman, thirteenth-century Spain
Rashi	Solomon ben Isaac, eleventh-century France

Modern Works

Abrahams, Israel. "Numbers, Typical and Important." In *Encyclopedia Judaica*, vol. 12. Jerusalem, 1972.
Ackerman, James. "The Literary Context of the Moses Birth Story." In

Literary Interpretations of Biblical Narratives, edited by Kenneth R. R. Gros Louis, James Ackerman, and Thayer S. Warshaw. Nashville, Tenn., 1974.

Albright, William F. "What Were the Cherubim?" In *The Biblical Archaeologist Reader,* no. 1, edited by G. Ernest Wright and David Noel Freedman. New York, 1961.

Alter, Robert. *The Art of Biblical Narrative.* New York, 1981.

Andersen, Francis. *The Hebrew Verbless Clause in the Pentateuch.* Nashville, Tenn., 1970.

———. *The Sentence in Biblical Hebrew.* The Hague, 1974.

Auerbach, Erich. *Mimesis.* New York, 1952.

Bar Efrat, Shimon. *The Art of the Biblical Story* [Hebrew]. Tel Aviv, 1979.

Beck, Harrell F. "Incense." In *The Interpreter's Dictionary of the Bible,* vol. 2. New York, 1962.

Buber, Martin. *Israel and the World.* New York, 1948.

———. *The Prophetic Faith.* New York, 1949.

———. *Moses.* New York, 1958.

———. *On the Bible.* New York, 1968.

———, and Rosenzweig, Franz. *Die Schrift und ihre Verdeutschung* [German]. Berlin, 1936.

Campbell, Joseph. *The Hero with a Thousand Faces.* Princeton, N.J., 1972.

Cassuto, Umberto. *A Commentary on the Book of Exodus.* Jerusalem, 1967.

Childs, Brevard W. *The Book of Exodus: A Critical, Theological Commentary.* Philadelphia, 1974.

Clements, Ronald E. *Exodus* (Catholic Bible Commentary). Cambridge, 1972.

Cohn, Robert L. *The Shape of Sacred Space: Four Biblical Studies.* Chico, Calif. 1981.

Cross, Frank Moore. *Canaanite Myth and Hebrew Epic.* Cambridge, Mass., 1973.

Culley, Robert. *Studies in the Structure of Hebrew Narrative.* Philadelphia, 1967a.

———, ed. "Oral Tradition and Old Testament Studies." *Semeia,* vol. 5 (1976b).

Daiches, David. *Moses: The Man and His Vision.* New York, 1975.

Daube, David. *Studies in Biblical Law.* Cambridge, 1947.

———. "Direct and Indirect Causation in Biblical Law." *Vetus Testamentum,* vol. 11 (1961).

———. *The Exodus Pattern in the Bible*. London, 1963.

DeVaux, Roland. *Ancient Israel: Its Life and Institutions*. New York, 1965.

———. *The Early History of Israel*. Philadelphia, 1978.

Driver, Samuel R. *Exodus*. (*Cambridge Bible*). Cambridge, 1911.

Exum, J. Cheryl. "You Shall Let Every Daughter Live: A Study of Ex. 1:8–2:10." *Semeia*, vol. 28 (1983).

Fishbane, Michael. "The Sacred Center: The Symbolic Structure of the Bible." In *Texts and Responses: Studies Presented to Nahum N. Glatzer on the Occasion of His Seventieth Birthday by His Students*. Leiden, 1975.

———. *Text and Texture*. New York, 1979.

Fox, Everett. "The Bible Needs to Be Read Aloud." *Response*, vol. 33 (Spring 1977).

———. "The Samson Cycle in an Oral Setting." *Alcheringa: Ethnopoetics*, vol. 4, no. 1 (1978).

———. "A Buber-Rosenzweig Bible in English." *Armsterdamse Cahiers voor exegese in bijbelse Theologie*, vol. 2 (Kampen, Holland, 1980).

———. *In the Beginning*. New York, 1983.

Frankfort, Henri. *Before Philosophy*. New York, 1951.

Fredman, Ruth Gruber. *The Passover Seder*. New York, 1983.

Friedman, Richard Eliot, ed. *The Poet and the Historian: Essays in Literary and Historic Biblical Criticism*. Chico, Calif., 1983.

Gaster, Theodor H. *Passover: Its History and Traditions*. New York, 1949.

———. *Myth, Legend and Custom in the Old Testament:* New York, 1969.

Geller, Stephen A. "The Struggle at the Jabbok: The Uses of Enigma in a Biblical Narrative." *Journal of the Ancient Near Eastern Society of Columbia University*, no. 14 (1982).

Ginsberg, H. L. *The Israelian Heritage*. New York, 1982.

Ginzberg, Louis. *The Legends of the Jews*. Philadelphia, 1937.

Glatzer, Nahum N. *Franz Rosenzweig: His Life and Thought*. New York, 1961.

Greenberg, Moses. "Crimes and Punishments." In *The Interpreter's Dictionary of the Bible*, vol. 1. New York, 1962.

———. *Understanding Exodus*. New York, 1969.

———. "Some Postulates of the Biblical Criminal Law." In *The Jewish Expression*, edited by Judah Goldin. New York, 1970.

———. "Exodus, Book of." In *Encyclopedia Judaica*, vol. 6. Jerusalem, 1972.

Greenstein, Edward L. "The Riddle of Samson." *Prooftexts*, vol 1, no. 3 (September 1981).

———. "Theories of Modern Bible Translation." *Prooftexts*, vol. 8 (1983).

———. "Biblical Law." In *Back to the Sources*, edited by Barry W. Holtz. New York, 1984a.

———. "Medieval Bible Commentaries." In *Back to the Sources*, edited by Barry W. Holtz. New York, 1984b.

———. "Understanding the Sinai Revelation." In *Exodus: A Teacher's Guide*, edited by Ruth Zielenziger. New York, 1984c.

———. "The Torah as She Is Read." *Response*, vol. 14 (Winter 1985a).

———. "Literature, The Old Testament as." In *Harper's Bible Dictionary*, edited by Paul J. Achtmeier. San Francisco. 1985b.

Gunn, David M. *The Story of King David: Genre and Interpretation*. Sheffield, England, 1978.

Haran, Menahem. "The Nature of the 'Ohel Mo'edh' in the Pentateuchal Sources." *Journal of Semitic Studies*, vol. 5 (1960a).

———. "The Use of Incense in Ancient Israelite Ritual." *Vetus Testamentum*, vol. 10 (1960b).

———. *Temples and Temple Service in Ancient Israel*. Winona Lake, Ind., 1985.

Hertz, Joseph H. *The Pentateuch and Haftorahs*. London, 1960.

Hyatt, J. Philip. *Commentary on Exodus*. (New Century Bible). London, 1971.

Isbell, Charles. "The Structure of Exodus 1:1–14." In *Art and Meaning: Rhetoric in Biblical Literature*, edited by David A. Clines, David M. Gunn, and Alan J. Hauser. Sheffield, England, 1982.

Jackson, Bernard S. "The Ceremonial and the Judicial: Biblical Law as Sign and Symbol." *Journal for the Study of the Old Testament*, vol. 30 (October 1981).

Kasher, Menahem M., ed. *Encyclopedia of Biblical Interpretation*, vols. 7–9. New York, 1967–1969.

Keil, Carl, and Delitzsch, Franz. *Commentary on the Old Testament in Ten Volumes*. Vol. 1, *The Pentateuch*. Grand Rapids, Mich., 1968.

Kikawada, Isaac. "Literary Convention of the Primeval History." *Annual of the Japanese Biblical Institute*, no. 1 (1975).

———, and Quinn, Henry. *Before Abraham Was*. Nashville, Tenn., 1985.

Kirk, G. S. *Myth: Its Meaning and Functions in Ancient and Other Cultures*. Berkeley, Calif., 1970.

Knight, Douglas A., and Tucker, Gene, eds. *The Hebrew Bible and Its Modern Interpreters*. Philadelphia, 1985.

Kosmala, Hans. "The 'Bloody Husband'." *Vetus Testamentum*, vol. 12 (1962).

Lauterbach, Jacob Z., ed. *The Mekilta de-Rabbi Ishmael*. Philadelphia, 1976.

Leibowitz, Nehama. *Studies in Shemot I and II*. Jerusalem, 1976.

Levine, Baruch A. *In the Presence of the Lord*. Leiden, 1974.

Licht, Jacob. *Storytelling in the Bible*. Jerusalem, 1978.

Lichtenstein, Murray H. "Biblical Poetry." In *Back to the Sources*, edited by Barry W. Holtz. New York, 1984.

Mendenhall, George. "Covenant Forms in Israelite Tradition." *Biblical Archaeologist*, vol. 17 (1954).

Meyers, Carol. *The Tabernacle Menorah*. ASOR Dissertation Series no. 2. Missoula, Mont., 1976.

Milgrom, Jacob. *Studies in Cultic Theology and Terminology*. Leiden, 1983.

Miller, J. Maxwell. *The Old Testament and the Historian*. Philadelphia, 1976.

Nohrnberg, James. "Moses." In *Images of Man and God: Old Testament Short Stories in Literary Focus*, edited by Burke O. Long. Sheffield, England, 1981.

Orlinsky, Harry M. *Notes on the New Translation of the Torah*. Philadelphia, 1970.

Paul, Shalom. *Studies in the Book of the Covenant in the Light of Biblical and Cuneiform Law*. Leiden, 1970.

Plaut, W. Gunther. *The Torah: A Modern Commentary*. New York, 1981.

Lord Raglan. *The Hero*. New York, 1979.

Rosenberg, Joel. "Biblical Narrative." In *Back to the Sources*, edited by Barry W. Holtz. New York, 1984.

Ryken, Leland. "The Epic of the Exodus." In *Literature of the Bible*. Grand Rapids, Mich., 1974.

Sarna, Nahum M. *Exploring Exodus*. New York, 1986.

Schneidau, Herbert N. *Sacred Discontent: The Bible and Western Tradition*. Berkeley, Calif., 1976.

Scholem, Gershom. *The Messianic Idea in Judaism*. New York, 1972.

Sellers, Ovid P. "Weights and Measures." In *The Interpreter's Dictionary of the Bible*, vol. 4. New York, 1962.

Sonsino, Rifat. *Motive Clauses in Hebrew Law: Biblical Forms and Near Eastern Parallels*. SBL Dissertation Series no. 45. Chico, Calif., 1980.

Sternberg, Meir. *The Poetics of Biblical Narrative*. Bloomington, Ind., 1985.

Talmon, Shemaryahu. "The 'Desert Motif' in the Bible and in Qumran Literature." In *Biblical Motifs: Origins and Transformations*, edited by Alexander Altmann. Cambridge, Mass., 1966.

Tigay, Jeffrey H. "On the Meaning of t(w)tpt." *Journal of Biblical Literature*, vol. 3, no. 101 (September 1982).

Turner, Victor. *The Ritual Process: Structure and Anti-Structure*. Chicago, 1969.

Ullendorff, Edward. *Is Biblical Hebrew a Language?* Wiesbaden, Germany, 1977.

Vansina, Jan. *Oral Tradition: A Study in Historical Methodology*. London, 1965.

Walzer, Michael. *Exodus and Revolution*. New York, 1985.

Weinfeld, Moshe. "Congregation." *Encyclopedia Judaica*, vol. 5. Jerusalem, 1972a.

———. "Covenant." *Encyclopedia Judaica*, vol. 5. Jerusalem, 1972b.